a.s. berman

CUBE

inside the making of
a cult film classic

BEARMANOR MEDIA

"CUBE" oct. '94

'i wanted to make a movie that took place entirely in hell.'

↘ Vincenzo Natali, Director, *Cube*

For Vincenzo Natali and Andre Bijelic, and the cast and crew who guided us through the cube one last time.

text
A.S. Berman ©2018

design
Pamela Norman
pnormandesigns.com

photography
Photo credits are on page 348. All photos and/or copyrighted material appearing in this book remains the work of its owners; every effort has been made to give credit. No infringement is intended in this work of journalism. *Cube: Inside the Making of a Cult Film Classic* is not affiliated with the cast, crew, production or distribution companies of the *Cube* film or its sequels.

publisher
BearManor Media
bearmanormedia.com

ISBN
978-1-62933-291-8

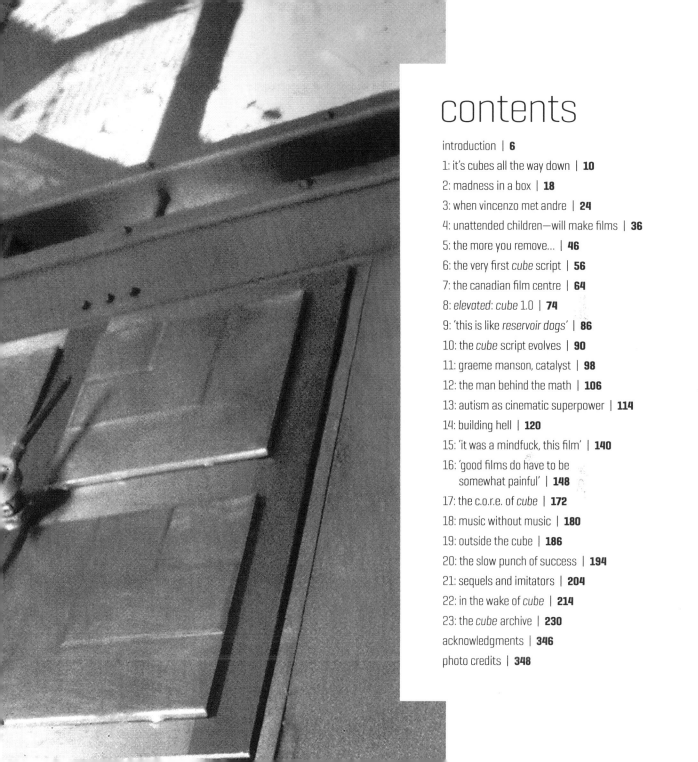

contents

introduction

CUBE DIRECTOR VINCENZO Natali's cult masterpiece belongs to another age yet somehow remains timeless.

Released in 1997 it was one of the last films to find its audience through video store rentals. I well remember discovering it on the New Releases rack at my local Blockbuster Video, even if I can no longer remember which city that video store was in. Netflix would kick off in April of the following year, paving the way for the video store's inevitable demise.

There was nothing particularly impressive about the *Cube* cover art, but the plot summary on the back was enough. (Be warned that this is as close to a dissection of the film itself as you're going to get, at least until we dive into the complicated evolution of the script in Chapter 10. If you've never seen *Cube*, find it and watch it. Really. Don't get me wrong, I've read many books about movies that I'll never see—I completely get that that's a thing—but trust me, this is not the type of movie you can easily do that with.)

"Six ordinary strangers awaken from their daily lives to find themselves in a seemingly endless maze of interlocking cubical chambers armed with lethal booby traps. Without food and water, they have a few days to live. None of them knows how or why they've been imprisoned, but they soon discover that each of them possess a skill that could contribute to their escape."

After the end credits rolled, it proved itself to be one of those rare films that left you with more questions than answers, and not in some Lynchian being-obscure-for-obscurity's-sake way. (Compare *Cube* to David Lynch's effort of that same year: *Lost Highway*.)

The year of *Cube*'s premiere was also one of the last to be virtually devoid of widespread web access as we know it today. There was no heading over to Wikipedia to get a broader perspective on what the hell you'd just seen, nor blogs worthy of the name subjecting it to the type of analysis that it received much later online. The flick had to stand on its own, unanswered questions and all. And it did. After two ill-advised additions to the franchise to the contrary, it does so still to this day which, quite frankly, is saying something.

'in some ways i feel i can't take credit for the concept of *cube*, it just felt like something that dropped into my lap out of the sky.'

↘ **Vincenzo Natali, director**

When this book was begun an embarrassingly long time ago, it was meant to be a celebration of *Cube* and what a handful of young Canadians accomplished with little more than a dream, a passion for cinema, and a pocket full of Canadian Tire money. For the most part that remains the case.

But somewhere along the way the film's dystopian vision of a future world in which people can be snatched off the streets and banged up indefinitely in an enormous complex without due process has sadly become a familiar phenomenon in the United States, especially if you were born someplace else.

Indeed, one of the most fascinating aspects of the film is the ease with which it can be viewed as a metaphor for the great oppressive forces, large and small, that rule our lives.

At the time of this writing, while watching the groundwork being laid for a one-party state in the United States, *Cube* feels less like a piece of escapist cinema and more a documentary of something we simply haven't found out about yet.

Ultimately, though, *Cube* is the story of a young director who managed to overcome a lack of money and his native Canada's own dearth of a film industry to create a movie that remained faithful to his original vision, and is still cherished to this day.

We are indebted to the director for allowing us to share his *Cube* sketches, storyboards and notes here (all artwork in this book is by Natali unless otherwise noted), along with personal photos, ads and other ephemera. Our hope is that through these and our exclusive interviews with members of the cast and crew, you will better appreciate *Cube* not just for its uniquely horrific cinematic vision, but as the against-the-odds creative achievement it truly is.

1: it's cubes all the way down

A CHILLY AFTERNOON in 2010 high up in Los Angeles' famed Hollywood Hills. Inside a modest three-bedroom house, an equally modest Vincenzo Natali gives the author an informal tour of his 1950s-style home, ending in an office tucked away downstairs.

Resting on a white corner desk sits a large-screen computer flanked by tall bookshelves. From floor to ceiling these boast volumes of every description, from graphic novels to large coffee-table books about Japan.

Across the brightly lit office from his desk sit black binders containing plans for entire cinematic universes, including the nightmare world of *Cube*. Sketches of frail-looking prisoners and brutal traps made all the worse by their fiendish complexity exist now only as relics, pale shadows of the celluloid fever dream they midwifed into our collective imagination in 1997.

If anything, current events have made the world of *Cube* seem that much more plausible now. That afternoon we're still a good five years away from the release of the so-called CIA "torture memos" regarding America's abuse of terror suspects, but state kidnappings and detention in foreign lands have already

Opposite: Natali in his then-Hollywood Hills home in 2010.

'I think part of my fascination with Japan is that I feel like it's a peek into the future. I've always been fascinated by science fiction. When you go to Tokyo, I don't think you can help but think of it as a future culture. It's probably because they're dealing with issues that we will be dealing with in the future.'

↘ **Natali**

cemented the term "extreme rendition" into our vocabulary. For all we know, there may indeed be an enormous cube-like prison somewhere in the Nevada desert churning away, desperately trying to squeeze from its prisoners the answers to questions long forgotten.

As for Natali, the director of *Cube* has lived in that universe of prisoners and futuristic death traps for so long, he doesn't need the sketches to refresh his memory. He can still recall the feelings of agony and elation that attended the creation of his first feature 20 years ago.

Exchanging One Cube for Another

On that May afternoon, Natali prepares a salad for photographer Mark Lipczynski and I as we casually look around his living room and drink in the majestic views his enormous floor-to-ceiling windows provide.

The Japanese influences that inform his personal aesthetic are everywhere, from the orderly white shelves that hold the DVD collection he shares with his wife, to the lack of all but the most minimalist ornamentation. (A 2-foot-tall Hello Kitty figure by the television and a 6-foot stuffed Teddy bear on the sofa being the only exceptions to this—his wife's influence possibly, but we are too shy to confirm.)

When Japanese distributor Klockworx snapped up distribution rights for *Cube* in that country, they invited the director to Tokyo. "And then I just fell in love with it. To me it's like Disneyland, except when I go to Tokyo it's *my* Disneyland. There's

Inside the
Cube-maker's Lair

This rare glimpse inside
the former Hollywood
home of Vincenzo Natali
provides a taste of his
unique influences.

↘ For additional content see
the Cube Archive, pp. 230-345

Hoichi the Earless

In the Japanese legend upon which this segment of *Kwaidan* is based, Hoichi is a blind minstrel who sings so well he is tricked by ghosts into singing for them in a local cemetery night after night. To free the man from the spirits, a priest paints the "Heart Sutra"—a piece of Buddhist scripture—all over Hoichi's body to render him invisible to the ghosts. When one of them appears once again to lead the singer to the cemetery, all he sees are Hoichi's ears, which the spirit promptly cuts off to take back with him in order to prove that this is all that he could find of the man—the priest had neglected to print the scripture on Hoichi's ears.

hardly a moment that goes by where I'm not floored by some incredible device or piece of architecture or fashion or something I see in the street. It's a magical place and I really love the people." In fact, it was there that he met his wife, Kana. "A lot of great things came to me from Japan," he admits.

As we sit down to lunch, we can't help but notice one piece of art that dominates the dining room. Hanging on the wall is a very unusual wedding present: a huge poster (*see previous page*) for the 1964 Masaki Kobayashi horror anthology *Kwaidan*. Here the disembodied head of **"Hoichi the Earless"** floats against a vivid rainbow background, his face covered in the holy writing that plays such a pivotal role in the traditional Japanese tale.

Hoichi is not so different from the characters who inhabit Natali's cube—he's simply another hapless victim of unseen forces. It is also here that we get to the heart of *Cube's* perpetual relevance. It is the narrative equivalent of a black hole—a metaphor for the human condition so perfect, no situation can escape comparison to it. Not even the director's own.

On the day we meet, Natali's fourth feature film, *Splice*, had just enjoyed its North American premiere at Sundance four months earlier. A $25 million sci-fi/horror picture executive produced by art house/blockbuster director Guillermo del Toro (*Pan's Labyrinth, Pacific Rim*), *Splice* marks the first time Natali's been able to break the $8 million budget ceiling, though he will tell me later, "They spent more money promoting *Splice* than we did making the movie. The ratio of what I was putting on screen vs. the actual resources I had to make the film was about

'even though that film is indebted to other movies of the past, it has things in it that i don't think i've ever seen before.'

↘ **Natali on** *Splice*

the equivalent of *Cube*."

Still, he should be elated. A $25 million feature boasting a U.S. theatrical release by Warner Bros. and based on a story he co-wrote—there aren't many directors who get this kind of opportunity.

Yet for all his years directing films and television, he exists in a kind of purgatory between struggling artist and jobbing director—something underscored by the up-close view he gets from his driveway of the famous 45-foot-tall Hollywood letters on Mount Lee in the Hollywood Hills. (He has since relocated to Toronto, though he still does some work in the US.)

Until Natali creates a film that pulls in massive amounts

'The real issue
with movies
is that they're
so expensive
to make that
they need to
reach a really
big audience in
order to truly be
successful. And
to do that you
have to have the
power of a studio
behind you.'
↘**Natali**

of cash, odds are not much will change. It's going to be years of helming other people's film projects, work-for-hire jobs on television, and occasionally contributing shorts to scrappy little anthology films like *The ABCs of Death 2*. There's the concern that all he's really done with *Splice* is trade a smaller cube for a slightly larger one in the overall Grand Cube that is the Hollywood system. Recall Holloway frantically trying to reach the cube's outer shell as she swings from the end of the prisoners' makeshift rope and you'll have a pretty good idea of what that must feel like.

Surely that must be the most frustrating part of being the man who created the perfect existentialist metaphor for life—you never really lose perspective of your own place in the cube.

"There's a very famous Australian aboriginal legend about how the world sits on the back of a turtle," says Natali. "And when someone asks the shaman, 'Well, what does the turtle sit on top of, he says, 'Oh, it's turtles all the way down.' "

A short pause and then...enlightenment.

"It's cubes all the way down."

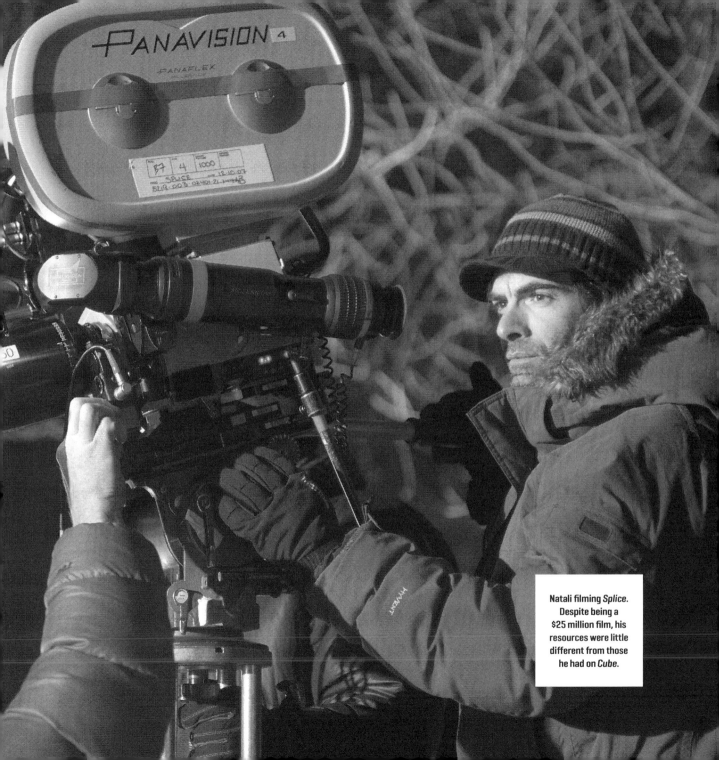

Natali filming *Splice*. Despite being a $25 million film, his resources were little different from those he had on *Cube*.

2: madness in a box

THE SPIKES, THE mesh slicer and all the other deadly devices lurking inside the cube on this day in 1996 may be harmless illusions whipped up by the magicians at special-effects house C.O.R.E., but the heat steadily rising within the 14' X 14' X 14' film set is the real deal. Any pride on the part of the creators over weaving an entire feature around a single set is gone now—they're paying for it. Everyone's paying for it.

When you have a budget of $30 million-plus, it's a small matter to conjure up hell in post-production today. When you're watching every penny with a mandate from above to keep it as close to the $750,000 (Canadian) mark as possible, you can't depict hell without inflicting it on your cast and crew.

The sweat on the face of Maurice Dean Wint (Quentin) was not put there by the makeup department; David Hewlett (Worth) has already bitten through two of the shirt buttons the characters are meant to use to stave off thirst. All the while, the mercury inside the set continues to rise thanks to light riggings packed with dozens of 100-watt bulbs that bring the enormous Plexiglas walls surrounding the small cast to life.

Opposite: A gleefully ghastly sketch of a *Cube* trap by Natali.

"I always like to think it's not the case, but the good films are the painful ones," cinematographer Derek Rogers will conclude philosophically 15 years later. "The ones that are too easy tend not to be as interesting."

Exhausted by grueling 12-hour days, the actors are in varying states of misery, yet try to cling to the humor of the situation because really, what else can you do?

The glowing floors of the cube chambers look appropriately futuristic on screen, but their wood and Plexiglas construction cause them to writhe beneath the actors' feet as they walk—it's like spending 12 hours each day walking along a hot plate with a will of its own.

I Melt With You

Every step brings a squeak that echoes inside the cube, an excellent way to get people's attention without having to say a word—just move back and forth repeatedly until they look at you with murder in their eyes.

The problem is so pervasive, the sound effects team created makeshift squeak silencers, or "sqilencers": large sheets of plywood covered by sound-dampening blankets. These were what the actors walked on any time the floor wasn't actually on camera.

While Rogers and Natali are setting up the next shot, the film's speechless Kazan—Andrew Miller—joins Hewlett and co-star Nicole de Boer (Leaven) in a spirited rendition of Modern English's 1982 hit "I Melt With You." The '80s Cube' has surfaced yet again, much to the crew's annoyance. "That kind of rotated

The Plot

A cop, a math student, a physician, an escape artist, an idiot savant and an enigma find themselves trapped in an enormous prison made of many cube-like rooms, without any idea how they got there. Moving from cube to cube in search of a way out, they encounter deadly traps that threaten their very existence, even as paranoia and madness eat away at their uneasy alliance.

Cube Face

Much of the misery and exhaustion you see on the faces of the characters trapped inside the cube are reflections of the long hours and miserable conditions endured by the actors themselves, and even the director, during filming.

from cube to cube," Miller admits, "because basically we did it whenever we were bored."

Hot and exhausted, Natali looks up from his notebook and laughs. This may not be the nihilistic vision of hell that he first dreamed up years before while scribbling out notes for his first feature film in a little Toronto townhouse in The Annex, but this is what he needs right now. This is his family.

As if on cue, co-writer Andre Bijelic wanders back to the set finishing off whatever he's been able to cadge from craft services' meager spread. Natali and Bijelic have been dreaming big together since elementary school. Fellow oddballs Hewlett and Miller joined them in their late teens, completing the quartet.

At that moment somebody curses, somebody else laughs, and without turning Natali and Bijelic know that the doors between cubes have gone wonky again. Second-unit supervisor William Phillips thinks he may have that particular problem licked, but it'll be days before they see what he's come up with. In the meantime, the director will have to juggle the shooting schedule yet again.

However frayed the actors' nerves, however much some of the crew gripe, Natali and Bijelic know something that the others do not. Had they gone with the former's original vision of the cube, things could've been much, much worse.

C$4,600

Amount spent feeding *Cube* cast and crew (craft services).

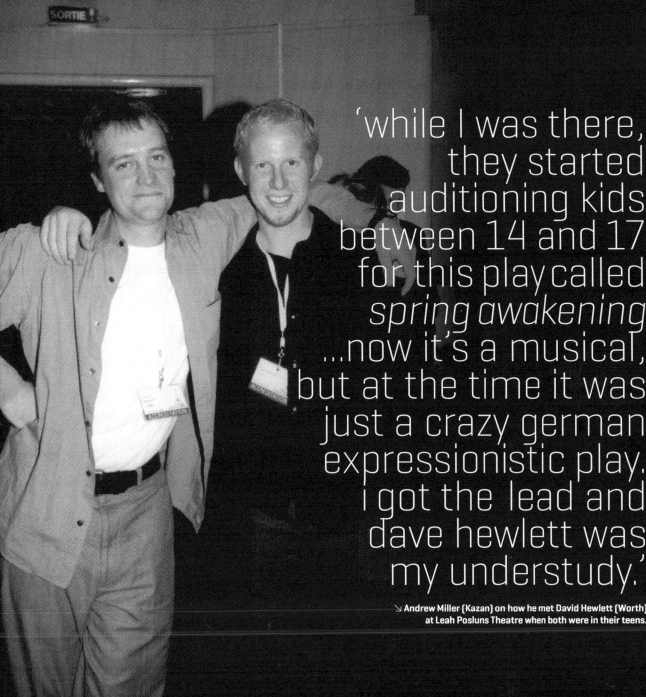

'while I was there, they started auditioning kids between 14 and 17 for this play called *spring awakening* ...now it's a musical, but at the time it was just a crazy german expressionistic play. i got the lead and dave hewlett was my understudy.'

↘ Andrew Miller (Kazan) on how he met David Hewlett (Worth) at Leah Posluns Theatre when both were in their teens.

3: when vincenzo met andre

A WARM SPRING day in 1993 on Atlantic Avenue in Toronto. Still trying to wake up, a 24-year-old Vincenzo Natali heads for the doors of the big brick building, and the whimsical polar bear that stands guard on the white sign above. How many people would kill to be in his shoes right now?

When he first landed a position as a storyboard artist's assistant at Canada's beloved Nelvana animation studio three years ago, there'd been that all-too-rare sense of having pulled one over on the universe. Somehow he'd found a job that merged the twin passions that had driven him since childhood—comics and filmmaking.

"That was the best job in the world for somebody like me," he says. "I had gone to film school briefly, quit, and then quickly realized I had made a mistake because once I left film school, I understood how expensive it is to make 16 mm movies. And in those days that really was the only way to do it. If you wanted to make a professional short film you had to shoot on 16; it wasn't like now where you can very cheaply pick up an HD camera and edit the thing on your laptop."

Opposite: Andre Bijelic ready to shoot (left) and Natali in the late '80s, somewhere in the Toronto sprawl.

'When I was a kid they made these holiday specials that I loved. They were progressive and they became quite famous. In fact so famous that George Lucas hired them to do the Saturday morning cartoons based on *Star Wars*. I think there was one called *Droids*, and there might have been an Ewok one. (They also did the infamous *Star Wars* Christmas special!) And they made a movie that wasn't seen very much but was really neat called *Rock and Rule*.'

↘ **Natali on Nelvana**

Still, however fun and educational his Nelvana job was, he would've rather been back in the cube.

Ever since the first wisps of the concept had entered his consciousness three years earlier, Natali had been going over it and over it in those rare moments of dead time that most people spend making plans for the weekend.

"It was the collision of two things that were rattling around in my head," he explains. "I wanted to make a movie that took place entirely in hell—I probably didn't even have a clear idea at the time—but in hell there was no context, no scene in the movie that begins *outside* of hell. You're just in this nightmare place from the beginning to the end. I think vaguely I had the notion that it would be a modern kind of hell. It wouldn't be a Dante's *Inferno*, but something very modern or postmodern. So it was that combined with the fact that I knew that, as a first-time feature film director, I would have very little money to make my movie."

From then on he brainstormed different scenarios in which he could shoot everything in a single location. It wasn't working. No matter what he came up with, it all ended up feeling very much like a stage play.

"I remember the moment vividly when I sort of tasked myself with coming up with a story. I went for a walk and sat down at the edge of a fountain in Toronto, and I was suddenly struck by the idea of 'What if one set could double as many?' Therefore I wouldn't have the kind of physical restrictions that one would normally have in a movie like that.

"My fear was it would become too much like a play or **My Dinner with Andre**. But if one set could double as many, then I could have my characters moving around and it would be a much more cinematic experience. So that led me to think of a maze composed of identical rooms."

From there one idea built upon the next pretty quickly. It would have to be a symmetrical maze, which meant a maze composed of cubes, and finally, one enormous cube.

Now three years of endless notes and doodles about this nightmare world had reached a tipping point, compelling him to begin work on a rough script—just lines of dialogue here and there. And always the ever-changing vision of the cube itself.

"I was probably 21 when I came up with the concept. I had this idea that many young filmmakers do at the time, which is I had to make my first feature film by the age of 25 because that's when Orson Welles made *Citizen Kane*—that's sort of the bar." He laughs. "Which I should point out I failed to do. I wasn't too far off the mark, though."

He would be 28 when *Cube* was finally released.

A Type of Film School

In a strange way, the three years Natali spent composing storyboards for cartoons such as *Beetlejuice, Eek! the Cat* and the prestigious *Babar* at Nelvana served as an intensive class in film direction.

"It was like film school. I really learned how to translate the written word into images. They would give you a script and

My Dinner with Andre

Louis Malle's 1981 comedy-drama stars Wallace Shawn (best remembered as Vizzini in *The Princess Bride*) and Andre Gregory discussing life and the theatre while sharing a meal at Manhattan's Café des Artistes. While a much-respected movie, its ponderous "talking heads" approach is clearly the type of play-like staging that Natali was anxious to avoid for *Cube*.

essentially say 'Draw it.' You select your shots and you figure out what the cut points are in advance of the animation actually being made. All this was being done under the tutelage of the animation director. I really learned the basics of classic narrative storytelling that way. And I got paid for it."

Paid for about half the year, anyway. Animation, like television, is seasonal work. In another month or so Nelvana would go on hiatus and he'd be laid off until the following season. Up till now he'd made enough at the studio to be able to use these enforced vacations to shoot his own 16 mm movies with his roommate, Andre Bijelic. This year, though, all his thoughts were on the cube.

His house on Roxton Road in The Annex was small and in a reasonably decent part of town bordering the University of Toronto. It was as if somebody had found a way to take the first 18 years of Natali's life and condense them into one house. His room wasn't all that different from the one he'd grown up in on High Park Avenue in downtown Toronto, the only child of Enrico and Gale Natali.

The couple had split up shortly after he was born in 1969 in Detroit. His father remarried and moved to upstate New York; his mother bundled the infant off to Toronto to make a new life for them both.

Though Natali would gain two stepsisters and a stepbrother from his father's second marriage, he grew up as an only child in his own little world, immersed in comic books and movies. That was until he turned 8 and got to know the equally insular little boy who lived one street away.

'In some ways Andre [Bijelic] is like a brother to me. I've had the weird experience of hearing his voice on an answering machine and thinking it was me.'

↘**Natali**

A World's-eye View

Born in the former Yugoslavia, Andre Bijelic was brought to Toronto three months later by his mother who had lived there as a teen; he would spend much of his early life continuing to travel.

Holidays were taken in Germany, Austria and the Caribbean, as well as driving vacations throughout the United States: South Carolina, Florida, and on and on. And at 21, he found himself present for one of the most pivotal moments in the 20th century.

"My mom got a job at this hotel that was a joint venture between this Canadian company and the Russians when they were trying to become more open, so she was living there [in the Soviet Union] for a few years," he remembers. "When I had graduated school she was like, 'Come over here for a while.' That's when I went to Italy and Greece, and then up to Russia; I spent a few months there. I was actually there when they tried to overthrow Gorbachev and the tanks were rolling in. I saw the very end of the Soviet Union, saw the flag going down over the Kremlin.

"It was kind of a surreal experience but I never felt like I was in any imminent danger. They never shut down the airport, which was a big thing. They never blocked CNN or anything so you could actually see what was happening, although what they *said* was happening and what was actually happening didn't seem totally in sync sometimes."

Years before these events (which Bijelic modestly describes

as "my little James Bond adventure at 21"), there was the child who grew up loving books, television and film.

A chance viewing of 1975's *The Return of the Pink Panther* on TV around the age of 9 finally nudged him over the line between movie fan and budding director. From then on, his father's Super 8 movie camera became his in all but name and Vincenzo Natali, the quiet little boy one street over, became his co-director, co-writer, and above all, production illustrator. Bijelic would write the script and Natali would make intricate storyboards.

Calling their outfit Adventure Films, the pair frequently swapped duties: sometimes Bijelic was the writer and Natali the director/cameraman, other times vice versa, yet Bijelic was always the editor. After a while, though, they simply did everything together. Nearby High Park became their back lot.

"Our filmmaking progression actually followed the progression of the history of film in a way," says Bijelic. "We started off with these silent films, just trying to do little tricks and special effects, and gradually evolved into trying to tell stories more, and started adding sound. By the time we were out of high school we were actually doing fairly sophisticated short films."

As their techniques improved, their films took on darker tones.

"I don't know why they were always about psychos," laughs Bijelic. "I guess it was that era. *Halloween, Friday the 13th*, all those movies that started coming out when we were kids." And it was fun.

Bijelic 'on location' in Toronto for Adventure Films. Initially he wrote the scripts and Natali storyboarded them.

Andre Lining up the Shot

Fueled by countless hours spent in The Eglinton Theatre, Bijelic (above and right) and Natali initially cranked out as many short Super 8 films as their finances would allow before moving on to 16mm.

↘ *For additional content see the Cube Archive, pp. 230-345*

It was also a welcome distraction from Bijelic's homelife as his parents' marriage was coming to an end. At 14 he and his mom moved from their home on Oakmount—just a street away from Natali—to Pacific, the next street over from their old home.

Cinema as Escape

The boys dreamed big, but they were children after all. Bijelic remembers their films being "terrible and short because those Super 8 reels are only 2-and-a-half minutes long. Somehow we'd scrape the money together—the $50 or whatever you needed to get the thing and shoot it."

The fact that children this young would part with enough cash to cover film and development costs speaks to one of the main drivers of their fantastic output—the crushing boredom of middle-class life.

"We got to travel a fair amount, both of us. And we certainly didn't want for anything," Bijelic admits. But in those pre-Internet days, "There really wasn't that much to do. You had TV, whatever happened to be on those four or five channels at the time. You had books and movies, and that was about it."

Living just a short drive from downtown Toronto, they had the usual distractions offered by any big city—movies, mostly. The best cinema in the city was The University Theatre at 100 Bloor Street West, the largest movie house in the country when it closed in 1986. (It was also the home of the Toronto International Film Festival.) It was here that the boys indulged their

Ginger Snaps

In 2010, *Cube*'s Andrew Miller (Kazan) completed work on a pilot script for a proposed *Ginger Snaps* TV series for The CW. Attached as executive producers were Marti Noxon (*Buffy the Vampire Slayer*) and Dawn Parouse (*Prison Break*). In the end, they declined to greenlight it. "It was incredibly disappointing because I'm a huge, huge fan of *Ginger Snaps* the movie," says Miller. "We really did a fun adaptation that would've made it an amazing series."

love of film. After it closed, The Eglinton Theatre (today The Eglinton Grand) became their preferred destination.

They were wrestling with the same stifling atmosphere that future screenwriter and Natali collaborator Karen Walton would find herself dealing with a few years later after her own family moved to the samey-samey suburbs of Sherwood Park, Alberta. She would grow up to communicate this feeling of middle-class soullessness in her smart and scathing script for the 2000 cult classic **_Ginger Snaps_**. (Natali would end up creating the storyboards for it, too.) As that film's director, John Fawcett, pointed out to the author in *The New Horror Handbook*, Canada is the world's second largest country after Russia, yet only has about 35 million people. This means a relatively small number of human beings separated by huge patches of open land.

Normally it might be years before children growing up in and around downtown Toronto gained a sense of this, of course, but Natali and Bijelic's travels, combined with their own social isolation growing up, underscored Toronto's relative smallness in the larger world. Just growing up Canadian in the cultural shadow of the neighboring US, whose TV and radio signals regularly crept into that country, one could be forgiven for feeling a bit separated and boxed in from the rest of the world.

Canada, in other words, as cube.

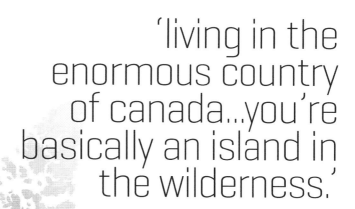

'living in the enormous country of canada...you're basically an island in the wilderness.'

↘ John Fawcett, director of the classic werewolf/
teen-angst flick *Ginger Snaps*. A similar sense
of isolation can be found in *Cube* .

4: unattended children—will make films

IT'S 1984. The long-haired young man sits at his desk in the classroom brooding, a pencil in his hand, the tie around his white collar looking particularly uncomfortable. The other students around him are hunched over their papers deep in thought.

Something isn't right. It's a math test which explains some of the tension; the on-screen world is black and white, which makes for a tension of its own. But it's the boy's face that sets us on edge—handsome but behind that dazed expression—it's not evil, exactly, more like something that's horribly broken. When he finally guns down his teacher a short while later, it will come as no great surprise.

Though boasting multiple locations, the tensest moments in the 20-minute 1984 Natali/Bijelic short film *Exam* take place in a single classroom—a detail whose significance won't be fully appreciated until the release of *Cube* 13 years later. It's a hell of a piece of work for a trio of teenage boys.

"We would probably be in juvenile detention if we made that now," laughs David Hewlett, who played the young gunman—his first collaboration with the filmmakers. "Nowadays that just

Opposite: Vincenzo Natali (left) on the set of the short film *Mouth*.

wouldn't go down well, but at the time it was like 'Look at how clever—they get their frustrations out by making these little movies.' "

But this was Toronto, after all, and in the '80s no less—school shootings would not become the teenage rite-of-passage they are today for another 15 years. Back then it was just three kids trying to recreate a bit of good old fashioned American film violence, though the ending is pure Canadian fair play: Hewlett runs away after the deed and gets hit by a car. The end.

"That was totally autobiographical," says Natali. "I was very poor at math."

The Royal St. George's School for Young Filmmakers

The scene is The Royal St. George's College playground in The Annex, an Anglican choir school. A 15-year-old student comes up to a boy a year older and says "Hey, you want to be in a movie?"

The older boy's been acting in school plays, occasionally dressing as women because it is a boy's school, after all. Films, huh? Seems the next logical step. Vincenzo Natali has found his muse; David Hewlett will appear in every film he makes from then on.

"I could be wrong but my hunch is I play Vincenzo in a lot of his movies," he says. "I've this theory that directors hire people who have some kind of connection with either themselves, their past, or people they know. You walk in a room and gauge what the director's like, and often you find that if you play up the parts that are similar to him, you end up getting the part."

Continued on page 42 >

All the Rage

In a weird retro-zeitgeist detail, the year after Natali, Bijelic and Hewlett shoot *Exam*, publisher NAL will bring out *The Bachman Books: Four Early Novels by Stephen King*. It's kicked off by the author's 1977 thriller *Rage*, in which high school senior Charlie Decker guns down his algebra teacher and takes the class hostage.

A young David Hewlett in the 1985 follow-up to *Exam*, *Johnny Roach*.

The Super 8 Four

Before there was *Cube*, there were four friends messing about with a camera. All photos are from the Super 8 short *Johnny Roach*.

1: A perfectly depressing setting **2:** Wheelchairs always make great camera dollies **3:** Andre Bijelic and James Paul, a high school friend who played an alien henchman **4:** David Hewlett in Johnny Roach. **5, 6** and **7:** Shooting *Johnny Roach*

4

5

6

7

All wisdom that will be gleaned in coming years. Right now the 16-year-old Hewlett just wants to move on with his life, to find the next hurdle to clear on his way to becoming James Dean.

"I didn't particularly like acting, I just wanted to be famous," he says. "What's funny about it is it's like anything else: When you get into it, you learn it's not about the end, it's about getting there."

And the St. George's school was an excellent road to take for anyone wanting to explore their creative side, especially in the 1980s.

"It was this under-funded private school, but the whole point of it was they had these great, crazy teachers who had different ideas on how things were done," he observes. "Hippyish in a way, I suppose, but they were all from odd places and odd backgrounds, but they were so inspiring."

There was the French instructor who insisted on being called Father Fraz, and drama teacher Father Michael, "a mad-actor-turned-priest from England," recalls Hewlett, "who was almost like a character in a movie."

One of those teachers, at least, *would* become a character in a movie. When it came time to shoot the short about the lethal math exam, St. George's English teacher Mr. Stephenson was enlisted.

"This guy used to teach us grammar using these incredibly violent sentences about the Easter Bunny being skewered, slashed and killed," the actor fondly remembers. "It was like having Roald Dahl as your English teacher—he was just fantastic."

Meanwhile Bijelic was enrolled at the local public school,

Humberside, though he and Natali would still get together over summer breaks **to make films**. And with the surprisingly benevolent help of St. George's, they were given carte blanche to use the school's classrooms, stage, lighting equipment—even the costume and makeup departments.

"I just can't believe they turned it over to us because we weren't even supervised," Bijelic reflects. "They just said OK, come in here on this date and go nuts." He laughs. "It was a different time. I don't think you'd get away with that now."

Shooting *Exam* on Super 8, "there were one or two days when we brought in just about anyone we could find and stuck them behind the desks, and we shot all the wide shots that way," he explains. "The rest of the time it was just four or five of us."

Despite years of devouring every magazine article they could find on movie makeup effects, it took a fair amount of trial and error before they were able to render Hewlett's killings to their satisfaction.

"We actually used firecrackers on a dummy torso," says Bijelic. "Then we'd stick a tube through it and load a water gun with chocolate syrup and spray it that way. [Mr. Stephenson] was a really good sport because we covered him in chocolate syrup."

The shooting of *Exam* coincided with a time when Bijelic had begun working in hotels—the $200-$300 he made was integral to the funding of their film projects. "While everyone else was off buying cars, we were pouring all our money into movies."

With the co-directors attending two schools, they had twice the number of students from which to draw when they needed

To make films

In addition to *Exam*, the one film that's still recalled by its makers is *Johnny Roach*, "about a struggling actor and his girlfriend who stumble upon an alien invasion plot spearheaded by leader Big Jim, who is more a used car salesman/infomercial pitchman than overlord," explains Bijelic. "And in keeping with something of a theme, it was overly ambitious for our resources, and was unfortunately never finished."

Mouth

Scenes from the short film *Mouth*. Above: David Hewlett. Right: The woman on the right is Natali's mom.

↘ *For additional content see the* Cube *Archive, pp. 230-345*

actors. While several kids entered and left their orbit, Hewlett was one of a select few who actually stuck it out. The filmmakers had long since outgrown the point-shoot-let's-see-what-happens phase—those who attached themselves to a Natali-Bijelic project had to be in it for the long haul.

Sometimes 14 or 16 hours would be gobbled up in the making of a single short—God knows how many setups that entailed. "We worked like dogs," says Hewlett. "Instead of dicking around in arcades and goofing around in the summers, we made movies.

"Vincenzo got his hands on 16 mil cameras—admittedly they were wind-up ones. You couldn't sync sound—it was like having a sewing machine going on the table in front of you. So everything had to be done in this very peculiar way because we had no resources or anything; it just forced you to be more creative."

By the time he landed his first professional role around 18, "I came into the room and I knew more than most actors at that point—I'd already been doing it for two years with my friends. I already knew about hitting marks. I knew about the way things worked. I *didn't* know some of the lingo because we didn't know that either—we had our own terms for things.

"We were very lucky in that we found a bunch of us who knew what we wanted to be when we grew up. We were always focused on the right thing. Any opportunity we had, we were either at movies, talking movies, making movies, writing movies—and we haven't really stopped." He laughs. "Still acting like idiot children."

'I think we would be in jail if we made that now.'

↘ **Bijelic on**
***Exam* (1984)**

45

CUBE
SCRIPTS
PART I

CUBE
SCRIPTS
PART II

CUBE
ART

CUBE
STORYBOARD

5: the more you remove the scarier it becomes

DURING THE SUMMER of 1993, Natali developed a particularly nasty bout of pneumonia which confined him to bed just as Nelvana was shutting down for fall hiatus. On Jan. 22, 1994, he completed the very first draft of *Cube* during "post-pneumonia recovery," he remembers.

He never had any doubt that he'd show Bijelic the finished piece. But his childhood friend wasn't one to sugarcoat his reactions to anything—if it was great, he'd tell him so. And if it wasn't, he'd tell him that, too.

"He's a very harsh critic," the director admits. "He's tough, he's brutal, but that's why I gave it to him. And he, in his typical very perceptive way, said, 'You know what's great about the idea for this script is that it's so simple.' He was the one who realized that we should take out anything from this story that is extraneous."

What's so striking in hindsight is that it was the very film-centric Bijelic who extolled the virtues of something every artist learns early on: To create a successful work of art, you first must erase all the sketch lines underneath. And there were many, many sketch lines buttressing *Cube* in that first script.

Opposite: Binders full of notes and storyboards for *Cube* give little hint at the hell imagined within.

The Cube on Roxton Road

A lot had changed since the two elementary school kids had shot their 2-and-a-half-minute epics in Toronto's High Park all those years ago. Though they'd been parted during their high school days "we still hung out and still shared the same group of friends for the most part, so it wasn't that big of a difference," Bijelic recalls.

After graduation, they ended up sharing a house at 548 Roxton Road in The Annex with four other people, even as their work lives began to diverge sharply. Natali had gotten his foot in the door at Nelvana while Bijelic was bouncing from job to job, the pair still managing to make movies on the side. "At that time I worked in a hotel, I was carrying luggage," says Bijelic. "I was valet parking, driving a delivery truck, and I was a bartender." He would work at a bar right through the shooting of *Cube*.

Natali, at least, was getting a crash-course in scene composition as a professional storyboard artist, but his friend saw no way out of his own cycle of menial employment.

And now Natali had gone off and written a script by himself about a bunch of people trapped in a maze with no idea how they got there, or how to get out. Bijelic couldn't have put his own situation better himself.

Years after *Cube* became a cult hit, the pair would downplay the influence their cramped situation in The Annex had on the writing of the script. Yet looking at their living arrangement, it's hard to completely dismiss its effect on the story they produced.

The townhouse on the right (as it appears today) is where the first *Cube* script was written.

21

How old Natali
was when he first
began developing
the idea of *Cube*.

28

How old he
was when *Cube*
was released.

The house was nice enough, standing as it did in an OK neighborhood in the Portuguese part of Toronto, says Natali, even if "it was a little rough around the edges in those days."

Like *Cube*, it housed six people from various backgrounds: one in the basement, two on the first floor, Natali and Bijelic on the second, and their friend Lawrence Nichols in the attic. "He was more into music than movies, although we roped him into some student films," says Bijelic. All shared a kitchen, living room and a single bathroom.

Says Natali, "I think Andre's right in that at that time in our lives we were feeling really confined, and to some degree frustrated because we were living in a crappy little place together and we were lonely and we didn't have girlfriends; we were just struggling as a lot of young people do. I think the movie took on those existential aspects to it—that's really what makes it resonate."

Stripping *Cube* Down to its Essence

When Natali finally let his friend read his first attempt at a *Cube* script, Bijelic realized there was an intriguing idea lurking within its pages. But it wasn't just about people trapped in a maze—there was a great deal more to it. Too much.

"It had all these crazy monsters, cannibalism, there was moss growing on the walls that people ate," Bijelic explains. "He asked me what I thought of it and I said I like the idea, the premise is interesting, but it didn't feel like it had much focus."

Says Natali, "When I wrote *Cube* originally, and I started

writing it alone, it was much more like **a Terry Gilliam kind of movie**. It was a group of accountants who were being sent to this place with no understanding of why they were there. In fact there was never an explanation, really—it was kind of absurd. And the *Cube* universe, while it was essentially the same notion of being a giant cube composed of many smaller cubes that are, in fact, a larger mathematical puzzle, it had these magical elements to it, too." (For a detailed look at the early drafts of *Cube*, check out pp. 231-243.)

While the passage of time has understandably dulled the director's memory of that first treatment, certain details remain. "There was a kind of minotaur in the maze—it was just a much more baroque version of the cube than what actually got made."

In short, this was Natali the graphic artist giving full vent to his visual imagination, dreaming up things that would be extremely cool to draw. But somewhere between the moss and the monsters, there was...something.

"I thought it would be more effective if he stripped it of all this stuff and just concentrated on a bunch of people who have nothing," explains Bijelic. "There's no food, there's no water, which gave it a time limit, a ticking time bomb, and just put the focus on how they get out."

The director saw the value in this critique at once. "The power of the story is that these people have been dropped into this place without anything other than the shirts on their backs," he says. From that point on, "We were thinking at the time that this was something that could've been made in the Soviet Union—it had

A Terry Gilliam kind of movie

The film Natali no doubt had in mind here is *Brazil*. In that 1985 sci-fi classic, a government employee (Jonathan Pryce) in a dystopian world finds his life turned upside down by political intrigues beyond his control, all the while dreaming of a damsel in distress. *Brazil* is also noteworthy for the battle of wills that ensued between Gilliam and his US distributor Universal over the latter's insistence on giving the film a happy ending. Ultimately it relented, releasing Gilliam's original cut. Check out Jack Mathews' book *The Battle of Brazil* for all the gory details.

that flavor of a Russian movie. Very stark and grim. And that was absolutely the right approach. That was really the birth of the *Cube* that got made."

'Writing *Cube* Felt...Like Archaeology'

By this time, both men knew where this was headed. For years they'd been putting together short films as they'd always done, but more recently they'd been finding themselves talking about doing their first feature together.

Up till then, they'd been writing and rewriting a couple of different scripts, mostly something called *Love Kills*, which Bijelic recalls being a sort of dark romantic comedy. It was a bit like the François Truffaut film *The Man Who Loved Women* [1977], says Natali, in that the protagonist dies. "And it was as far away from *Cube* as you can imagine."

Bijelic adds, "Nothing really came together that well, probably because neither one of us likes those types of films as much as sci-fi and suspense."

It was a particularly frustrating time for both—Natali was working long hours at Nelvana, storyboarding other people's visions; Bijelic was working at a hotel and spending less and less time behind the camera. Neither could see things changing anytime soon.

The duo drafted a second, pared down *Cube* script early in the summer of '94 that did away with a lot of the more outlandish elements. On June 21st, Natali wrote another version on his own "because I felt that we were onto something special and I

'i wrote the first draft [of *cube*] partly because i just wanted to be the one to write it, knowing that andre would improve on it vastly.'

↘ **Natali**

wanted to be the one to take the first crack at it," he says.

However, it was the next draft, this one written by Bijelic alone in July, that Natali says "galvanized" the film. "And that was very good. In some ways the script changed only superficially from that point onward. It was Andre's draft that [made] it into something really strong." (Bijelic would go on to write all subsequent drafts until the pair teamed up with Graeme Manson later on.)

The moment Bijelic began peeling away the details from the *Cube* script, both men suddenly realized what they had—not just something that would be much easier to film, but a concept that was intriguing enough to carry them through the development process. Says Bijelic, "It felt like something that could work."

Adds Natali, "We knew that going from my Gilliam draft, we were going to do something pared down and more realistic.

'We were thinking of the cube being somewhere between a Rubik's Cube and one of those 2-dimensional puzzles that you slide around to make a picture, where there's always one hole left.'

↘**Natali**

But the first step after that was figuring out the puzzle. I believe it was Andre who came up with this whole idea that one of the rooms would function as a bridge, and that would be a very important realization.

"To me, writing *Cube* felt as much like archaeology as writing," the director adds. "It felt like we had stumbled upon something that had already existed and our job was really just exhuming it from the earth."

Because their bedrooms were on the same floor, the two would hash out the details in conversation, each jotting down notes as they refined the scenes. "We were usually in Vince's room because he had the nicer one," says Bijelic. "He had a big window."

He also had the nicer computer, a Mac PowerBook laptop (borrowed from David Hewlett, as it happened). "*I* had an ancient pre-Windows word processor," says the *Cube* co-writer. "A late '80s PC, just yellow text."

Very quickly it became clear that the script they were putting together wasn't just something they intended to shop around, it was something that, if worse came to worst, they could probably shoot themselves on 16 mm. Perhaps even more importantly, the subject matter—unlike the aborted rom-com—was intriguing enough to carry them through the whole production process.

The pair who'd created so many short films together growing up were about to develop their first feature; both were 25.

                    RYKER
Tell us what you do know.

                    ELLIS
As you have probably surmised already, this
place is designed on the principals of
symmetry. All the rooms are perfect cubes. In
fact, the entire structure is one big cube
composed of smaller cubes. It is surrounded by
an outer shell. The key to getting out is to
pass through that shell.

                    LANG
How big is it?

                    ELLIS
Twenty rooms across and twenty stories high.

                    RYKER
How do we avoid the traps?

                    ELLIS
I...I'm not sure. There are parts that I can't
remember. The concussion seems to have
affected my memory. It has something to do
with the numbers on the walls.

                    RYKER
We've gone that far on our own.

                    ELLIS
They have some kind of significance. If only I
could remember.

                    DRAKE
Quit holding back, Ellis.

                    ELLIS
I'm not holding back. I want to get out of
here as much as you do.

                    LANG
Maybe I can help you. I was a cryptographer
for the bureau of investigation. I specialize
in number codes.

                    ELLIS
What's a bureau member doing here?

'Believe me, you can ask as many questions as you want, but you will never find any answers.'

⬊ From p. 38 of the first *Cube* script

6: the very first *cube* script

THOUGH NATALI RECALLS writing the first iteration of *Cube* in the vein of a Terry Gilliam film, today it reads more like Douglas Adams' *Hitchhiker's Guide to the Galaxy*, rounded off with some of the dry humor Gilliam and the rest of Monty Python made famous. Squint and it's easy to mistake our protagonist, the Worth-like Jeremy, for *Hitchhikers'* Arthur Dent—an everyman dropped into the most absurd of situations. His wisecracking Ford Prefect through it all is Ethan, a fellow accountant—*everyone* in this *Cube* is an accountant—a no-nonsense American with a cutting wit.

Down the Rabbit Hole

If the following scenario seems like a mishmash of hard-to-follow happenings, that is only because the script reads that way, too. The story opens much the same way the film does, with an Alderson-like fellow frantically making calculations in a little book while using a small, cube-shaped object to orient himself in the maze. Suddenly a terrifying roar echoes through the structure, forcing him to open a door that he isn't entirely sure of. Instant-

Opposite: Vincenzo Natali writing the first draft of *Cube* with a companion.

ly, five barbed hooks on chains shoot out and bury themselves in his flesh, pulling him inside. The door automatically slams shut and...title card. Both the hooks and the minotaur-like beast prowling the maze smack heavily of 1987's *Hellraiser*. (The mesh screen from the opening moments of the *Cube* shooting script will make an appearance much later in the first version.)

We next find ourselves in a Toronto house where we meet Jeremy and wife Zoe, who gives us what could very well be the tagline for *Cube*: "Things are boring when they make sense." There's clearly a rift between the couple, with Jeremy's anal retentiveness over his wife's inability to use the same dish twice feeling like a nod to the tensions at Natali and Bijelic's place on Roxton Road.

Leaving to perform an errand we'll find out more about later, Jeremy is stranded when his car breaks down in an industrial area. Ultimately the accountant is lured into the cube by a mysterious child who runs away with his briefcase.

From the moment Jeremy meets Ethan inside, it becomes more of a two-hander than the ensemble piece we're familiar with. That's not to say they don't pick up additional characters along the way, including a passive-aggressive cannibal who's been in the maze a very long time.

Ultimately, Ethan gives his life for Jeremy, Jeremy dispatches the cube monster and the little-boy creature that got him into this mess in the first place, finally stepping through a door into... what? As in the final film, we simply don't know.

Glimpses of *Cube* and *Hypercube*

Despite having a wildly uneven tone and dialogue that occasionally reads like what it is—a burgeoning writer testing out his comedic chops—there are hints of our *Cube,* too. Perhaps most compelling are two lines spoken by Jeremy to Ethan (both on p. 36 of the script):

> JEREMY
> Ethan, how long have you been here, stuck in the maze?
>
> ETHAN
> It's hard to say. Long enough to shatter any allusions that I may have once held about logic and order in the universe.
>
> JEREMY
> Funny, I got the same feeling when I conducted an audit of the municipal government's spending policies.

And

> JEREMY
> Well, someone built this place. The maze has to be here for a reason.

Taken together, we catch a glimpse of the Worth we know—a drab worker bee who dutifully toiled away in the background building something for the government he will later be consumed by.

Oddly, Natali also predicts the basis for the Andrzej Sekuła-helmed *Cube 2: Hypercube* with Ethan explaining the cube:

> ETHAN
> This is us. A couple of two dimensional guys living on a piece of paper. One day, some mean, three dimensional motherfucker comes along and punches a pencil through the paper.
>
> Being two dimensional stick men, we can't see the three dimensional pencil. All we see is a hole in our paper world.

this first draft demonstrates a striking tension between quirky college humor and a filmmaker flirting with, if not fully embracing, avant-garde cinema.

Indeed, in this version the cube's center (rather than the edge) is said to be the portal through which they must pass to return home...though this comes from the calculating lips of a cannibal.

Perhaps the greatest difference between the first and final scripts is the former's focus on the relationship between Jeremy and Zoe. Though the couple are only glimpsed together at the beginning, we understand their marriage is a complicated one. While there's the temptation to say it's been shoehorned into the script, we discover that Jeremy's affair with the wife of his business partner, and her subsequent blackmail of him, indirectly led him to the wrong place at the wrong time: the entrance to the cube.

From rooms filled entirely with open umbrellas (!) to the center of the cube itself containing a beating heart in a rusty cage—a powerful image—you can practically feel the director straining at the leash. At times humor and art rudely collide: the minotaur thing (dubbed a "Xenochrosteptuloc" in the script) that's been pursuing them this whole time, for example, turns out to be an old man in a suit.

There is also more of a sense of the cube as limbo, at least as far as Jeremy is concerned; a feeling that he must walk its deadly corridors until he has come to terms with his own marital infidelity. In the *Cube* that we know, the only expiation for sin is death.

'...Remember, if Life is Just a Game, Then in the End, Everyone Loses'

Finally, the rules to this cube read more **like those of a video game** than the finely tuned universe of the *Cube* we know. Prisoners navigate their way through the maze using calculations, certainly, but also a mysterious pocket model of the cube that never receives a lick of explanation. Toward the end, even this is set aside for a special door whose coordinates can only be read once Jeremy has consumed a drug-like fruit from a tree. It's this contrast between scripts that allows us to see the compelling message of the one that was ultimately shot: Everything we need to navigate the cube (read: life) can be found within.

Despite this contrast, the philosophical heart of *Cube* can be found in this very first attempt: a brutal, nihilistic pessimism that screams its frustrations at the sky, and knows before it's finished that there will be no reply. The last word on this, and on this very first script, goes to Jeremy:

"All this pain and suffering, it doesn't have any meaning. All those lives wasted. They were wasted for nothing. There is no plan. There is no scheme. There is no grand design."

Like those of a video game

During the writing of the scripts, Natali and Bijelic occasionally questioned whether they were actually writing a film or a game. As the director told Slashfilm.com in 2010, "I actually wrote an outline for a game, in fact. I also thought it would be interesting because, in addition to dealing with the traps, you'd have to deal with the other people."

The Breakfast Club

Just because Natali, Bijelic and co. made movies when they were young doesn't mean they didn't have a good time.

1: Left to right: Kelley Doris (Bijelic's wife), Andre Bijelic, Andrew Miller, David Hewlett and Anne Schwitzer, their French attaché in Paris **2:** Natali and Doris **3:** Left to right: filmmaker Carol Clusiau, Natali and Hewlett.

1: Miller and Hewlett
2: Natali, shot at the Roxton Road townhouse he shared with Bijelic during the writing of the *Cube* script 3: Left to right: Bijelic, Miller, Doris and Hewlett

↘ *For additional content see the* Cube *Archive, pp. 230-345*

7: the canadian film centre

IN 1994 ANDRE Bijelic's hotel gig came to an end, even as he was still struggling to get his own draft of the *Cube* script into some kind of shape. "I thought of the unemployment payments as being an arts grant," he says with a laugh.

Vincenzo Natali's storyboarding job at Nelvana, too, came to an end as usual for the fall. "They would employ me for about six months out of the year and then they would go on hiatus, at which point I would go on unemployment insurance and work on my own movie," he explains.

This year was different. All they could think about now was *Cube*—there was neither time nor interest in shooting anything else.

In the fall, once they had the script in good shape, they began shopping it around.

"There was a low-budget company called Norstar who showed some interest," Natali remembers. "At that point I was thinking *Cube* is never going to get made because Andre and I had some interest from various production companies in Toronto, but nobody had really stepped up to the plate. It bounced around a little bit in that B-movie world, but they always want-

Opposite: With the founding in 1988 of what came to be known as the Canadian Film Centre, director Norman Jewison helped jump-start numerous careers.

ed—in my eyes—to cheapen it a little bit. I got to a point where I was half committed in my own mind to doing it [on a shoestring budget] on 16 mm with my own money somehow."

Unwilling to spend another six months hanging out in this *Cube*-like limbo until Nelvana started up again, Natali applied for a place at the Canadian Film Centre.

The Canadian Film Scene

There's really no diplomatic way to say it: Most Canadian feature films prior to the 1990s—particularly English-language ones—were **poorly funded**, poorly made and poorly treated.

Sure, there had been exceptions—mostly genre flicks. There were Bob Clark's offerings, including 1974's *Black Christmas* (arguably the first slasher film) and 1981's *Porky's* (the ur-*American Pie*). George Mihalka's 1981 slasher *My Bloody Valentine* was another. Then there was Sandor Stern's underappreciated 1988 creepy classic *Pin...* (starring David Hewlett), not to mention David Cronenberg's wave of body-horror pics, back when Cronenberg was still Cronenberg.

Doomed from the beginning to languish in Hollywood's shadow, Canadian directors initially avoided sinking their meager funds into features, concentrating instead on far-less-expensive-to-produce documentaries. As a result, there was only one viable model for them to follow: slip over the border to work in American television.

Toronto's Norman Jewison set the standard, parlaying a gig at CBS directing specials (Judy Garland's "comeback" special in

Poorly funded

Filmmaking in Canada has always faced an up-hill battle economically as there simply aren't enough people in the country to finance a thriving film market. Compare its overall 2012 population of 34.9 million to the US's 313.9 million that same year. Canada's entire population is usually within a few million of that of California alone.

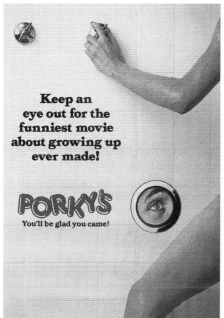

Prior to the '90s, the only Canadian films that found an audience outside that land were genre pics. (*Cube*'s David Hewlett starred in *Pin* above.)

1961 being a highlight) into working on Tony Curtis and Doris Day movies, before making his groundbreaking 1965 Steve Mc-Queen drama *The Cincinnati Kid*. From there he went from hit to hit, including Oscar winners *In the Heat of the Night* (1967) and *Fiddler on the Roof* (1971).

Yet it was only after the release of his Oscar-winning 1987 Cher-starrer *Moonstruck* that Jewison moved forward on an idea he had been nursing for some time—the creation of a training ground for Canadian filmmakers.

The Filmmaker Factory (North)

Designed to be the Canadian equivalent of the successful American Film Institute, the Canadian Centre for Advanced Film Studies as it was then known opened its doors in 1988 offering advanced classes in directing, producing and scriptwriting.

Students were given four to nine months to learn from leading industry professionals, who would ultimately include directors such as Ethan Cohen (with brother Joel, *No Country for Old Men, Fargo*), Judd Apatow (*Anchorman: The Legend of Ron Burgundy*) and Ivan Reitman (*Ghostbusters, Stripes*). Under their tutelage, students were able to make several short films using equipment and materials acquired through the Centre.

Though he was never officially enrolled, David Hewlett knew his way around the place. "I did a lot of acting with those guys, a lot of the people who went through when it first started. I was actually acting in the first year that they had that set up. We had these directors coming through and it was at the point where

Colin Brunton (left) honed his filmmaking chops producing *Roadkill* (1989) and *Highway 61* (1991), the twin features that put maverick Canadian director Bruce MacDonald on the map.

they'd basically been given the house which is now the actual film centre. I remember getting there early one day and hopping in a window because someone had forgotten to let us in—it was before they'd set anything up."

In 1992, under executive director Wayne Clarkson, the institution rebranded itself as the Canadian Film Centre and greatly expanded its scope with The Feature Film Project. This finally allowed students to create three feature films each year.

The choice of Colin Brunton as the project's first executive director made it clear how CFC viewed its role: the centre was there to stop the brain drain by instructing budding filmmakers

'A guy submitted [a feature film proposal] a couple of times but his films were huge in scope. So I tried to explain all the things that were costing too much money for us. He finally comes back with a shit-eating grin and says he's got it, it's all in one location. The location was a working carnival.'

﹀ **Brunton, executive director, CFC's Feature Film Project**

in how best to make small films on small budgets, rather than grooming them to work in the studio system over the border.

"They wanted me for my rep of being able to put all the money on screen while working with not much," says Brunton. "And they liked my sensibility. When I got the job and was told my responsibilities, I thought it was just awesome. It was like running my own little studio, and I was going to help new filmmakers make cool films—films unlikely to get funded in any traditional way."

Brunton honed his filmmaking chops producing *Roadkill* (1989) and *Highway 61* (1991), the twin features that put maverick Canadian director Bruce MacDonald on the map. (He'd met MacDonald, along with the likes of Atom Egoyan, Peter Mettler and Patricia Rozema, when he joined the film co-op LIFT.) It was during the making of these two films that he first came across Natali.

"He was doing storyboards for other people," Brunton says. "He worked near us on Adelaide Street. It was clear, however, that he wanted to make his own films."

By the time Natali was accepted to CFC in 1995, Brunton had already shepherded a few films through The Feature Film Project. One, *Rude* (1995), was a character study set in the inner city starring *Cube's* Quentin, Maurice Dean Wint. Says Brunton, "One reason I loved green-lighting *Cube* was knowing that I was going to leave the Centre, and I was going to go out with a bang."

"They were making some great shorts but there was no platform for people to see those back then," says Hewlett. "And

Colin Brunton

Lacking anything resembling a corporate studio system, all Canadian film is, in a sense, indie film, breeding a make-the-most-of-every-dollar mentality. Still, Colin Brunton came from an even more ragtag sensibility than most, having emerged from Toronto's late-'70s punk scene.

Having managed The New Yorker rep theater for two years, he followed owner Gary Topp to the Horseshoe Tavern in 1978, where he made the handbills for every act. Topp and partner Gary Cormier had transformed the venue into a punk and new wave mecca, presenting acts such as The Cramps, Talking Heads, Suicide and The Police.

At the end of 1978, when word came down that the music being featured was not to the owner's liking, "the Garys" said to hell with it, and invited their favorite local punk bands for a going-away party that was quickly dubbed "The Last Pogo."

"I was only working there part-time and driving a cab, and trying to get work in the film business," remembers Brunton. "I came in one night after smoking a joint in my cab coming down Spadina [Avenue], and heard about the concert they were planning. I blurted out that I was going to make a film about it.

"The next morning, clear-headed and sober, I *still* thought it would be a great film to make—historical. I had taken a weekend filmmaking course, and even though I had no money and really no knowledge of how to make a film, I contacted my teacher, Patrick Lee, and asked if he'd help."

The resulting short documentary, *The Last Pogo*, recorded the Dec. 1st show featuring seminal Toronto acts such as The Mods, Teenage Head and The Cardboard Brains among many others. With more than 800 fans fueled by the music, illegal substances, and righteous anger over the death of the only decent punk venue in the city, the event quickly devolved into a near riot, with police and firemen clashing with audience members. "Myself and my crew, save the sound recordist, were kicked out by the cops," Brunton recalls. "So I only have the riot on audio; we snuck back in later and shot footage of the aftermath.

"The spirit of the punk scene—you can do anything—was in my wheelhouse," he explains. "I made this short film; left me in debt for a decade." In 2013, Brunton created a full-length documentary on the Toronto punk scene: *The Last Pogo Jumps Again*.

Among the acts featured in Brunton's *The Last Pogo* were Teenage Head, The Viletones and Cardboard Brains.

the feature films leading up to *Cube* had never found audiences. And then Vincenzo came in with this passion for films that had a commercial angle as well, which I think is something that's often missing from Canadian films."

Certainly Brunton realized that if the program was ever going to live up to its intended purpose—turning out Canadian directors who stood a chance in the industry—they'd have to push the envelope a bit now and then.

Says Brunton, "The odd thing was that I had sole authority to green light a project. As long as I thought it could be done, and thought it would be good, it was good to go.

"That said, I still had to pitch it to an advisory committee made up of other producers, as well as a stakeholders' committee made up of reps from all the unions and suppliers. Finally I had to convince the board of directors. So while I did have sole authority, I had to allow myself to be challenged by all of these people on the creative, business and practical aspects. Remember how much Albert Brooks sweated in *Broadcast News*? That's me at some of those meetings. And I had to report back to them on the progress. That is where I learned the terms 'mea culpa,' and 'mea maxima culpa.'

"In the four years I was there, I got to make five groups of people's collective dreams come true. What I hadn't thought of was all the heartbreak I would cause: I had to turn down a few hundred other groups of people. Some were very upset with me, but most took it in their stride. I had to turn down Michael Ondaatje [author of *The English Patient*], for one. I couldn't do it

'It always bugged me that [the Canadian Film Centre] didn't train actors—just everybody else. They do now though.'

↘ **Guadagni (Holloway)**

by email — it was Michael Fucking Ondaatje — so I phoned him. I hadn't even completed my first sentence: 'Hey, Michael, so I got your script...' And he cuts in and says, 'Let me guess. I can't write screenplays, can I?' 'Uh...sort of?'"

Holly Dale's *Blood & Donuts* (1995) probably made for some excessively Albert Brooks-style sweaty meetings. Though perhaps not so bad seen through the eyes of a post-*Twilight* audience, Dale's story of a newly awakened vampire falling for a donut-shop worker is a problematic movie, hamstrung by sleepy performances and an inability to strike a balance between humor and serious exploration of the "human condition." (To be fair, this is something that won't really be mastered in Canadian film until 2000's *Ginger Snaps*, beautifully written by CFC alumna Karen Walton and directed by John Fawcett.) Even an on-screen performance by Canada's best-known genre director, David Cronenberg, fails to move the needle.

Though it would ultimately find a small audience on home video, the movie didn't do well at the box office and suggested to the CFC that genre pictures were not the way forward.

This was the atmosphere in which Natali found himself on entering the Canadian Film Centre.

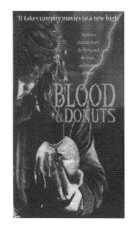

Poor reception to *Blood & Donuts* may have left the CFC reluctant to finance another genre flick.

8: *elevated*: cube 1.0

IT'S 1996 AND 10 days since shooting began on *Cube*. If these 14-foot walls of blue, green and white aren't seeping into the dreams of the cast and crew by now, it's only because the grueling 12 hour days haven't left much time for sleep. That's to say nothing of the *red* walls, which pretty much soak in through their pores, stirring their blood and making everyone more irritable than they might otherwise be.

Cinematographer Derek Rogers isn't the first person on the shoot to see the whole thing as one big science experiment. But unencumbered by having to learn lines or manage egos, he's one of the few to see the bigger picture. And he can't quite shake the feeling that he's been here before.

'If Alien Made it With Pumpkinhead'

Rewind to one year earlier. Almost from the moment Vincenzo Natali enrolled in the Canadian Film Centre he was pitching *Cube* to Colin Brunton, even though he hadn't yet applied to The Feature Film Project.

Opposite: David Hewlett and Vickie Papavs share a moment of horror in Natali's 1996 short film, *Elevated*.

Trapped in an elevator

Director M. Night Shyamalan would take his own stab at this concept by coming up with the plot for 2010's *Devil*. After years of cinematic missteps, Shyamalan ratchets up the tension by having the characters come to realize that one of the people trapped in their elevator might be the devil himself. As Natali points out, there are only so many story lines, and many hit on the same ones eventually. "I've found that I've worked on ideas I thought were totally original only to discover that someone else was doing exactly the same thing, or had done the same thing long ago." He laughs. "I'm willing to cut him some slack."

"I made a very aggressive and fancy presentation that included a presentation book and storyboards," the director recalls. He'd even constructed a model of the cube itself out of foam core. He still has the book; the model has since been lost to time.

"It was a very ambitious looking movie technically and they had a very limited budget," he says. "And I think Colin's primary concern was 'Is this an independent movie?' Because the script that Andre and I wrote was a little less quirky and a little more of a straight ahead science-fiction movie. At any rate, he passed on it. I was coming to him as a student—I hadn't made my short film there yet."

That short film was *Elevated*, a 17-minute exercise in tension and claustrophobia that would change everything.

Written by Natali and future *Ginger Snaps* scribe Karen Walton, the entire film consists of just three characters **trapped in an elevator**—a dry-run for *Cube* on a number of levels.

Ellen (Vickie Papavs) and Ben (Bruce McFee) who would go on to play a startling number of cops and security guards on television) are in an office elevator on their way down to the parking garage when they pick up Hank (David Hewlett) who scrambles inside, tells them he's "security," and frantically hits the button for the top floor. Only after that do the other two see that his white shirt is covered in blood. "It's OK," he reassures them, "it's not mine."

After making introductions he tells them there are monsters down below—their only hope now is to reach the top floor.

Shot on 16 mm, the short is remarkably effective thanks in

part to the clever dialogue. (Typical example: "It was like—did you see *Pumpkinhead*? Yeah, obscure. Or *Alien*, *Alien* the movie?... If *Alien* made it with *Pumpkinhead*—it's fuckin' outside!")

Yet what truly holds your attention are the tight close-ups, creative framing and use of lighting—particularly the "emergency lighting" that kicks in after the power goes out—as well as camera angles that lend just the right amount of tension to key scenes. (The exact same shot of Ellen on the elevator phone in the foreground while Ben restrains Hank over her shoulder will be seen again in *Cube*.) Many of those elements were down to cinematographer Rogers.

"Early on, Vincenzo was like let's just hand hold it all," he remembers. "I was a big fan of all the early American indie films from the '70s. Those guys were all just hand-holding everything because they had no time to use the dolly, so I was into that whole aesthetic."

Initially they scouted potential locations to shoot—"a whole bunch of us went on like 50 elevators," says Rogers—but soon realized that to get the angles and mobility they needed, even handheld, they "needed an extra foot or two."

Fortunately for a passionate cinematographer like Rogers, the challenge of shooting in so intimate a space was like catnip.

"I wanted to do big films," he says. "And I wanted to make small films look big. That was the whole thing with *Elevated*: How can we make things look big and dramatic with no money?"

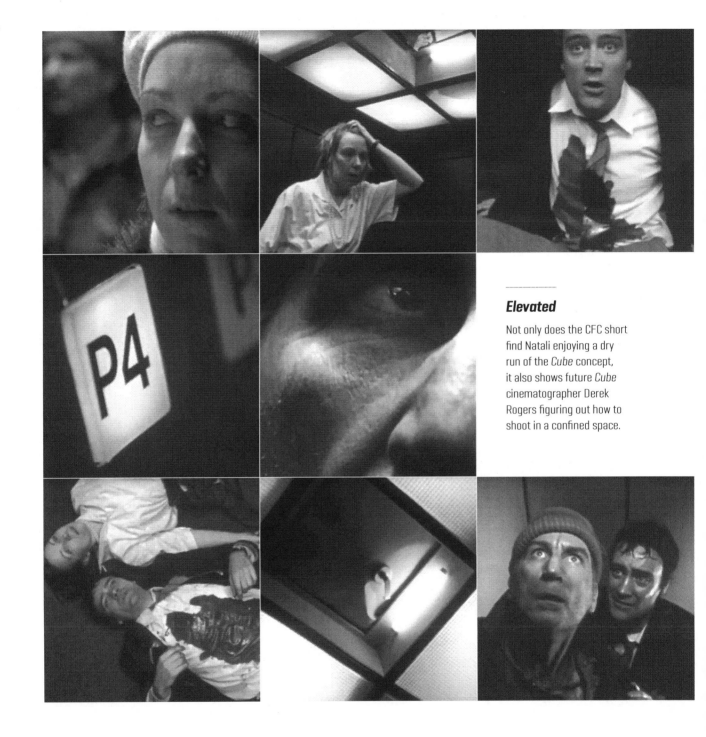

Elevated

Not only does the CFC short find Natali enjoying a dry run of the *Cube* concept, it also shows future *Cube* cinematographer Derek Rogers figuring out how to shoot in a confined space.

'I Come From a Lot of Energy'

Rogers is the polar opposite of Natali: a man of strong opinions forcefully expressed. And whereas the director had been making films from an early age with a filmmaking career firmly his goal, Rogers came to his calling slightly later in life.

Studying film at Ryerson Polytechnic University in Toronto, he met documentary maker Adrienne Amato, who asked him to shoot her short film *Forgotten Mother* in her native Zimbabwe. (Amato would later marry Rogers and, as a psychotherapist, go on to use film as a means of therapy for psychiatric patients.)

Early on his gift for lighting a scene earned him a reputation among directors for having European film sensibilities. In 1994, Rogers shot "this really wild black and white first feature"— *Stories of Chide the Wind: Soul Investigator*—written, directed, produced by and starring Hong Kong filmmaker Kal Ng.

Citing influences as varied as George Lucas, Steven Spielberg, Yasujirō Ozu, Robert Altman and Lars von Trier, Ng put everything he had into *Investigator*, which Rogers describes as being "about a Hong Kong man who comes to Canada and gets very depressed and lost in suburbia. It was an Asian take on bleak suburban Canada in the winter." Total cost: $40,000, with Amato editing the film. "It did really well on the art circuit and at the Berlin Film Festival," Rogers recalls.

"The first thing I did for Vincenzo was a short about a guy that has a huge dildo that he loves. When I read the script I said, 'This is utterly stupid.' So I went and did it and I think we just connected on the level that he had all this energy, and I come

'They were created with the purest intentions, which was to showcase the voices of the emerging director and writer. The gain for an actor in these scenarios is that you become an integral part of the process; it's a full-on collaboration. No one is getting paid to be there, so their involvement hinges on their belief in the project.'

↘ **Papavs on her roles in CFC short films** *Elevated* **and Audrey Cummings'** *Burgeon and Fade* **(2007)**

from a lot of energy."

That's an understatement. Five minutes into your first conversation with Rogers leaves you with the impression of a man living so far on the edge of his own passions, your only options are to help him realize his vision or get the hell out of the way—an SAS drill sergeant with a weakness for Kubrick.

After discovering that Natali shared the same fondness for the maker of *2001: A Space Odyssey* and *The Shining*, Rogers threw himself fully into the "dildo movie," tackling something like 75 setups for what amounted to an experimental video short.

"I think that was a kind of bonding," says Rogers. "And for me it was realizing that he has such a strong visual sense. I was just looking to do crazy shit."

'It's All About Intimacy'

Natali, too, was "looking to do crazy shit," and knew that having *Exam* star David Hewlett involved would guarantee at least one person he could count on to do what needed to be done, no questions asked. The only challenge now was how to make an elevator exciting enough to watch for 17 minutes.

"I learned how to work in a small space with a camera; how the tiniest of reactions can be enough to convey the moment," says Papavs of her work on *Elevated*. "The camera was the fourth person in that elevator."

Very quickly Rogers realized that lighting was going to be key—back to their old friend Kubrick again.

"Kubrick to me was the first commercial filmmaker who took

'Poor Derek Rogers [center] worked like a dog! Second Unit would show up as Main Unit wrapped and Derek would be soaked with sweat having hauled a 35 mm camera on his shoulder for 12 hours.'

↘ **William Phillips, second-unit supervisor**

the lighting out of the studio context," he says. "My favorite reference for that was *Clockwork Orange* [1971], the opening shot in the bar. If it had been a US studio picture, all the lights would've been hanging from outside. What does he do? He puts it on the widest lens possible, gets right in the guy's face, and then he pulls back and you see everything—floor, ceiling—and he's lit everything from within the set."

This was a good eight years before Ridley Scott's use of light tables in *Alien* (1979), he's quick to point out. "Before that **nobody lit from within the set.**"

Rogers' Kubrick fixation can also be found in the tinny Muzak-like diegetic music that plays throughout *Elevated*, evoking the ghostly party music that pervades key scenes in *The Shining*.

Without much of a setting to ogle, the key to ratcheting up the tension in *Elevated* lay in the forced intimacy that comes with mixing wide lenses with long ones.

"We talked about how to create a different look, and the only way was to build a set and pop the walls," says Rogers. "At the beginning we pulled the wall out so we could use some long lenses because they give more of a compressed telephoto effect. You start using wide lenses, you start pushing a wide lens into someone's face. And Vincenzo gets that. Terry Gilliam gets that. Even Spielberg kind of gets that. It's all about the intimacy. With Vincenzo, he's so visceral and visual, and for me I'm channeling Kubrick through him; I started to re-understand the idea of intimate space."

'Letting It All Go Insane'

Aside from anything else, *Elevated* was the first film that Natali managed to create without Andre Bijelic; an undeniable line separating the countless movies they'd made together as children from the professional film career to which the former aspired. Yet it was all those years of shooting footage in High Park with his childhood friend that had prepared him for working on a minuscule budget.

Nobody lit from within the set

Derek Rogers explains "The old Hollywood films couldn't do it because the ASAs [film speeds] were too low. But by the '70s and Kubrick, all of the sudden the film stocks were higher and you could put in lamp [lighting]. You watch *The Shining*, my favorite film of all time, and all the chandeliers are just photo floods."

"*Elevated* was all about restraint," says Rogers. "In Canada we come from that whole documentary thing and that no-money thing. I'm a big fan of all of Cronenberg's early Montreal films—like *Rabid* [1977] and *Scanners* [1981]—which were made for nothing. You learn to work in the limitations, and that's what Vincenzo is all about. I think it's about sticking him in a box and letting it all go insane."

However, if anyone got a crash course in filmmaking, it was Rogers himself. Relatively seasoned as he was before he shot Frame One on *Elevated*, the experience of working hand-held on that tiny set fundamentally changed the way he looked at the intimacy of space. Being forced to instinctively dream up the new angles and lighting needed to hold an audience's attention in one setting would stand him in good stead for years to come.

"It evolved my career in how I shoot everything, and I shoot docs, dramas, it doesn't matter what I shoot. I just look at it from that point of view of how am I going to make that work? I never say 'no' to a director, so if they put me in a room, it forces me to come up with crazy shit."

Completed in 1996, *Elevated* was released the following year and received a Genie Award nomination (for Best Live Action Short), and won David Hewlett the Golden Sheaf Award for Best Performance at the 1997 Yorkton Short Film & Video Festival. At the age of 28, the actor had already honed his now-trademark quirky intensity. As Papavs recalls, his presence was just as vital off camera as on.

'I was on a movie and I was trying to convince the art dept. to do a bar with the 'Kubrick glow,' and it became such a big thing because they wanted to build this fancy thing and the budget came back at $20,000. In the end I just got a grip, grabbed some black card and did this really fast. You've gotta have this mother of invention thing going on, and I think that's what *Cube* was.'

↘ **Rogers**

'you learn to work in the limitations, and that's what vincenzo is all about. i think it's all about sticking him in a box and letting it all go insane.'

↘ **Rogers**

"Although I had had years of theater experience behind me, this was one of my first forays into acting for camera. It was a little scary for me—this was all such a new medium and I had to adjust my approach to the work. In theater you often have three weeks of rehearsal before you are in front of an audience. With film you are in front of an audience from the first moment the director yells 'Action!'

"But being with David was comforting because he had many more hours under his belt, and by being able to watch him I was able to negotiate my way through the days of shooting. He is a wildly talented guy, very inspired and full of confidence. His friendship with Vincenzo was also wonderful to witness because they had a shorthand that was highly entertaining. They made each other laugh at every turn, which created a very buoyant and friendly set—I loved watching it all. There were a lot of laughs, especially when they would talk about their school days."

Three years later, *Elevated* would take 3rd Place in the Best Short Film category at the hugely influential Fantasia Film Festival. By then, of course, *Cube* would already be capturing awards in Spain, Korea, Brussels, France...and Canada.

Still, for the people who worked on it, *Elevated* was its own career highlight—a testament to the tension and manipulation of space that can be accomplished with a handful of people and very little money.

"My strongest memory was watching Vincenzo make quick decisions," says Papavs, who auditioned for the role of Ellen in response to an open call to Toronto agents. "At one point they were behind schedule and he went off by himself for a few minutes to figure out what setups he could cut—what he could sacrifice—without compromising the story. He was razor-sharp focused, and without a hint of stress was able to make some very tough decisions. There was so much riding on this short film for him, but he handled it with such professionalism and grace. I learned a lot watching that moment."

Confides Rogers, "I think I've shot 60 short dramas. At that time I had done like 12, and some have done pretty well and won some little awards and all that, but that one really stands out for me. It even plays on Air Canada every once in a while."

It turns out that the airline began its "enRoute" in-flight "film festivals" in 2008. "I think two years ago I looked down the aisle and saw two people who had it on—it was really exciting," he says. "And of course, it's a precursor to *Cube*..."

DON'T LOOK FOR
A REASON.

842 646 943

94 576 438

5 672 84 782 543

581 768 291 57

545 581 756 29

212 816 753

LOOK FOR
A WAY OUT.

CUBE

9: 'this is like reservoir dogs'

WITH THE COMPLETION of *Elevated*, something had changed. Natali felt it. Bijelic felt it. More importantly for the fate of *Cube*, Colin Brunton felt it, too.

"At that point I was getting the feeling that *Cube* would never be made," Natali admits. "And ironically *Elevated* was the thing that made Colin realize what *Cube* could be."

Some members of the production team recall Brunton being less gung ho about making *Cube*. In view of the maelstrom of personality clashes that was to come, this "us vs. them" attitude was only to be expected. As the man with his finger on the CFC checkbook, Brunton was bound to become the focus of that tension. "I guess it's all a matter of perception," he says now, "but I *loved* the project!"

Lifeboat

Now a graduate of the Canadian Film Centre, Natali once again set to work pitching *Cube* for The Feature Film Project.

Says Brunton, "The script was great. The story was original. And it could be done on the meager budget we had. I had com-

Opposite: The cover for the *Cube* press book.

Lifeboat

It's pretty surprising just how closely *Cube* tracks with this minor classic, written by John Steinbeck from an idea by Alfred Hitchcock. After an allied ship and a German U-boat sink each other, several British and American soldiers and civilians (and the occasional German) cling to life in the titular craft. While they get along at first, differences major and minor soon tear the group apart.

plete faith in Vincenzo as a filmmaker. *Elevated* helped convince the people *I* had to convince that he could pull it off."

Yet there was still a major challenge that threatened to queer the deal.

"Two things that don't go together very often—especially at that time—were independent film and visual effects," says Natali. "Now that's changed because you can do extraordinary things on your own little PC at home, but that was not the case then. Digital effects were much more costly than physical ones at that time. So [Brunton] had every reason to be a little bit suspicious about it.

"But I also remember him saying 'This is like *Reservoir Dogs*,' it's the perfect model for an independent film because it's so contained. But invariably with *Cube* there was always this dichotomy between having these very limited elements on one hand, and on the other hand having these very extravagant, ambitious visual effects."

From the very beginning, Natali's cinematic reference for *Cube* wasn't another sci-fi flick but Alfred Hitchcock's 1944 classic **Lifeboat,** starring Tallulah Bankhead and William Bendix.

"Part of the reason simply was because it's a very cinematic movie in the most confined space imaginable," he says. "But it was also impressive to me because I found the characters so engaging. Through the course of the film you discovered secrets about each of them; each character reveals themself to be something you didn't initially expect them to be. I thought that was really wonderful and unusual, too, because most movies are just busy getting people from Point A to Point B—you don't really get that much time with them, that degree of intimacy."

'A Runaway Train'

There was one very big factor working in *Cube*'s favor: The Feature Film Project's funding schedule.

"The way they were structured was they would make three movies in one cycle, and they had made two of the movies and they didn't know what to do for the third one. I think we were sort of their best and only option," says the director.

"I just don't think that Colin in particular either liked the script or really understood it that much," Bijelic adds. "I remember there was one meeting where going out of it I felt really bad. It felt like things were not going to turn out well. I think he said something like, 'You should be able to take this whole cube thing out of it,' so it'll be a bunch of people sitting in a room talking, like Sartre or something. To me that was like taking the shark out of *Jaws*." Brunton doesn't recall suggesting this.

Natali admits, "It took a little bit of effort on our part to make him see the light. But once he did, he was 100% behind the project."

Says Bijelic, "In the end I think he became more enthusiastic about it as it went along. I think it was Francis Coppola who said something like 'A movie becomes a runaway train. It takes forever to get going, but once it's in motion it's a hard thing to stop.'"

'*Cube* was a kind of Chinese puzzle box, really—it had this appearance of being oh so simple. It's just one set and six actors—what could possibly go wrong?'
↘ **Natali**

89

CUBE
OCT. '94

McNEIL

HOLLOWAY
'CUBE' NOV. '94

10: the *cube* script evolves

THERE IS SOMETHING almost supernatural in the complete transformation of Natali's first solo *Cube* script into the one Andre Bijelic wrote six months later. Gone are the self-conscious quips and life-sustaining moss. What we have instead, from the very first sentence of the second draft, is essentially what we get on screen.

Sure, the characters are slightly different; they're all men, for a start. Yet the women are certainly here in spirit. Brainy puzzle solver Leaven is Lang, a male former cryptographer for the government's "bureau of investigation." Holloway is Ryker (occasionally spelled "Riker" in future scripts), both being doctors and willing to work with the others to get through their shared nightmare.

Cut to the Chase

After the tone, the greatest change in this script is the complete jettisoning of any and all scenes outside the cube. In the process, we lose the unnecessary character development of the protagonist. No marital troubles, no guilt feelings, just bam—a sudden belly flop into hell.

Opposite: An early *Cube* uniform design by Natali. Note the unused character name, McNeil, on the lapel.

↘ *For additional content see the* Cube Archive, *pp. 230-345*

As before, we begin with our Alderson character, aka the first "sacrifice." This time out his name is Morris, and he quite literally falls into the cube from an upper level. Emerging naked and wet from an artificial cocoon (a detail that would've been right at home in Natali's inaugural draft), the poor devil slips into a prison-style uniform and proceeds to wander through the maze until ultimately being cubed by the wire mesh trap—cue title.

Next we find our "Worth" character, "Brooks," delivered into the cube under similar circumstances. After he's wounded by a brush with the *Hellraiser* chains (carried over from the first script,) we realize we're not in for another hour and a half of witticisms and oddities—this time we're solidly in thriller territory.

Prisoners in Cell Block C

The unfortunates who find themselves in this cube aren't accountants as in the earlier script, but all have had a brush with the Powers That Be on the outside. This leads Cox, the Rennes-like escape artist Brooks encounters early on, to muse, "What the hell is this place? It certainly isn't like any prison I've seen before." To which Brooks replies, "Maybe it's an execution."

He persuades Cox to join forces with him by informing him rather menacingly that he was a "tactics specialist in the army," and admits that the last thing he recalls is being sentenced to death and given a needle that "was supposed to be lethal. I guess they have more interesting plans in store for me."

Observes Cox, "Well now that you're legally dead, I suppose they can do whatever they want to you."

Blythe: Why would anyone go to the trouble of constructing this if there was a way out?

↘ **From p. 34 of Natali's second solo script (7/21/94)**

Other characters they meet include:

Ellis: An unconscious man who appears to be in his 60s. Upon awaking, he admits that he helped design the cube. (Compare to Worth's confession in the final film.)

Ryker: A former doctor. (Like Holloway.)

Drake: A hit man. (Quentin in the film.)

Blythe: An apathetic type who nevertheless has a keen analytical mind when pushed to use it.

Lang: A cryptographer for the "Bureau of Investigation." (Leaven, essentially.)

Egan: An idiot savant who's a whiz with numbers. (Kazan on screen.)

A Near Thing

In many ways this version of events is what we ultimately get in the shooting script.

Bijelic's influence can be felt most in the way he steers the whole concept away from fantasy toward a grittier reality. The roaring of the minotaur from Natali's first attempt becomes the groaning of the structure itself that we come to discover is actually the moving of rooms inside the cube. The ability to graze on edible moss is replaced with the grim reality of trying to escape this deathtrap before the prisoners die of thirst or starvation. (The famous "button trick" from the movie fails to make an appearance, however.)

Some characters in this version will be consolidated later on. Ellis and Egan, for example, both function as a Kazan-like

— CHILLION PRISON - SWITZERLAND
— BRIDWELL — WORKHOUSE (1557 LONDON

Rennes - France   PENN
Aubum - U.S.   — AUBURN — NEW YORK 1868
                                 Prisons
Simbirsk - RUS.   — JOLIET
Pskov - RUS.   PENITENTIARY — ILLINOIS
                                         1900
Tobolsk - RUS   — CLINTON PRISON — NEW YORK
PJM - RUS.   — RIKERS
Wilno - RUS.   ISLAND — NEW YORK
Joliet - U.S.   — LEAVENWORTH
Oakalla - Can.   — KULANI PRISON — HAWAII
Butner - U.S.   — DARTMOOR — PORTLAND
                                         ENGLAND
Folsom —   .848

written by   — BETHLEM
Vincenzo Natali ASYLUM
          &
Andre Bijelic

          — FOLSOM PRISON

          — "CLINK" PRISON SOUTH-
                 WARK
                 LONDON
                 (12TH century
                 — 1780)

          — BRIXTON PRISON (1821)

Quentin
Riker
Worth
~~Leaven~~
~~Butner~~

CUBE

Morris =
Arnold =
Ford =
Ellis =
Egan =

With this first script revision we already see Natali casting about for prison names to be used for the names of *Cube's* characters.

First Revision
July 23, 1994

burden to the others, eventually proving their worth at the end as Kazan does.

In other cases, character backgrounds are tweaked ever so slightly to avoid pat explanations for the violence to come. In this script, Drake is a hit man, his homicidal rage in the cube sparked by the discovery that Lang's work in the outside world led to Drake being sentenced to die in the cube. In the film, the Drake character, Quentin, is a bullying cop who seems to snap from the pressure of their situation alone.

But let's return to Ellis, whose elimination from the film is a welcome one, creatively speaking. In this version he is a veritable whirlwind of exposition, revealing everything from the fact that the cube is made up of smaller cubes 20 rooms across and 20 stories high, to the fact that the whole structure has an outer shell. The only thing he doesn't know is how to avoid the traps, owing to a convenient bump on the noggin received when he was dumped into the device.

By and large the various mathematical discoveries the group makes are already in evidence here, with notes like this one appearing a few times in this script:

*THIS SECTION WILL BE INSERTED AFTER DAVID HAS GIVEN US ALL THE NECESSARY INFORMATION.

(The David in question is mathematical consultant Dr. David W. Pravica whom we'll meet in Chapter 12.)

Though we don't learn very much about the sadists behind this whole bizarre experiment (if experiment it is), Ellis does reveal that its purpose is "to test endurance, resourcefulness and so on. We're being monitored all the time. The purpose is to see if we can solve the puzzle." And in keeping with the finest traditions of the building of secret lairs, he also informs us that everyone else who worked on its construction disappeared, presumably sacrificed to the cube as well.

Finally, the third act plays out pretty much the way we get it on screen, with one startling exception. Moments after admonishing Blythe to stay positive, Brooks—presumably our David Hewlett "Worth" audience-identification character—is promptly decapitated by the next room he enters.

The rest is all here: the sound-activated spikes, Ryker's (Holloway's) valiant attempt to reach the cube's outer shell by swinging out on the end of a shirt rope, and Drake purposefully letting go of the unfortunate's hand. Here, too, we get the discovery that they've been traveling in circles (or have they?), Lang providing the calculations necessary to avoid traps, and a final melee that leaves the Kazan-like character the only one left alive, perched on the threshold of....what?

If you are a die-hard *Cube* fan, the only reaction you can have after reading this script is the shouting of "You're *so* close!" Fortunately for Bijelic and Natali, it was close enough for the Canadian Film Centre.

Early on we see the
explanation of the
cube puzzle, right
down to the moving
rooms.

                         LANG
          But how do you explain Cox. He didn't just
          stroll in here.

Blythe's face lights up.

                         BLYTHE
          Maybe he did!

                         DRAKE
          You've gone completely loony, Blythe.

                         BLYTHE
          That's it! We didn't come to him, he came to
          us!

                         LANG
          What are you talking about?

                         BLYTHE
          What if the rooms are moving. What if they
          were shifting all this time, so that the
          configuration of the rooms was always
          changing. That would explain why Cox is here
          now, when he should be way behind us.

                         LANG
          That would also explain why the formula
          stopped working. When the rooms were static it
          worked, but once they started moving it
          failed. THAT is the missing variable.

                         BLYTHE
          And that's why the room shook when we nearly
          dropped Ryker. That's what those strange
          rumbling sounds are. They're rooms shifting!

                         LANG
          That's what the cube is; A big moving puzzle,
          and each room is a piece!

Lang jumps to his feet. He rushes over to the room's engraved
numbers. The others crowd around him.

                         LANG
          I've got it! I know what these other numbers
          are now! They are all the permutations of this
          room!

                         DRAKE
          What? Permutations?

11: graeme manson, catalyst

FINALLY IN THE summer of 1996 the Canadian Film Centre approved *Cube* for takeoff, though the board still wasn't happy with what Natali and Bijelic had put down on paper so far.

"Basically they said we like this script a lot but we think the characters could be fleshed out. We want you to bring on another writer," the director recalls.

Much of the problem stemmed from having to figure out just who the people trapped in the cube were supposed to be. In his earliest drafts, Natali had seen them as accountants inexplicably banished to this nightmare world—one of those lunges into the absurd that felt like there could be some profound meaning in there somewhere. But once he and Bijelic began to tackle the script together, they quickly realized just how limiting absurdity could be on screen.

In the script that ultimately won CFC approval, the individuals inside the cube were actually criminals banished there for their crimes, "so it was very much a purgatory," Natali says. "They had all done bad things in their lives and were fighting their way through the darkness to the light. The problem I had

Opposite: Graeme Manson joined the *Cube* script-revising process about the time the CFC became involved.

with the criminals was that invariably it seemed like we had to explain what their crime was—I didn't want to be too specific about what kind of society we were in. I also had a harder time relating to them."

The writer they ended up bringing on to help them was someone Natali knew and liked from the Centre: Graeme Manson. Best known today as the writer and co-creator (with *Ginger Snaps* director John Fawcett) of the Canadian sci-fi series *Orphan Black*, Manson at the time was just starting out in the business. Very quickly he began to give the *Cube* characters unique personalities.

"I think if I had to break it down to its most simplistic form (and it's not really fair because it wasn't this simple), I came up with the concept and wrote a script that didn't work," Natali explains. "Andre came in and he found a way to make that concept work as a movie, but the characters were somewhat limited. I think it was Graeme who really made the group dynamic between the characters fully realized and fleshed out. And we were all there. There was never a point in the process, except the very beginning where I wrote that first draft, where it was just one writer in a room."

Once Manson was on board, the three began deconstructing the story to discover together the one element that would keep an audience glued to their seats for an entire feature film—the characters. It was a process that quite nearly destroyed *Cube*.

'To write a perfect script is just about the hardest thing anybody can do. I think that's evidenced by the fact that there aren't a lot of movies out there that are that well written.'
↘ **Natali**

INTRO KAZAN
TOO LATE (?)

- BRING WORTH IN
   EARLIER TOO (?)

- WORK ON
   KAZAN'S DIAL.

- URINE PAN
   OFF?

At the third script revision, Bijelic and Natali were still considering the inclusion of a "good explanation for maze (something ironic)."

MAKE IT VERY
CLEAR THAT
IF THE-I
ESCAPE THEY
WILL
SURVIVE.

<u>CUBE</u>

screenplay by

Andre Bijelic & Vincenzo Natal

101

GOOD
EXPLINATION
FOR MAZE
(SOMETHING
    IRONIC)

SPFX

MAKE·UP FX

Third Revision
November 6, 1994

STUNTS

Canned Films
548 Roxton Road
Toronto, Ontario
M6G 3R4
(416) 538-8560

'A Really Scary, Frustrating Process'

By the time Manson became involved, Natali had managed to scrape up enough money to leave the group house at 548 Roxton Road, thanks in part to his first bit of paid television work on a Nickelodeon sci-fi/comedy series called *Space Cases*. His new digs...a peanut factory.

"It was actually a really nice place," he says. "It had a shared bathroom, but I had my own apartment for the first time in my life."

It was at the peanut factory that he, Bijelic and Manson held their script meetings, and where Natali set to work on storyboarding the action of *Cube*. Though they were still in the process of hashing out who the characters were, the director already had a good sense of what the film would look like, and of the bloody carnage the cube's soon-to-be-infamous traps would leave in their wake.

Concentrating on the kills was certainly much easier (and more gratifying) than going over who the victims were yet again with the other two members of the triumvirate. Natali had been mulling over the *Cube* story on and off for six years now—long enough to realize that without a massive special effects budget, the film's success was contingent on engaging, believable characters doing engaging, believable things.

Now that the project had been green lit, they'd also picked up a story editor, Hugh Graham, "who was kind of like the experienced guy in the room," the director says. "He came in and, in a very gentle way, acted as a mentor over the whole process."

Gradually, Manson helped transform the victims into characters boasting unique personalities, mannerisms and motivations, even if the last would only later become apparent to the audience. It was through this writing process that Natali and Bijelic finally abandoned the idea of their being criminals in favor of something a great deal more interesting.

"If they're people who've been thrown in the cube for no cause that we can discern, that was more compelling," Natali says. "As a filmmaker, I personally could relate to those characters better."

This was exactly the kind of development he welcomed, but it came at a price. To truly get to the heart of the story, the three of them had to thoroughly take it apart and rebuild it into something stronger and more easily filmed. Now that the Centre had cleared *Cube* for takeoff, the clock was ticking.

"The movie went into production super fast—like way too fast," Natali says now. "We were rewriting with Graeme as I was prepping. I seem to recall we had six weeks from the moment the Film Centre said 'OK'—six weeks before we had to shoot. It was this mad scramble to rewrite the script and design the sets and prep everything at the same time. That's part of the reason why it was such a stressful experience. I almost backed away from it.

"I remember there was a point where I thought this isn't good enough, I should say no to this. It was Andre who said, 'No, you've got to do it, you may never get this chance again.' And so I stuck it out and we made it. But it was scary because

6

Number of weeks the team had to rewrite the script, design the sets and prep everything before shooting *Cube*.

20

Number of days Natali had to shoot it.

'My agent told me they wanted to see me. I was shooting *We the Jury* across town and it was eating up all my summer and I missed my kids. Twice I had to schlep to the Canadian Film Centre to read for Vincenzo. [That place is a real schlep.] I was a bit cockier and more confident than usual because I had work and I figured they were lucky to get me all the way out there. I wasn't desperate for it—so I probably read well.'

↘ **Guadagni**

often when you rewrite a script, you have to take a step back before you take a step forward. So the initial rewrite, it felt like the script was getting worse. Not that Graeme wasn't doing a good job, but you had to deconstruct certain things. It lost some of what was in those fine-tuned drafts that Andre and I did. Eventually we got it back but it was a really scary, frustrating process because I didn't know for sure if this was the right way to do it."

There was another problem staring them in the face. The schedule gave them just 20 days to shoot everything in the "multi-roomed" cube...that hadn't even been built yet. If they'd had more experience shooting features rather than tons of shorts, they might've jacked it all in then and there.

"We committed to do this thing," says Natali, "but no one really had a plan that worked."

natali 'mailed me the script and said we just wrote this... for you and dave; you're going to win a genie award because you're playing autistic...'

⬊ Andrew Miller (Kazan)

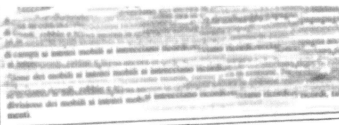

IL RESTO DEL CARLINO 16/11/2000

Imprigionati in quel Cubo

Il cubo di Rubik. Un'ingegnosa applicazione della matematica. Ruotare le facce del solido, formato da cubi più piccoli, colorati e semoventi, per ottenere la stessa tinta su ogni superficie. Una piacevole sfida all'intelletto umano? Se si è fuori. E se ci si trova al suo interno? Ce lo racconta **Vincenzo Natali** con il suo film **Cube** (Canada, 1997).

La pellicola è stata proiettata alcune sere fa in via Mascarella 44 nell'ambito della Rassegna **Matematica e Cinema** organizzata dal Dipartimento di Matematica dell'Università degli Studi di Bologna. Sala Mascarella gremita di persone, soprattutto giovani, col fiato sospeso. E c'era una buona ragione: il film.

Claustrofobico, angosciante e vertiginoso, "Cube" narra le vicende di sei persone rinchiuse, senza ragioni plausibili, in un enorme labirinto, una specie di cubo di Rubik dagli scomparti semoventi, disseminato di trappole micidiali. Alla ricerca di un'ipotetica via d'uscita, i prigionieri si spostano da una stanza

Continua il ciclo di film su cinema e matematica

all'altra capendo in breve che la chiave della loro salvezza è la giusta interpretazione matematica della costruzione metallica. Dall'iniziale collaborazione, si passa, con lo svolgersi del film, ai conflitti e persino alla pazzia. Incidenti e follia sfoltiscono il gruppo a poco a poco.

Soltanto uno riuscirà ad uscirne vivo.

"Vincenzo – ha chiarito dopo la proiezione **David Pravica (nella foto)**, consulente matematico del film – voleva girare una pellicola interamente in un ambiente chiuso. Era inoltre suo interesse ricostruire una sorta di microcosmo sociale e mostrare le interazioni tra personalità molto diverse le une dalle altre."

Alla domanda che non poteva mancare: "Perché quelle persone sono nel Cubo?", Pravica ha risposto: "E' un mistero. Natali non lo ha mai detto neppure a me."

Il prossimo appuntamento è fissato per stasera con la proiezione del film «Morte di un matematico napoletano» di **Mario Martone** alla quale seguirà un dibattito con **Carlo Sbordone**, presidente dell'Unione Matematica Italiana. I principali interpreti di questo film sono **Carlo Cecchi, Anna Bonaiuto, Renato Carpentieri, Antonio Neiwiller** e **Toni Servillo**

Camilla Sandri

Sulla tastiera di Battel

Entra nel vivo la sedicesima edizione dei Concerti del Circolo della Musica (direzione artistica: **Sandro Baldi**). Domani alle ore 21, presso la Maison Française de Bologne di via De Marchi, 4 si esibirà il pianista **Giovanni Umberto Battel**. In programma la musica pianistica del primo Novecento: stili popolari americani e russi nel repertorio colto. Il programma prevede anche l'esecuzione di uno dei pezzi più difficili della letteratura pianistica: i Trois mouvements de Pétrouchka di Stravinskij

12: the man behind the math

THOUGH *CUBE* HAD become an all consuming passion for Natali and Bijelic, they still maintained a healthy social life. The former was dating Tamara Pravica at the time. "A bunch of us used to go out to dinner and talk about school and science and movies," remembers her brother, David. "Somewhat later my sister told me that Vincenzo was having problems with the ending of his movie. Supposedly she came up with the idea that [Kazan] should be the only one to survive the cube. I thought that was a great suggestion."

But this was far from the only contribution the Pravica family would make to the film.

Born in Toronto and raised just beyond the Greater Toronto Area in the village of Kleinburg, David Pravica found himself drawn to the subject of nuclear power in the 1970s, seeing it as a means to wean society off of its dependence on foreign oil. "Nuclear power plants offered the hope of a future world based solely on electric power—this drew me into physics," he explains. "But after some time I found that it was the *mathematics* of science that I enjoyed most. Besides, nuclear energy was getting a bad rap."

Opposite: *Cube* math mastermind David Pravica (pictured) was interviewed by media from as far away as Italy about his work on the film.

'I remember [Natali] visiting my sister one winter, and when I entered the living room I shrieked because there was a rubber hand lying on one of the Christmas boxes.'

↘ **David Pravica**

At the time the *Cube* script was being revised, Pravica was studying and teaching mathematics at the University of Windsor.

"The mechanism that Andre was looking for when the film was first discussed had to somehow use prime numbers," he remembers. "This was because he had taken a course in mathematics where primes were discussed. However, he wanted a way to introduce a surprise into the story that the characters did not, or could not, expect. I knew that the point of the various sets of numbers was to provide a clue to the plot.

"It took me a while, but I finally decided to use one of the biggest surprises in number theory, which is that the power-of-primes in a large number can be an important feature of that number. These features are extracted using the Von Mangoldt function. Thus I tried to build that in as the surprise."

Explaining Math to a Mainstream Audience

Perhaps the most genius-in-hindsight aspect of *Cube*'s math is that the numbers the prisoners discover are in fact coordinates of a given room's place inside the vast mechanism, as well as an indication of its preprogrammed movement through it.

"This was a tall order," Pravica admits, "and it turned out to be a trickier problem than initially imagined. I used some concepts from group theory, which is often used in models of finite-step phenomena that cycle back to a starting point.

"Keep in mind that all the realizations had to happen, initially, so that the math student [Leaven] could figure it out in the simple, initial cubes, but for the cubes near the end, only a computer

Nosferatu, the Mouse and Me

'I remember one poster [among many] at Vincenzo's place for the 1979 movie *Nosferatu*," says Pravica. "I remembered the movie because I saw it one night in 1985, in my small, rat-infested dorm room in Toronto while working all night on my last math assignment of the spring semester. [The movie was a morbid distraction to a challenging set of problems in fluid dynamics.] Every so often a cute mouse would peek over the edge of my cot, which distracted me from both the movie and the math. However, I got terribly ill soon after and it took me that whole summer at my parents' house to recover. I think I had the plague! Since surviving that ordeal, I try to be positive and joyful in life, but Vincenzo always had kind of a morbid sense of humor.'

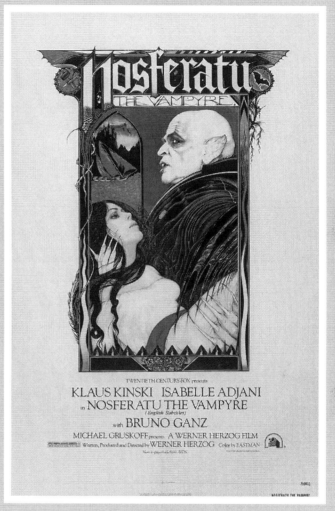

'I suck at math. Terrible at math. Vincenzo and I, I think, were probably in the same math class together. I just goofed around most of the time. People would stop sitting next to me as we approached exams. They would sort of move away from my seat at the back of the classroom because they knew I was never actually going to get any of the work done.'

↘ **Hewlett**

could figure it out or, of course, a savant [Kazan]. One possible exaggeration was that the numbers are not too big to figure out if you know about Euler functions like a math student should. I tried to put some of that in there, too."

After several discussions with Pravica, Natali and Bijelic began sending him parts of the script containing notes asking him to fill in the blanks, both in terms of numbers and mathematical explanations.

"My concern was with the flow of the plot, while avoiding inconsistencies," says Pravica. "At some point near the end of the refinements, there were some changes that I hated having to make because I thought of them as disruptive to what we had already discussed. However, the authors were very patient with me."

To organize his thoughts, he even wrote a small computer program, "but due to time constraints, I had to abandon a full working model. If we had Excel back then," he muses, "that may have helped."

As gratifying as it was for Pravica to see his area of expertise given the big screen treatment, he naturally would've liked to have gone into the numbers further still. That said, he concedes there's really only so much mathematics to which you can subject a mainstream audience.

"The calculations that [Leaven] was doing could have come out clearer, and I would have liked to have seen that. But not all people appreciate the beauty of mathematical discovery, so I have to respect the aesthetic choices of the producers."

And as with any film, there are always people who seem to de-

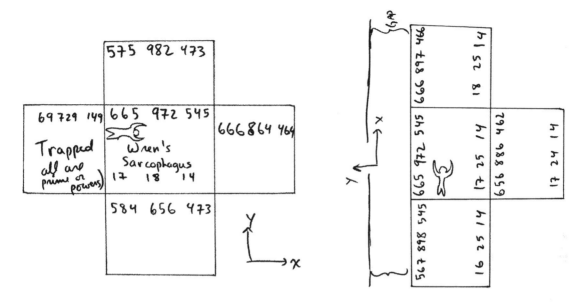

rive a perverse satisfaction from pointing out errors and inconsistencies, which can often be explained by the hectic moviemaking process itself. Burkard Polster and Marty Ross' 2012 book *Math Goes to the Movies* offers up some typical examples.

Looking at Chapter 6 of that book Pravica explains, "I see here that it says that '...some inconsistencies were introduced during the shooting and editing.' What I remember as the most glaring issue was that [Leaven] spoke one number but the number displayed was different. It's just one of those things that happens when there's time pressure.

"Another issue was when I wanted to make a change in one of the numbers that was displayed. I was told (by Andre, I think) that the number plates were rather expensive to make and they had

Cube math: David Pravica finally published a full explanation of the mathematics of *Cube* in the article *"Cube:* The Math Paper," co-written with Heather Ries and published in the book *Mathematics, Art, Technology and Cinema* in 2003.

Pravica has the final word on Cube's math during the scripting stage.

↘ For additional content see the Cube Archive, pp. 230-345

FINAL COMMENTS

① Factorization $\# = P_1^{n_1} P_2^{n_2} \cdots P_\alpha^{n_\kappa}$ (fatteri per numeri primi)

$\alpha = \omega(\#)$, $n_1 + n_2 + \cdots n_\alpha = \Omega(\#)$

$P_i \rightarrow$ prime numbers (numeri primi)

If $\#$ ends in $0, 2, 4, 6, 8 \rightarrow 2$ is a prime factor.

If $\#$ ends in $0, 5 \rightarrow 5$ is a prime factor.

If sum of digits in $\#$ is $3, 6, 9 \rightarrow 3$ is a prime factor.

i.e. $651 \rightarrow 6+5+1 = 12 \rightarrow 1+2 = 3$ ✓

$$3\overline{\smash{)}651} \quad \substack{217}$$

If sum/difference of digits is 0, then divisible by 11,

$13310 \rightarrow 1-3+3-1+0 = 0$ ✓

② fattore, fattoriale, prime fattors, prime fatteriale

③ My Social Insurance Number from CANADA was used in the film

④ Look for golden plate with mathematics writing.

⑤ Some other slight problems with the numbers due to poor communication.

⑥ music → oppressive film.

Maybe "Laudate Dominum" from

W.A. Mozart's

"Vesperae Solennes de Confessore"

would have been good as part of the sleeping sequence, possibly a part of a combined dream.

already all been made. After I heard that I stopped even thinking about making any major changes and only focused on weeding out any inconsistencies. Even that turned out to be difficult."

By this time the mathematician had also moved to North Carolina for work while the film team remained in Toronto.

"When I talked on the phone with the authors they wanted to send me material for the script, so I told them my address," he says. "Unfortunately, they heard the address wrong. They mailed it to 'Queenwood Drive' when it should have been 'Greenwood Drive.' That mix-up cost a couple of weeks. Other little delays added up until there was a crunch at their end. Ultimately they got the project done and I really admire them for having completed what they set out to do."

Finally, like many involved in *Cube*'s creation, Pravica was amazed to see just how deeply the film ultimately resonated with audiences around the world.

"I thought that the script was for a film school project," he says. "Thus I was just a student helping out a couple of other students. Even when I was told that their script had been chosen as one of the ones that would be made, I thought that it would be filmed on Super 8 or videotape—you know, a typical Canuck production. But when I got the first video cassette of the film with all the acting done and some outlines of the animation, I started to get a sense that it was going to be a much more professional product. Even then I never imagined that it would get the exposure and interest that it did."

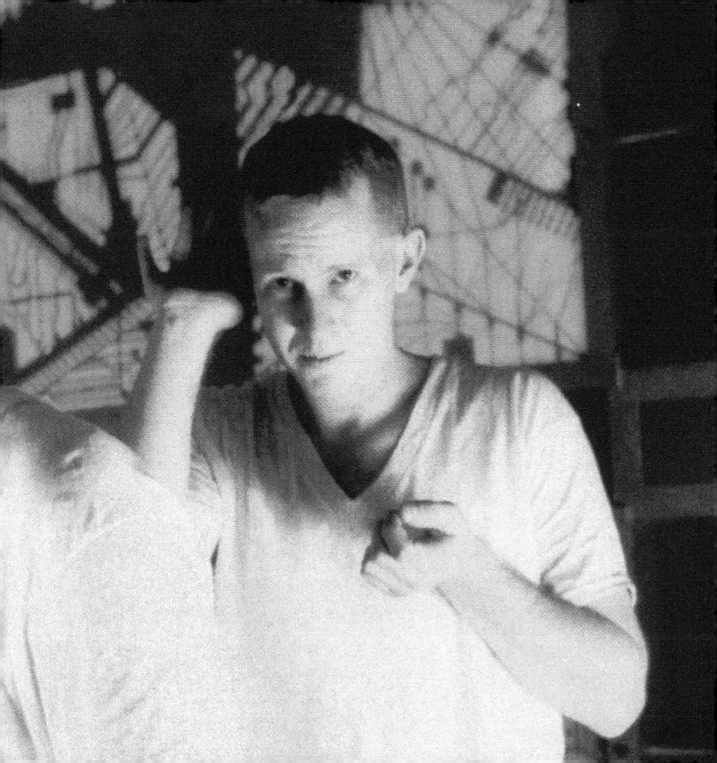

13: autism as cinematic superpower

WITH *CUBE*'S MATH nailed down, there was now only one more plot point in need of research.

"Vincenzo and Andre knew the character [of Kazan] was autistic, but didn't really know what autistic meant," says Andrew Miller. "So they just said to me, 'Look, we're busy—can you just figure this out? We know he has some sort of handicap and we think it's autism and we've seen *Rain Man* but just...do it.'

"I didn't know anything about autism," he says, and he wasn't confident enough as an actor to wing it. (Also it should be noted that this was 1996, shortly before the web came into its own.) "I'm not a good enough actor for that. I needed to really get a sense of it to craft my performance—I couldn't really make it up. Vincenzo knows everything about everything, but because he didn't know much about this, there was really no one to guide me and I was petrified of the movie coming out and misrepresenting autism in any way. It just seemed like I would be the biggest asshole in the world if I was half-assing it, which is my tendency. It felt like I needed to really be on top of it because after shooting, I knew there would be responsibility."

Andrew Miller: "Luckily for me, the Kazan character didn't have the same growth that the other characters did, so I got off a little bit easier than they did."

ECU K.
SLOW ZOOM OUT

A.

STICKS · ZOOM

B.

C.

HOLD

D.

Kazan proves himself a
potentially deadly liability
in these scene sketches by
Natali.

Living in LA at the time, Miller began his research there.

"There are a bunch of autistic groups in LA that are amazingly generous with actors. (I think people call them up 10 times a week for guest spots and movies.) I ended up with the celebrity autistic group, because Dustin Hoffman had been there and Elisabeth Shue, I think, had been there—it was like a revolving door. I was the loser—you're not famous remotely—so they were a little disappointed in me. But they were really great and I hung out with them for a long time.

"They couldn't have been more welcoming but they were asking about the project because everybody was very savvy. I was like, 'Well, it's an independent film.' 'OK, is it Steven Soderbergh?' 'No, it's this guy Vincenzo, it's in Canada.' It sounded like I was scamming them, so that made me feel bad.

"So we're sitting in a big group the first day I was there and there were people exhibiting clear signs of autism and there were people who weren't, and I thought the others were their guardians and parents or brothers and sisters. I believed that for days. Only later did somebody tell me that everybody was autistic, including the people who were running it, and I was the only guy who wasn't. That was pretty intimidating."

Arriving in Toronto just before shooting commenced on *Cube*, Miller paid several visits to a halfway house for "fairly high functioning" autistic people, he remembers. "They would take them to work at restaurants before they opened, sorting and cleaning things up, and those guys were amazing."

It was around this time that the actor met a kid in the subway that would have a great impact on his portrayal of Kazan. "I kind of based a lot of Kazan on him, some of his movements. He was the guy who said to me early on that 'When *you* sit in the cafeteria and you're eating, you just eat and you may recognize that things are going on around you, but you're concentrating on eating and the conversation you're having. When I sit in a cafeteria, all I can hear are the clanging of the silverware and the insanely bright lights and it feels like people screaming in my ear all around me, and that's the problem.' That was him explaining autism to me as best I could understand it, and that was a huge thing for me in terms of trying to figure out who Kazan was."

Autism in *Cube*

Even at the time of this writing in 2018, it's extraordinarily difficult to discuss autism in terms of a plot device without fear of straying into gross insensitivity. While virtually any other disability is up for grabs, cinematically speaking, with little uproar, autism still sets society's teeth on edge. This is likely because it strikes us in the two places where we are most vulnerable: it afflicts the very young and it attacks the center of who we are as individuals—our minds. As a result, those who've been somehow affected by the disorder are particularly sensitive to it being depicted as some kind of super power—it feels both cheap and woefully inaccurate.

And yet in the character of Kazan *Cube* uses autism in a very human way. Yes, at the end Kazan functions as a virtual human

'None of the people in *Cube* were method actors to the point where they were staying in character over the course of the day, let alone a month's shooting.'

↘ **Miller**

computer, giving the others their best hope for avoiding the trapped rooms by computing the powers of prime numbers in the metal tags beneath the doors. But this turns out to be something of a MacGuffin, as the film is only ostensibly about escaping the mechanized prison.

What *Cube* is really about is how people cooperate, how that cooperation falls apart, and how adversity brings out the best—and worst—in human beings. It is the helpless state in which Kazan's disability has left him that tells us everything we need to know about the other prisoners. Those who refuse to leave him behind are the good people, those who want to ditch him at the first opportunity are the baddies. And the baddies, in this case, are basically Quentin.

Finally, it is Kazan's autism that makes the final shot in the film so impactful. If any other character had stepped tentatively into the light of that open door, we would feel that individual's relief, but nothing more. It is only through Kazan's seeming innocence that we experience this scene as something more—a rebirth.

For his part, Miller was relieved and heartened by the response to his character.

"At the time people couldn't have been nicer," he says. "There weren't any official statements by autistic groups, but when we premiered at the Toronto festival, someone stood up and said my brother's autistic—thank you for making a film. What I heard the most from both autistic people and the family and friends of autistic people was there had been movies about

It is Kazan's autism that makes the final shot in the film so impactful. If any other character had stepped tentatively into the light of that open door, we would feel that individual's relief, but nothing more.

autism and someone dealing with it, but there had never been just a movie with a character who was autistic. All the people in the cube had these different problems, and Kazan was just one of them. I got a lot of 'thank you for bringing autism to a movie as a character quality rather than the big drama.' "

Andre Bijelic
watching the cube he
co-created with Natali
come together on set.

14: building hell

ONCE HE RECEIVED the go-ahead from the Canadian Film Centre, Vincenzo Natali had six weeks. Six weeks to build a set, cast and crew the film, and hammer out once and for all how on earth they were going to make one set seem like many on screen. And how they were going to keep it all under **$750,000-plus Canadian.**

The crew, at least, were drawn from the Centre, which both made things easier by ensuring that people understood that everything was being done on a shoestring budget, and made it more difficult in that those who ended up being chosen fostered a certain sense of entitlement. At least that seems to have been the case considering how things eventually went.

Welcome to the Easy-Bake Oven

The greatest obstacle right out of the gate was the planning and fabrication of the actual set—in a very real sense it would be the star of the movie.

Toronto production designer Jasna Stefanovic had cut her teeth as assistant art director on television shows in the late '80s like *My Pet Monster*, a cartoon that happened to hail from

121

$750,00-plus Canadian

Says Colin Brunton, "The cash budget of all the films I did at The Feature Film Project was $400,000. If you add in donations by suppliers and deferrals by crew, the 'real' budget would be around $750K to $1 million."

'As an actor, the hardest thing to learn I always found was you don't get a run at anything. Rarely do you get scenes that you get to go from one point to another emotionally. Often you're cutting because of lighting, because of blocking, because of camera issues, whatever.'

↘**Hewlett**

Natali's own alma mater, Nelvana. More importantly, she was no stranger to the sci-fi/horror genre with art direction work on movies such as *Prom Night IV: Deliver Us from Evil* (1992) and *The Psychic* (1991) helmed by *My Bloody Valentine* director George Mihalka, and began her run as an art department trainee on the set of Cronenberg's *Dead Ringers* (1988).

"Jasna and I knew each other long before the CFC," says Natali. "I met her because she was a friend of David's Hewlett's girlfriend at the time, an assistant director. I made this little 16 mm film called *Mouth* (1992) that David was in and I needed a production designer. She did an amazing job. Jasna's insanely brilliant. I remember with that particular film, it takes place in (I guess you'd call it) a post-apocalyptic basement. So we went on these garbage raids. We'd go out at night and steal people's garbage to build our set. That's the kind of person Jasna is—we had lots of fun. And of course she went on to have a very successful career—she production designed *The Virgin Suicides* for Sofia Coppola, *Tideland* for Terry Gilliam…"

What she came up with for *Cube* was a piece of filmmaking genius in itself—one full, 6-sided cube and a half (3-sided) cube connected by a hatchway. "At that point she had done feature films but they were very small movies," says Natali. "She worked a lot with a company called Norstar, did kung fu movies, all kinds of craziness." Her prior work included *Boulevard* (1994) and kickboxing extravaganza *Operation Golden Phoenix* (1994).

Initially, Natali thought seriously about making all the walls on set white, eliminating the audience's ability to tell which "room" the characters happened to be in, claims cinematographer Derek Rogers. Natali has no memory of this.

"I certainly remember in the script stage we identified the rooms with a color," says the director. "It would be interesting to look back at some of the earlier scripts and see if they all did that or not; probably the earliest ones did not. When we were making the movie we were certainly talking about the rooms having different colors. I think it was embedded into the whole concept fairly early on because we knew if we were cross cutting between two different rooms and they were absolutely identical, that could be potentially very confusing, so there had to be some visual way to delineate them."

Says Rogers, "What it meant was this huge laborious thing of having to figure out how to create those colors. In the script there's something like 50 rooms that they go through, so I knew that everything had to be lit from outside. The whole idea was how to create backlight that you can change the color on, and that you can also then change the tone of all the lights, the luminosity levels, and do it really fast."

The cinematographer hit upon the idea of sliding colored gel frames—basically tinted plastic wrap—between the lights and frosted Plexiglas panels to make each room a different hue. But, he says, "I was trying to figure out how to backlight all this Plexiglas when somebody just told me that's what they do with light boxes. Photographers will just put a light bulb underneath. So it was like ah ha!"

Cube production designer Jasna Stefanovic has worked on everything from *Josie and the Pussycats* to *The Virgin Suicides.*

1,841

Number of 100-watt bulbs that were used to light up the cube.

C$9k

The approximate cost of the colored gels required to color all the rooms on the *Cube* set.

The crew commenced hammering together 2-x-4-foot wood frames to hold the Plexiglas sheets with a slot in between to accept the color gels. It would take about 20 minutes to completely change out all the gels on set, according to Rogers, though Natali remembers it being closer to an hour.

"Once we had done the pre-lighting and had all the gel frames ready to go, it was quite efficient," says Rogers. The gels alone cost them about C$9,000, he recalls, but were instrumental in pulling off the one-set-for-many concept by which *Cube* would ultimately rise or fall.

Surprisingly, the cinematographer says "the Film Centre really fought us on the gels. I was like Vincenzo, if we don't get the gels, we have a white film. I think the audience aren't going to do an hour-and-a-half in white rooms."

To further break up the monotony of the similar cube rooms, Rogers says he decided that each would have a "key wall."

"Each room had a different wall that was brighter, so that would give it a different feel to it. The floor in some of the rooms was really bright." The red room, for example, was lit from below, the blue room from above.

In total, 1,841 100-watt bulbs were placed behind them, all on dimmer packs. "The whole set had thousands of bulbs," Rogers explains. "Four walls, floor and ceiling. I think we blew a couple of dimmer carousels because we didn't know what the fuck we were doing, but we finally figured it out."

All the heat generated by these light bulbs transformed the small box in which the cast and crew labored into a tiny hell

Cinematographer Derek Rogers: 'We made 2-x-4 wooden frames and literally put hundreds of bulbs on different dimmer packs behind each one."

THE CUBE SET

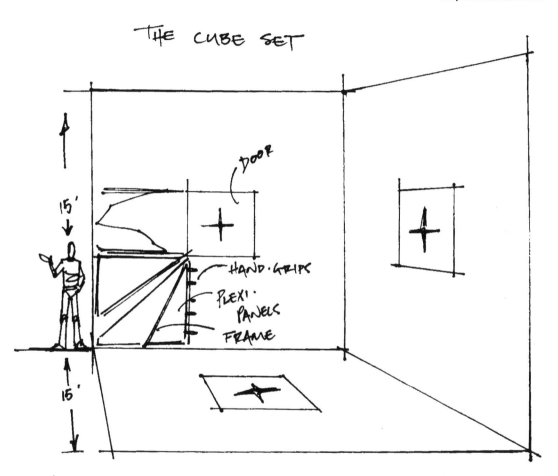

DOOR

HAND-GRIPS

PLEXI-
PANELS
FRAME

15'

15'

ALL WALLS - FLOOR & CEILING ARE IDENTICAL
EACH CONTAINS A WORKING HATCH DOOR.

I Remember...

'...Vincenzo showing me the set and how skeptical I was that they could make it look like lots of different cubes just with lights.

...Sitting with the other actors in the dressing room, Maurice [Dean Wint—Quentin] studying his part really diligently and systematically. His script was orchestrated and calibrated with highlighters.

...David Hewlett, C-shaped, curled into the back of the sofa, working on a computer. There weren't a lot of computers around then. David knew *Cube* was going to be successful judging from the number of 'hits' it had received—he could have been talking Greek.'

↘ Guadagni

they quickly dubbed the "Easy-Bake Oven."

"Once we started doing our scenes, I still had to light the actors," Rogers adds. "All the lighting of the actors was done from the inside, that was all a cheat using cheap IKEA lights—I used whatever I could. So if one room was all lit from below, I just put all the lights on the floor; if it was a top-lit room then we would hang a light from above. Actually, you couldn't really hang things in there because it was just a fucked-up set."

By this point it's pretty clear that the common perception of *Cube* being the product of a bunch of never-shot-a-foot-of-film students is just plain fantasy. As executive producer Colin Brunton puts it, "they weren't really 'film students.' Almost all of them had worked in the business in one way or another. In a funny way, the learning curve for them was 'Hey, here's your money—do whatever you want.' 'Uh—say what?!'"

Door-lemma

Natali began work on *Cube* fully intending to shoot scenes in order by simply lining up his heavily detailed storyboards and transferring them to celluloid—bam, bam bam. That plan fell apart by the end of Day One.

There were two reasons for that. The first was the obvious-in-hindsight practicality of having to shoot every scene that takes place in the same cube "room" at the same time. Already so hamstrung by shooting 12 hours each day, there was no compelling reason for them to shoot a few scenes in Room 1, redress it as Room 2, and then redress it back again later as Room 1 again

Let There Be Light

Top: Above Natali, you can see the banks of light bulbs that help bring the cube to life. Right: A glimpse of the cube from outside the set reveals just what a work of genius the *Cube* set actually was.

↘ For additional content see the *Cube Archive*, pp. 230-345

when each transformation took an hour to get the color right, never mind the lighting.

In Andrew Miller's experience, movies are seldom shot in order anyway. In the case of *Cube*, this was especially hard on Hewlett. "I think Dave's complaint, which is legitimate, was more about the physical task of learning lines. Everything Dave ever plays, he's just constantly explaining things to people. Dave always has more lines than anyone because he's always like, 'Look, here's what it is...' He's always got to talk about something, and he talks faster than anybody. It's just a pain in the ass learning lines. The truth about Dave is he'll find something to whine and complain about no matter what's happening. If they had done it in order he'd be like 'I can't believe I have to do it in order.'" Miller laughs. "I would gladly say all this to his face, as Vincenzo would. Dave's not happy unless he's unhappy."

The second reason scenes weren't shot in order was because of something that quickly became the bane of cast and crew for the entire 20-day shoot.

"The biggest problem we had making that movie was that the doors didn't work," Natali says, sounding nearly 20 years later like he still can't quite believe it. "That seems like a small thing, but actually when you consider the whole movie is about people opening and closing doors, it was a nightmare. It almost shut down the production."

David Hewlett recalls, "We either couldn't open the doors, or you'd open the doors and they'd drop off the wall. It was no one's fault, it's just the logistics of a low-budget film. You have the time

C$43k

Amount budgeted
for *Cube* set
construction

to build them and shoot it, you don't have the time or money to test much. You have to build it and just hope for the best."

Cube itself may boast no one hero narratively speaking, but during its making one man became everyone's hero and, in the words of Andrew Miller, "is the guy who saved *Cube*." That guy was second-unit supervisor **William Phillips**.

"We had engineers coming in saying, 'We're shutting down production, we have to figure out these doors, it's a disaster!'" Miller remembers. "And then no one could figure out anything."

Says Phillips, "The doors were supposed to close by automatically rising up and sucking into the cube wall. From what I could tell, the designers planned to pull the doors up with invisible filament wire, like fishing line, but the doors were just too damn heavy! It never worked."

The people from JJamb [sic] Productions who'd originally designed the doors tried to solve the problem as best they could, but luck simply wasn't on their side.

"We were just a bunch of goofballs in second unit. While the main unit was stressing every minute, we were having fun filming fire, boots and small, improvised practical effects. And it came down to us to figure out" the doors, says Phillips. "In a way I had an advantage over the original designers because I think they probably had in their mind a particular way this was going to work. And when it didn't work that way they couldn't really separate themselves from it to figure out how to do it differently. I looked at it from the position of what have I got? How can I make what I've got work? They had these runners that went up the side and some

William Phillips

Credited as "the door doctor" on *Cube*, Phillips later shot second unit for Natali's *Cypher* (2002) before going on to become a writer-director in his own right. David Hewlett starred in his 2001 thriller *Treed Murray*, and appeared in his next feature: *Foolproof* (2003), photographed by *Cube's* Derek Rogers.

sort of counter runner that ran into the hole and that's all I had."

After a bit of agonizing, Phillips began to see a way forward using a piece of wood he found on set.

"I figured if we used the scrap wood as a temporary base, attached a pulley to it and ran a strong rope hidden down behind the door, we could hoist the door up from the bottom instead of pulling it up from the top. It worked! We got the door to close properly provided—and this was the big proviso—you couldn't shoot it head on or else you'd see us hauling it up. But if you filmed it from a slightly lower angle, we'd be hidden and the door looked totally automatic."

Already brushing the ceiling of their C$750,000 budget, Phillips had to essentially pull this rescue off without spending a dime.

Having made himself available to the production as a general runner of errands in addition to his second-unit work, he'd spent a lot of time going back and forth to Canadian Tire (roughly equivalent to Walmart or Target in the US).

"I'd go regularly to **Canadian Tire** with my Ziploc bag with production petty cash in it buying this and that, and every time I would go I would get Canadian Tire money back. [Coupons that can be used as currency in that store.] So I had this wad of Canadian Tire money. I don't know what the number was—was it 20 bucks? But that turned out to be the budget I had."

With those vouchers he bought the pulleys that would ultimately save *Cube*.

Says Phillips, "When I first got it to go, we did it a couple of times and then dragged Vincenzo into the cube and said 'Check

Canadian Tire

Canadian Tire was an unknowing micro-investor in *Cube* thanks to William Phillips' use of Canadian Tire money to fix the film's door woes.

OUTER SHELL

BRIDGE

EXT. CUBE

Deleted Scene:
The Space Between

The cube "was always supposed to be a magnetic system, kind of like a monorail," says Natali. "That's what those big strips of metal are that grid across the outside of each specific cube, which I think is fairly plausible.

"One of the few scenes that was cut out of the film is where the characters encounter a space between the rooms early on, and they don't really understand what it is because they don't realize at that stage that the rooms are actually moving. We built that. We cut it out because it was slowing things down. Also I had

to shoot it so simply that it was composed of maybe 2 or 3 shots because I didn't have enough time, so I don't think it was particularly well done.

"If you get the old DVD version I think you can see that scene, that there was a deleted scene section. But we were very vigorous about making the puzzle aspect of it work, and that was always the intention — to never be ambiguous about how they figure a way out of the cube. We would only be ambiguous about who was behind the cube and what its purpose ultimately was."

this out.' He just looked damned relieved. 'Thank God some-thing works!' Without it, it was going to be a really tough sell cinematically."

"The challenge was believing that our pretending to be strug-gling with those hatch doors—which were made of, like, balsa wood—would read on camera with the right sound effects," says Nicky Guadagni. "I learned that yes, with the right sound effects you can make balsa wood come off like the door of a safe."

Adds Miller, "It looked pretty rickety, like that can't possibly work. But I'll never forget seeing the first shots with the sound of the door—it had that *Raiders of the Lost Ark* kind of sound of doors shutting—and I'm like 'Oh my God, those doors seem so heavy!' In fact it was these two guys yanking on these little strings."

"My dad's an engineer so maybe there's some engineering in my blood or something," Phillips speculates. "But trust me, I'm not the only person in the world who could've figured that out. Maybe it was three parts practical improvisation and one part **MacGyver**."

'The Only Thing that Doesn't Require Doors is You Talking'

Already overwhelmed by the tight shooting schedule and working out which scenes he could afford to drop if necessary, doors that wouldn't open or close properly were the last things Natali needed. Not sure what else to do, he dropped all the door opening/closing shots from his shot list, hoping they could somehow solve the prob-lem as they went along. This also meant juggling scenes around to fill the gaps...and putting some old friendships to the test.

MacGyver

The 1980s series *MacGyver* (rebooted in 2016) starred Richard Dean Anderson as the titular secret agent Angus MacGyver who could get out of any situation simply by cobbling together something cool out of whatever parts were lying around.

"I got a phone call on the first day of shooting at midnight, and we were back in at 6 the next morning," says Hewlett. "And it's Vincenzo saying look, can you learn all of your dialogue by tomorrow because basically the only thing that doesn't require doors is you talking." He chuckles. "As a friend, you're able to take liberties to some extent. Film is such an irritatingly collaborative process."

Adds Miller, "What [the other actors] quickly realized is 'Oh, Dave and Andrew are really good friends with the director, which means he can ask them to do all the worst things. Like hold that body position longer or be upside down. Whenever there was something horribly shitty to do, it was always me and Dave doing it. Or can we just do another take? Smash him on the head again! At that point they're like OK, it's fine to be the new person because he's a little more respectful of us."

Back to the scene Hewlett had to learn by the next morning. It was Worth's lengthy confession, finally admitting to the other characters that he's known more about the nature of the cube than he's let on. This is the film's turning point, losing him any sympathy he had from the female characters and stoking Quentin's anger to the boiling point. It's also the one glimmer we get of the tremendous bureaucracy that must've put the whole enigmatic mechanism in motion in the first place.

"That's also classically Canadian, which I loved about *Cube*," says Hewlett. "It was like 'No, screw you, there is no leading man!' Our hero is also our villain. The loser coward, my char-

Continued on page 137 >

'Maurice Dean Wint [Quentin] gave me a coffee cup with 'Holloway' written on it—it was from Holloway prison in London, England, where his sister worked, I think. It was so thoughtful of him to give me that—and you could tell he was chuffed to have thought of it.'

↘ **Guadagni**

133

Grind, Grin, Repeat

For all the malfunctioning doors, tight shooting schedules and light-rig-induced heat, the core cast and crew never lost their sense of humor, nor their dedication to the creation of something many had thought impossible to film.

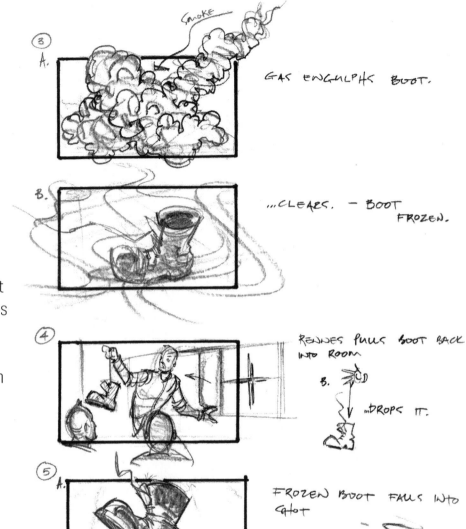

③
A.

GAS ENGULPHS BOOT.

B.

...CLEARS. — BOOT FROZEN.

> 'I got a great pair of black boots I couldn't afford—the ones we throw into the next cube. They stuck with me for years and years.'
> ↘ **Guadagni**

④

RENNES PULLS BOOT BACK INTO ROOM

B.

...DROPS IT.

⑤
A.

FROZEN BOOT FALLS INTO SHOT

B.

SHATTERS ON IMPACT.

acter, sort of becomes the reluctant hero, which I think again is kind of Canadian. We don't go running around grandstanding and being heroic in any way, but sort of hope that in our own way we'll make a difference."

Masterfully lit from above by Derek Rogers, Hewlett's confession evokes a thousand crime-drama back-room scenes. It's also 10 pages of dialogue, and Natali wanted Hewlett to memorize it all that morning and perform it before the camera throughout the day without rehearsal.

"So all of the 'there's no way out of here' monologue—the whole big breakdown speech—he's like yeah, we're gonna do that tomorrow," says Hewlett. "OK, so off you go."

The Cube Exacts its Pound of Flesh

Nightmare though they were, stubborn doors weren't the only technical problems bedeviling the production. Indeed, almost as if cognizant of the film's plot, the set proceeded to nip at the heels of cast and crew in a thousand different ways.

Gaps between the floor panels were a constant tripping hazard, meaning actors had to somehow keep the floor in sight without the camera picking up that this was what they were doing.

"It was like a nightmare getting around because you've got people twisting their ankles every time they try to walk over one of the rung sections," says Hewlett. "The actors were like that's it, we've got to put something in these holes here because we're going to kill ourselves."

Miller admits, "The beauty of playing Kazan was that I could always look down and see where I was going. It felt like Derek was holding a camera walking backward every day all day, so he was more susceptible to those kinds of injuries. Ultimately a lot of our injuries were just climbing up and down the rungs because we're in our stupid pajamas the whole time. There was a lot of bruised knees and feet. Like running back and forth in the cube, you would always hit a rung that would hurt, but I don't remember anything death-defying."

The wall rungs weren't much better. They'd climb up and down from the vertical room doors take after take, the bars biting into their palms, becoming ever more painful after the first couple of days of shooting. Finally a production assistant came up with the idea of wrapping the wall rungs with pipe insulating foam, which eased things tremendously—they just had to remember to remove it when actors weren't actually climbing lest it find its way into a shot.

"You're just learning as you go along," says Hewlett, "and about the day before you wrap is the day you usually get stuff right."

Even cinematographer Rogers rendered up his pound of flesh to the voracious cube. Bijelic says, "I remember he fell off the stage because it was raised so that people could get in and out. He was backing up and went right off it. After that, they always had somebody spotting him, making sure he wasn't going to do *that* again."

'i was fascinated by david hewlett— he seemed to sink into chairs, not sit on them, and he gestured like a smoker—like someone who has a fag in his hand at all times. he'd quit his 2-pack-a-day habit by then and took up running but he still had all the body language of a smoker.'

↘**Guadagni**

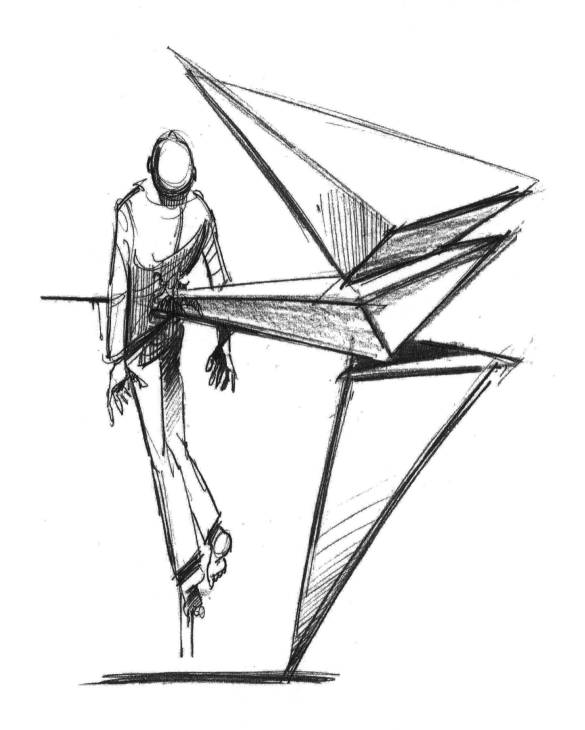

15: 'it was a mindfuck, this film'

WHILE PROMOTING *CUBE*, Natali and Bijelic often characterized their own cramped living conditions at the time of its writing as giving the film its claustrophobic edge. It was a convenient observation, and as we've seen there was some truth in it. What no one said publicly, however, was that a lot of *Cube*'s tension was also derived from the tempers that flared just off screen.

Extremely kind and positive by nature, the director had to be prodded by the author with stories heard elsewhere before finally admitting that the production's challenges hadn't been confined to painful climbing rungs and stubborn doors.

Push-Pull Mutiny

Even after it was green lit by The Feature Film Project, *Cube* was a hard sell for the Canadian Film Centre. This was not the art-house fare that many thought the CFC should be producing, and there wasn't a lot of love for science fiction there, either.

"There's always a cult following of people who are into these sort of films, but the establishment here is very anti-science fiction, or they were back then," says cinematographer Derek

Opposite: An unrealized *Cube* trap sketched by Natali.

Rogers. "They just see it as trash."

And with a budget of $750,000 Canadian (half in deferrals), no one was quite sure how a sci-fi film could be made on the cheap without looking like complete garbage. "If I had been in that position and I had looked at that script, I'm not sure I would've made it, either," Rogers admits. It seemed too ambitious, the scale of it. And the year before they'd turned it down."

He suspects that it was this fear that led several members of the crew to resent their work on the movie from the very beginning of filming.

"It's the classic thing with every film that if the people at the top don't believe in it, then everything filters down. And I think there were a lot of negative vibes filtered down to the film set, which was so ironic because you have a young director who's obviously so brilliant. It doesn't take any brains to realize that this guy at least has the enthusiasm, the sincerity, and the energy to do something crazy."

On being asked about this schism years later, Nicky Guadagni (Holloway) says, "You're actually telling me something I didn't know. There was just a day I recall when I felt 'discord'— factions. I'd never noticed that happening on any other set but maybe it had and I was just on this set enough that I noticed. Egos, sighing, eye-rolls, agitated voices—all that stuff. Vincenzo must have made it clear that the actors were to be protected from those goings on."

It should be said that years later, Natali still politely declines to discuss what happened next, saying simply, "I don't want to

142

blacken anyone's reputation."

Yet to fully appreciate what an accomplishment the making of *Cube* was, you have to understand all of the challenges that it faced, and this was a big one.

The way Rogers remembers it, a rift quickly formed between a core group of 10 or so people, creating a division right down the middle. On one side, Natali, Bijelic, Rogers, Phillips, Manson, Stefanovic and the actors—people who saw *Cube* as a tremendous artistic and production challenge waiting to be tackled. On the other, a crew made up of people who felt they had one shot to show the CFC what they could do, and they were being given a project they couldn't possibly pull off convincingly owing to a tiny budget and a too-ambitious vision of what *Cube* was supposed to be.

Says second-unit supervisor Phillips, "People get afraid, and that's when they're at their most disagreeable. There's a great quote that typifies on-set stress: 'Never underestimate other people's insecurities.'"

"There was a mutinous feeling right from square one," says Rogers. "There were a couple of people on the shoot that shouldn't have been there. There was someone on it who—I don't know why he was there; it wasn't like he was getting paid. He really had no respect for [the director]. Right from the beginning he was making cracks, making fun of the set, making fun of the film, making fun of Vincenzo. And it was like what is going on—fuck off! But we were young. I would never tolerate that now, even if it was a volunteer situation."

'[Producer] Betty Orr was sweet and tolerant of me being 5 minutes late most mornings—especially when I bribed her with a hash brown from McDonald's. I had a 4 year old, a 9 year old and an 11 year old—I didn't have time to eat breakfast so I'd stop at McDonald's on my 15 minute bike ride from The Annex to Wallace Street where the studio was.'

↘**Guadagni**

Yet Natali maintains, "It's not fair to attack somebody if they don't get a response.* But believe me, he really made my life miserable.

"I think what happened was he was just afraid because it was his first movie [in this position] and he thought that we weren't going to pull it off, that it was going to be very hard. So his first defense mechanism was to say 'I told you so' and then throw up his arms and be miserable and make everyone else miserable. To protect himself he tried to turn the crew against me, so it was very unpleasant. I desperately wanted to fire him but the producers wouldn't fire him because they were afraid the bond company would step in and it would just be a huge disaster. That was a big part of the difficulty of making the movie."

It also convinced Rogers—if he needed convincing—that handheld was the only way to go on this one. They had enough problems without getting fancy with their shooting.

"My gut to Vincenzo was we can't lay track in here—we have no time for that," he says. "I remember the very first day, one of the crew members (who turned out to be part of the mutinous crew)—I said can you set up a flag for me and I timed him—it took him 20 minutes to set it up. I turned to Vincenzo and I said no more flags, we're not even going to use the grips, let's just handhold as much as we can. So that's what we did."

As the cinematographer recalls, everyone was getting paid about C$500 a week, with the core group handing their checks

* *The crew member in question could not be reached for comment, therefore the author has declined to name him here.*

'second unit had zero budget except for pizza, and even then they'd get up our nose if we ordered three pizzas instead of two.'

↘ **William Phillips, second-unit supervisor**

145

back to Natali to help fill holes in the budget. And though Rogers still bristles at the animosity that grew amongst the more mutinous members of the crew, he admits that there was a lot to discourage people who didn't believe in the project as deeply as *Cube*'s inner circle. "It was a 20-day shoot—it wasn't enough. They had locked us to 12-hour days, which wasn't enough."

Natali concedes that "It was very strict. We simply could not go one minute over 12 hours—probably 11 hours plus lunch. We could not do one minute of overtime—the plug was pulled."

Every night they'd go out for noodle soup and discuss what they'd managed to accomplish, and what still had to be done.

"Then halfway through the film [Natali] started saying we're not going to make the 20 days," says Rogers. "We had gone

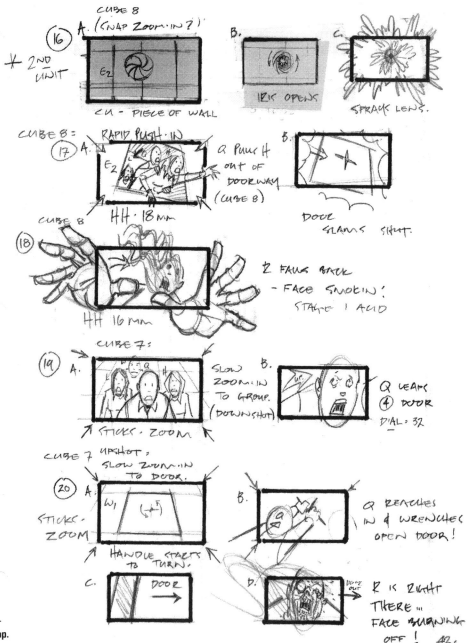

Natali's storyboards for *Cube* are particularly detailed when it comes to the effects of each trap.

through the shot list and he was pretty good at knowing what he could discard, but he really didn't think he was going to get the film done."

Of course Natali being Natali, his shot list wasn't merely a shot list at all but vast storyboards of every scene, emphasizing exactly which visual elements would be lost from the completed film every time he discarded one owing to a lack of time to shoot.

"When I was very young my ambition was to become a comic book artist for Marvel Comics," he says. "I even made a submission to them and was rejected. I had also always used storyboards making little short films when I was a kid and that remains a big part of my process. In some respects it's the most gratifying part because it's the moment when I actually start to see the movie, and what I'm seeing and what I'm able to draw is the perfect version of that film. It's not in any way hampered by the realities of budget or weather or personalities or all the things that usually make a film so difficult. It's a kind of wonderful, pristine moment."

Which made every cut scene all the more painful when he had to put the storyboarded version aside due to time constraints.

"Going into the third, and then into the fourth and final week was that real tension," says Rogers. "So the core of us started working harder and harder, and there were some great people like Bill Phillips trying to figure out the doors." He laughs. "It was a mindfuck, this film."

'In one shot, a boot is thrown through the door and it lands right on the lens. We shot this by placing the boot on the lens, running the camera in reverse and yanking the boot back through the door.'

↘ **Phillips on one of the shots of which second-unit was most proud.**

16: 'good films do have to be somewhat painful'

BORN IN THE states but growing up in Canada, Vincenzo Natali enjoys dual citizenship and has been living in both countries since 2000. In a profession notorious for breeding tin pot dictators, he remains uncompromisingly affable and polite. "I would say my temperament is Canadian," he says. "I'm a child of Toronto."

Doubtless the rigors of the industry have roughened up those smooth edges somewhat over the years, but back in 1996 he was definitely in Clark Kent territory during the making of his first feature.

Many pinpoint a single day on set that changed things—a moment when all the weeks of having his crew undermine his work finally took their toll. Those who tell the tale these days do so in the proud and amused tones reserved for all loss-of-virginity tales.

"It was quite a drama," admits cinematographer Derek Rogers. "As we know, Vincenzo is just a polite, well-spoken, sensitive individual. We reached the third or fourth week and the crew at this point was really saying out loud, 'This is going to be a clunker' [of a film], making jokes. We'd talked about trying to fire [a crew

Opposite: The 'cubing' of Alderson in the first few minutes of the film was accomplished with practical effects that still impress today.

'If you ever want to lose the magic of film, just come to a film set. It's just the most ridiculous process because the way things have to be fixed and the way things are done and it's so temporary. There's no magic.'

↘ **Hewlett**

member] and we were told we couldn't fire anyone, that's not how it works at the Film Centre; we're all working for nothing.

"Then the people started not coming back after lunch, or coming back late. One thing about a crew: You get there on time and you come back from lunch on time. If you don't, then you don't work in this business, that's how it works. You have to be there at call. So half the crew started not showing up. They were coming in five, 10 minutes late. Then it stretched to longer than that.

"Vincenzo was talking to me and saying, 'I don't know, it's not going to work, I don't know what to do.' And I just said, 'Fucking get mad! You have to get mad!' The executives at the Film Centre aren't doing it. Your producers aren't doing it—they're too sweet because they don't have the experience, but someone has to."

Talking to the self-assured, no bullshit cinematographer today, you'd never think that there was ever a time that Rogers had been the go-along-to-get-along type. But like everyone else in the business, he has his own loss-of-innocence story.

"I hadn't worked on that many films, but I'd worked on one with a horrible producer who just yelled at everyone, so I understood the concept of getting mad. We're Canadians—we're very sweet people. We get mad but we're repressed. The anger's in there but we have to be provoked. And I felt it was my job to provoke Vincenzo.

"I said, 'Just get out there and start swearing; get mad!' He looked at me: 'I can't get mad.' 'You have to just show that this is it or we're not going to get the film done.'

Natali and Hewlett: One of the great director-actor teams in modern film.

"So the mutiny-type crew didn't show up, there was no one there. The six or seven of us were all standing there ready to shoot and he just started screaming—he had a total outrage. He started throwing things—it was amazing, actually. It was amazing to see someone who is so nice, but at the same time is so focused on getting this film done. I enjoyed the fact that I had provoked him to get really angry and crazy—it was a loss of virginity."

"He kicked a chair and he looked at me and said, 'Oh fuck! I broke it,'" says Rogers. It, in this instance, was Natali's toe. "But it turned the tide. People were starting to come back in and when they saw him screaming, they were really shocked and upset because they had never seen this man mad—ever. And he was so angry. He was like a crazy puppet—his hands were flying up in the air, he was nuts!

"Then the tide did change. He spoke a little more elegantly. He said, 'Listen, I'm making this fucking film with you or without you.' The core came back and we pushed on. I think Bill Phillips' wife—**I guess she had medical training**—taped up his toe and Vincenzo soldiered on."

"What I do remember," adds Phillips, "is he kicked the chair, and I think the next day everything was wrapping up and he kind of made this brief announcement. Something along the lines of 'I'm sorry I lost my temper...but not really.'

"In a way that's Vincenzo all over in that he does not lose his temper, almost ever. And of course when he does, what happens? He wounds himself. It is a very difficult process and making a low budget movie like this—there's a certain bureaucratic pressure that comes from doing it under the umbrella of the CFC, things you can and can't do. It's a tough, tough road."

Adds Rogers, "I think this toe story is all about him losing his directing virginity."

Natali remembers, "When we finished shooting, [CFC Founder] Norman [Jewison] sent me a bottle of champagne and a note that said, 'You broke your toe but at least you didn't break your heart.' I'll never forget that—it was a really magnificent gesture."

"I'm so incredibly proud of Vincenzo on that film," says Hewlett. "He had a hell of a time shooting that film; some of the crew

I guess she had medical training

Phillips confirms that his wife, retinal surgeon Dr. Jill Hopkins, examined Vincenzo's toe on set and sent him to the ER (after wrap!) to get X-rayed and treated.

were very, very resistant to him as a director and I felt he dealt with it very well. It was nice to be there to see it all happen and to help. Andrew and I, given the parts we had in that film, were able to exert a certain amount of pressure and help our friend make his movie. That was fantastic for us."

The irony of making a movie about people slowly going crazy in a confined space while all of this was going on is not lost on the director.

"We definitely felt while making it that it was a case of art imitating life. We were making a movie about six people trapped in a cube, but the reality was we were closer to 36 people trapped in a cube. We had the cast and the whole crew crammed in this very small space, and we were all going crazy and getting on each other's nerves. It was a very unpleasant experience. I have to say it's about the hardest thing I've ever had to do in my life."

The Cubing of Alderson

Even if Natali had enjoyed the most cooperative of crews, it's doubtful that they could've tackled in only 20 days every shot the director had so painstakingly storyboarded. They'd bought some time by putting off a few of the most ambitious scenes, but when Day 20 arrived, they were completely up against the wall.

"We didn't have basic scenes," says Rogers. "We didn't have the opening scene of the movie: the bald guy getting cubed. We hadn't shot that. I kept saying, 'Aren't we going to shoot that?' It was an effects thing; it was taking them a while to figure it out."

And no wonder. By any measure, the cubing of Alderson

'At the time *Cube* was really tough, but looking back it was a fricking breeze compared to things I've done since. It was back in the good old days when you actually had 20 days to shoot.'

↘ **Hewlett**

153

'We loved him. There were a lot of adults in that play and we were all these young, relatively new, actors. Some of the adults were nicer than others, but he was one of the great ones.'

⬊ **Miller on working with Julian Richings [Alderson] in the play** *Spring Awakening* **as a teenager at Leah Posluns Theatre.**

(Julian Richings)—the pre-title sequence that introduces us to the harsh world of *Cube*—was also the most ambitious and effective scene in the entire film. As such, it required an extraordinary amount of preparation.

"It wasn't that it took a long time to shoot," says Louise Mackintosh, who crafted all of *Cube*'s makeup effects alongside her husband, Raymond, and Russell Cate. "It didn't involve any actors so we could do it afterwards and there was no problem with overtime."

However, the sheer complexity of the effect required them to build several different pieces: the actor's head and shoulders, an arm, and a full body. "I remember after one meeting with Vincenzo we went to a bar and said, 'OK, how are we going to do this?'"

They did it by creating dozens and dozens of small foam and latex cubes, she explains. "Each one of those little cube parts had the internal organs sculpted right into it. So if you were to pick up one of those pieces and turn it over you would see there's a piece of rib, there's some of the liver, there's a bit of the lungs, all of those things were there. It was all put together kind of like a Jenga game with fine wires through it so that when you pulled the wires out of the bottom, the entire thing crumbled.

"I'm not even sure that it was necessary, it was just fun. I thought that if you're going to put this cubed body together and it has plain, straight foam sides (because it had some foam in it), it would've been a letdown. If any real movie nerd were to slow that down and look at it frame by frame, they're not going to see

Continued on page 163 >

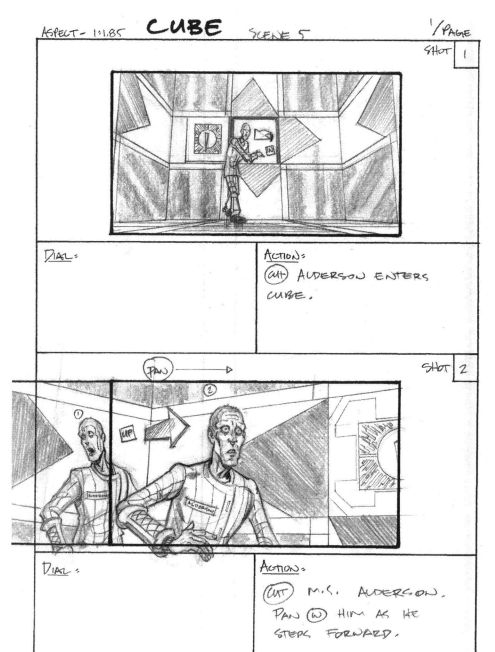

ASPECT- 1:1.85 **CUBE** SCENE 5

SHOT 1

DIAL:

ACTION:
(CUT) ALDERSON ENTERS CUBE.

PAN →

SHOT 2

DIAL:

ACTION:
(CUT) M.S. ALDERSON. PAN (W) HIM AS HE STEPS FORWARD.

The Cubing of Alderson

Natali's storyboards for this, the very first trap he devised, are stunning in their detail.

The Cubing
of Alderson

[continued]

Natali: "I remember
at the time Andre
and I thought the
only way to do [the
cubing of Alderson]
would be digitally.
This would be when
digital effects really
were in their infancy."

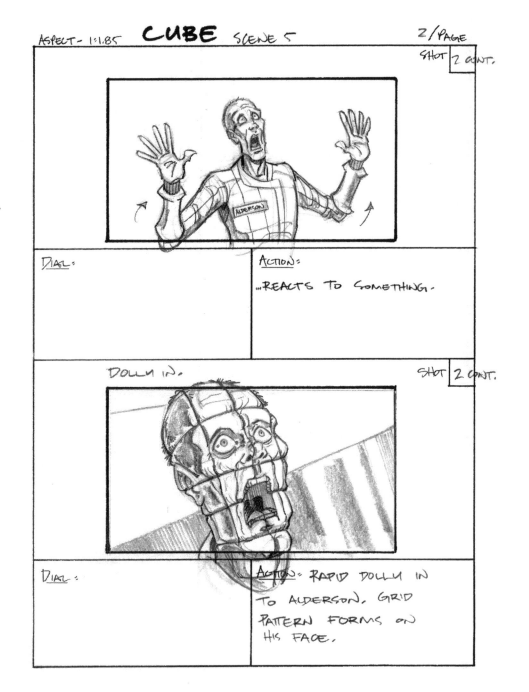

ASPECT- 1:1.85   CUBE SCENE 5   2/PAGE
SHOT 2 CONT.

DIAL:

ACTION:
...REACTS TO SOMETHING.

DOLLY IN.   SHOT 2 CONT.

DIAL:

ACTION: RAPID DOLLY IN
TO ALDERSON. GRID
PATTERN FORMS ON
HIS FACE.

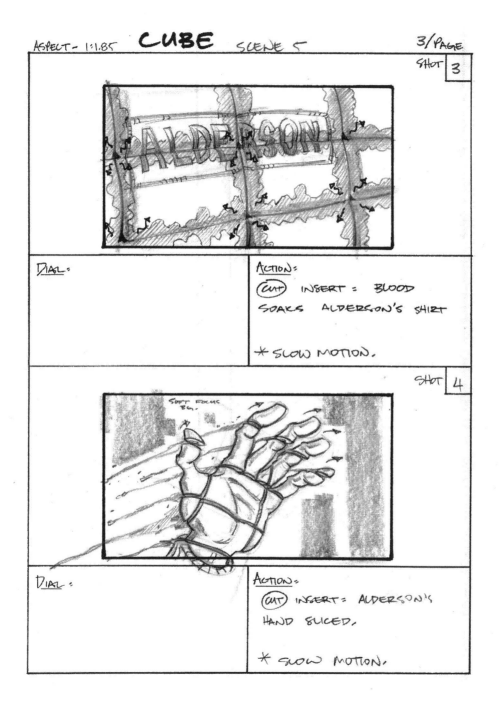

SHOT 3

DIAL =

ACTION =

(CUT) INSERT = BLOOD
SOAKS ALDERSON'S SHIRT

* SLOW MOTION.

SHOT 4

SOFT FOCUS
BG.

DIAL =

ACTION =

(CUT) INSERT = ALDERSON'S
HAND SLICED.

* SLOW MOTION.

Natali: "Long before
the Film Centre was
involved, we went to
one or two effects
houses in Toronto
and had them price
this stuff out."

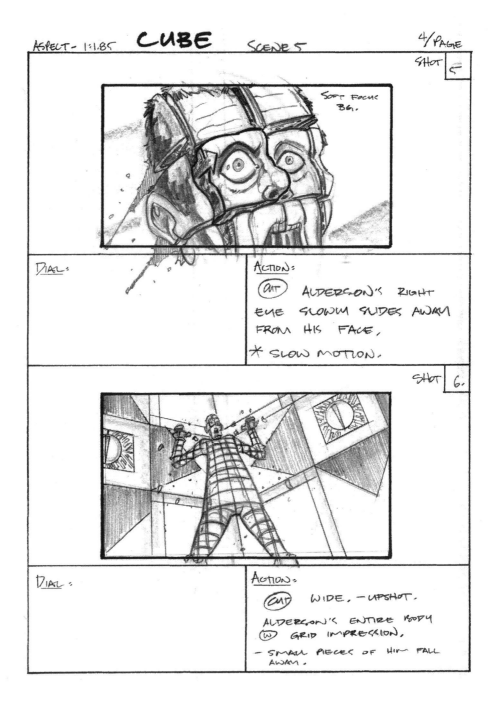

ASPECT - 1:1.85   CUBE   SCENE 5   4/PAGE

SHOT 5

SOFT FOCUS BG.

DIAL:

ACTION:

(CUT) ALDERSON'S RIGHT
EYE SLOWLY SLIDES AWAY
FROM HIS FACE,
* SLOW MOTION.

SHOT 6.

DIAL:

ACTION:

(CUT) WIDE. — UPSHOT.
ALDERSON'S ENTIRE BODY
(W) GRID IMPRESSION,
— SMALL PIECES OF HIM FALL
AWAY.

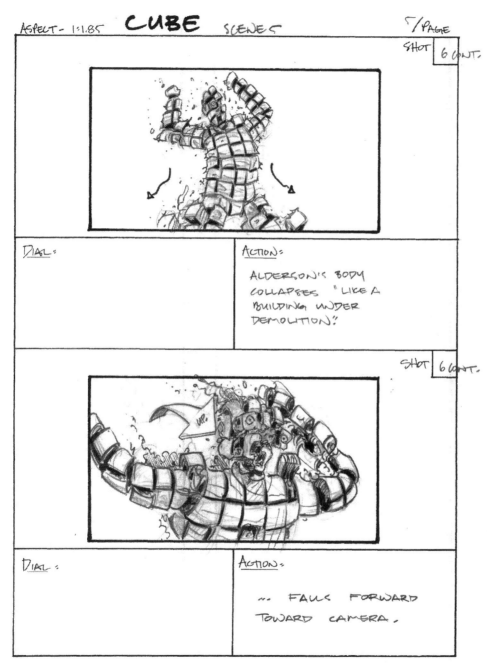

SHOT | 6 CONT.

DIAL:

ACTION:

ALDERSON'S BODY
COLLAPSES "LIKE A
BUILDING UNDER
DEMOLITION."

SHOT | 6 CONT.

DIAL:

ACTION:

~ FALLS FORWARD
TOWARD CAMERA.

'Julian Richings [Alderson] has got a face for sci-fi. If you just pass by some sci-fi set, you'll see Julian in some crazy makeup being a monster of some kind. It's like 'the aliens have landed and there's Julian.' 'Don't go in that house in the woods; there are creepy brothers there, and one of them's Julian.'

↘ **Miller**

The Cubing of Alderson
(continued)

Natali: "If we had done it [digitally] I'm willing to bet it wouldn't have held up nearly as well as the physical version of it did."

160

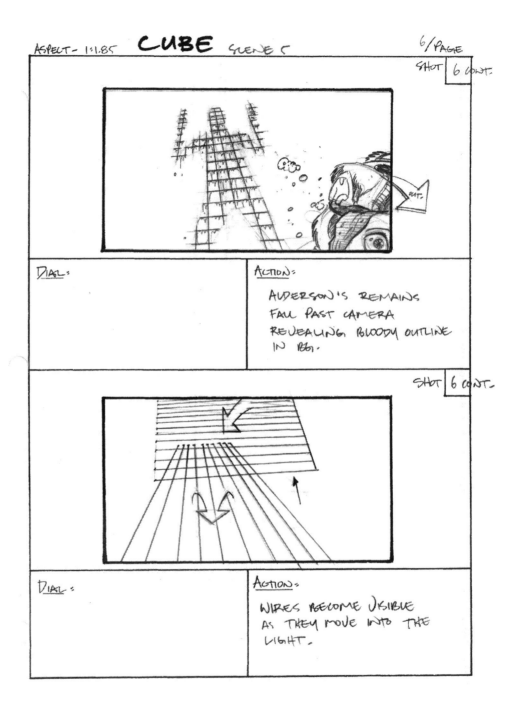

SHOT 6 CONT.

DIAL:

ACTION:
ALDERSON'S REMAINS FALL PAST CAMERA REVEALING BLOODY OUTLINE IN BG.

SHOT 6 CONT.

DIAL:

ACTION:
WIRES BECOME VISIBLE AS THEY MOVE INTO THE LIGHT.

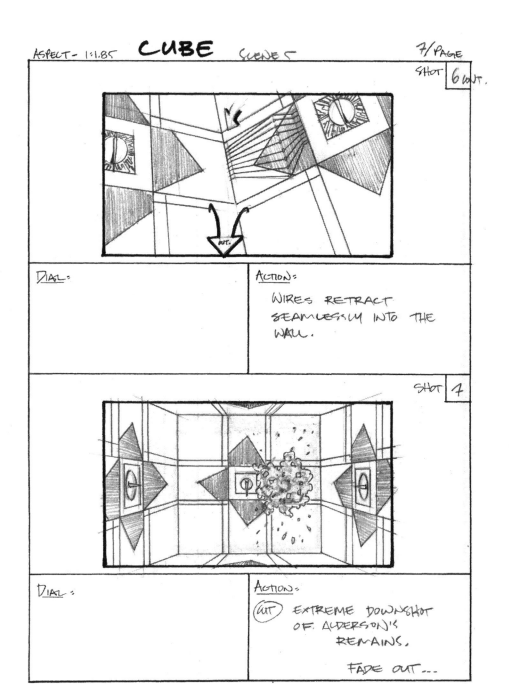

DIAL:

ACTION:

WIRES RETRACT
SEAMLESSLY INTO THE
WALL.

SHOT 7

DIAL:

ACTION:
(CUT) EXTREME DOWNSHOT
OF ALDERSON'S
REMAINS.

FADE OUT...

The Practical Effects Team

1: Russell Cate works on the Alderson dummy while Raymond Mackintosh watches **2:** Bloodying up Wayne Robson **3:** Left to right: Louise Mackintosh, Raymond and Cate (photo taken by actor Jeff Bridges) in their workshop during the making of Terry Gilliam's *Tideland* in 2004

↘ For additional content see the Cube Archive, pp. 230-345

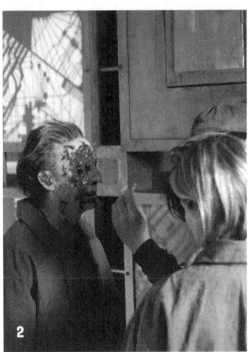

any foam rubber anywhere, they're going to see the real thing."

Natali recalls the entire sequence being shot in one take at around 3 in the morning on the very last day of the shoot.

"That was such a beautiful scene; I was always proud of that shot," says Rogers. "It starts on this eye. He gets up and Vincenzo wanted the camera to circle all the way around, so for the first time we'd see that he's imprisoned in a cube. And that's the first time I really understood the sense of space. So we put the lights on the floor to light him and then everything was backlit. We didn't have Steadicam, we didn't have circular tracks, so I just handheld it. We shot with an Aaton 35 mm camera; it had its problems but it's really tiny. When we were getting ready to shoot, I was concerned because all of the 35 mill film cameras were so heavy at the time: the BL3, the BL4—the Moviecam, I think, had just come out. But there weren't too many lightweight sync cameras except for the Aaton."

Looking back on it, it's hard to overestimate just how crucial that opening sequence was to the success of *Cube*; it's probably the one scene that absolutely everybody remembers 20 years later.

Says Hewlett, Natali "knew that if he could get people in the first five minutes of that movie, that was going to cement it. If you have a good beginning and a good ending, it almost doesn't matter what happens in the middle. I say that only because we couldn't make it up with digital effects, there was only a couple in that whole movie, but they were well chosen, well executed."

'Vincenzo is very Kubrick-like in his approach to filmmaking, I think. He's not as big an asshole as Kubrick was. As far as I'm concerned—and this applies to actors, too—you can be as big a pain in the ass as you want, as long as you're brilliant. If you're not brilliant then I've got no time for you at all.'

↘ **Hewlett**

163

Cost of our materials

Natali and producer Mehra Meh were "kind of glum" when they first approached the Mackintoshes. "They had already talked to another studio where they were told the effects would cost a million dollars," says Louise. "But Raymond and I said we would do it. They were buoyant when they left. Then we went to the bar to talk about how!"

The 37-hour Day

The Canadian Film Centre had been very strict on the 12-hour cap it placed on the actors each day, but the same did not apply to crew members such as those in the effects department.

"We agreed to do it for **the cost of our materials** and over-head, and every year or so we get $12, $13, $22, depending on how much [the films] made," says Louise Mackintosh. "Working with Vincenzo, I don't think overtime has ever entered into it with me or with Raymond because we like Vincenzo so much, we love working with him. He's so enthusiastic and he has such a great vision. He's the kind of guy you want to please, you want to give him what he wants."

"So we got to the very last day of shooting," Rogers recalls. "Vincenzo was so worried. He kept saying, 'I don't have enough time!' The Film Centre was li ke, 'You're finished after 12 hours, that's it. We're tearing down the sets the next day.' And we were like, 'What? You can't do that!'"

"We got to 12 hours and we'd been negotiating with the Film Centre saying the people who want to stay can stay, but the peo-ple who want to go home can go home—can we do that? Yes, you can do that. So we made an announcement and half the crew left, which was really interesting. All the mutineers basically left and the rest of us stayed—we had about 15 people. Then people just started dropping out and getting tired. Vincenzo is so nice, so he was: 'Just go, it's fine, it's fine.' I think we ended up with like four or five people at the end."

Continued on page 168 >

The Longest Day

The last "day" of filming took a whopping 37 hours and pushed cast and crew to the breaking point. Says Natali today, "I could only have made *Cube,* under the circumstances, completely independently. That movie would never have been made in the mainstream, it just wouldn't have been possible."

One of the tensest moments in *Cube* as it is rendered in Natali's storyboarding.

Opposite: Maurice Dean Wint and Nicky Guadagni preparing to shoot Quentin's dropping of Holloway.

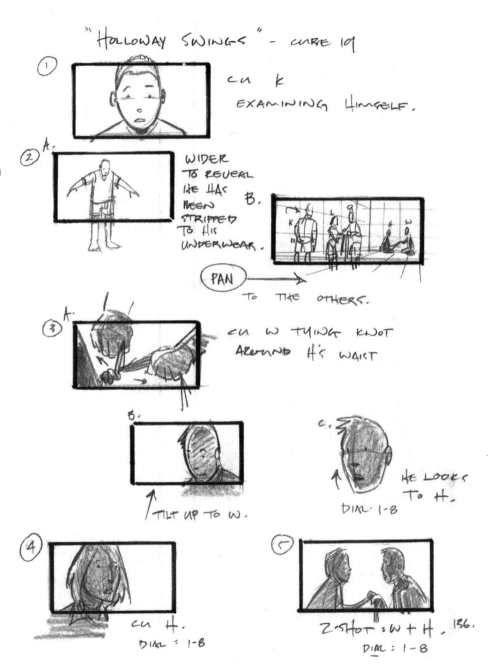

"HOLLOWAY SWINGS" - CUBE 19

1) CU K EXAMINING HIMSELF.

2) A. WIDER TO REVEAL HE HAS BEEN STRIPPED TO HIS UNDERWEAR.

B.

PAN TO THE OTHERS.

3) A. CU W TYING KNOT AROUND H'S WAIST

B. TILT UP TO W.

C. HE LOOKS TO H. DIAL 1-8

4) CU H. DIAL: 1-8

5) 2-SHOT: W + H. 136. DIAL: 1-8

'They were all far more film acting savvy than me and I just tried to keep up with them. Holloway did have some advantages though—she got to quip 'single bullet theory,' swallow a button by mistake, stick up for the autistic kid, get socked by the cop, sacrifice herself for the group and dangle before dying—who could not like her? She seemed to like herself, too.'

↘ **Guadagni**

Somewhere between hours 25 and 37 is when Louise and Raymond Macintosh worked their magic on what would become the very first effect we see in the completed film: the cubing of Alderson.

Natali says, "I honestly don't remember when that idea came up but it just seemed like a really shocking image, and of course it was metaphorical for the whole movie so a good way to start."

"We shot it slow motion," Rogers explains. "There's a shot in that film where you can see the flickering of the light bulbs, all these imperfections. But it was really hard—I just couldn't focus.

"I think on the last couple shots we were like 'Vincenzo, focus!' There was six of us and we were all looking through [the camera] to make sure that things were focused because we were shooting 35 [mm]. When you shoot for 37 hours and you have to really function, it becomes *the* battle. But to me it's the best memory I have of any film I've worked on—those last five hours.

"It was 'What's the next shot?!' It wasn't like 'Aw fuck, what's the next shot—have you got enough?' And then he said, 'I think I'm done.' He had all his lists. 'Are you sure, are you sure?' 'No, no, I could do one more.' 'OK, OK, let's do it.'"

Says Andrew Miller, "We're all there and we've lost half the crew and no one had slept and everyone was kind of pitching in and we all felt like student filmmakers. We vowed to have real budgets. For us it's been the same way every movie since. I guess it's just unavoidable and you end up spending as much money as you have and constantly need more. Nobody's ever like 'Yeah, we've got an extra million dollars, what do you want to do with it?' I guess it's just the nature of the beast."

"We've all done 20-hour days and 22-hour days, but 37 fucking hours," marvels Rogers. "It was just a test for the respect and love for [Natali]. I'm not advocating everyone works 37 hours, but it *made* that film. Good films do have to be somewhat painful."

Arguably some of that pain shows up on screen in the performances. Whether or not that's true, David Hewlett believes that it's the earnestness with which the characters approach their situation that makes *Cube* work. While there may be a lighter moment here or there, the characters never forget or gloss over the direness of their predicament. "You can't be flip about it. Often there's this sense now with a lot of these movies—even the actors approaching the movies—you've gotta believe the people are in trouble. If you don't believe they're in trouble then we don't care. There are too many cool hip lines and shrugging off danger, then no one feels that peril. What was great about that film was that the performances were kind of big and terrified. Everyone was so terrified the entire time, you could never forget that you were uncomfortable and that you were going to die."

Though audiences came for the kills, they ended up caring for the characters, something almost unheard of in horror movies today. This was mostly down to little moments sprinkled throughout that allowed us to see them for who they really were.

"I remember Vincenzo ran out of time the last day and cut the scene where Worth ties the rope around Holloway and we have quite a *tête-à-tête,*" says Guadagni (see storyboard on p. 166). It was one of the best scenes in the script and I was looking forward

Sleep deprived and jubilant, Natali and Hewlett unwind at the *Cube* wrap party.

'we did a commercial later where [vincenzo] had to get mad at somebody and he did. i think he learned that lesson that you have to be assertive. it's very hard for canadians to do that.'

↘ Rogers

to it as her final chapter. It bothered me like crazy. I may have begged him. Yes, I think I begged him. I also tried to sound older and very wise. That he was making a big mistake—cutting out the scene with heart. And to his great credit he found the time and overtime bucks to shoot it and it's a beautiful scene."

And with that it was over. Bleary-eyed and dazed from nearly two straight days of shooting, yet still high on the adrenaline it had taken to wrap things up, the few people left knew they'd never get to sleep immediately after wrap...so they went to the movies: Tim Burton's $70 million WTF flick *Mars Attacks*.

"We liked our film better," Rogers says with a chuckle. "We all fell asleep."

17: the c.o.r.e. of *cube*

HAVING WRAPPED SHOOTING on *Cube* in early December 1996, Natali and John Sanders began the grueling editing process early the following year. The greatest challenge now facing them: neatly splicing together live action with the visual effects created by C.O.R.E.

'$10,000 Would've Gotten Them One Shot'

Since his start in the '80s, visual effects master Robert Munroe has racked up an impressive CV, including work on everything from the 2013 Robert Redford one-man-against-the-elements flick *All is Lost* to modern classics like the first *X-Men* film and *The Tudors* television series. And yet, he says, "it's funny because people see my credit list and they go, oh you worked on that, you worked on that—oh, you worked on *Cube*?!"

Back in 1996 *Cube* was just another project trying to find someone to inject a little VFX magic into its production, and C.O.R.E., Munroe's effects studio, was already stretched pretty thin as it was. In the process of wrapping up their work on Guillermo del Toro's *Mimic*, his team of 25 or so people were

Opposite: An early cube-wall illustration by Natali.

'Eye candy puts asses in seats like no other department. You take a look at the box office successes... When you get a visual FX artist or the FX crew or supervisor and they're putting their heart and soul into it like Richard Parker in *Life of Pi* or *Benjamin Button* or Dren in *Splice*, your work takes on a whole new meaning.'

↘**Robert Munroe**

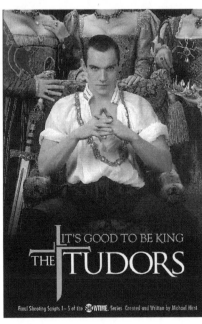

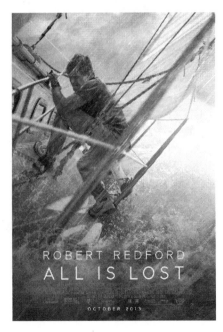

also plugging away at TV shows including *The Outer Limits*, *PSI Factor: Chronicles of the Paranormal* and *Lexx*. This also meant that there would not be anybody working exclusively on *Cube*, as "there was a lot of other work we were doing simultaneously," he explains.

But first, Natali would have to pitch him on the project.

"I have to say that Vincenzo and Mehra [Meh], his producer, were two of the most prepared filmmakers I've ever met in my life. Vincenzo came in with a script, with the bible, with his sketches, with his storyboards—everything," Munroe remembers. "He came in so well prepared, and I had just come off a movie working with another director who was also extremely well prepared, and that was Guillermo del Toro.

"After they left, my in-house producer called Mehra and said what kind of money do you have for the visual effects, and he was told they had $10,000 set aside," he says with a laugh. "$10,000 would've gotten them one shot."

Points in favor of working on *Cube*? "This guy was going to be quite the talented young filmmaker, and the production company behind it was the **Canadian Film Centre**, and we'd always wanted to be associated with the CFC—[founder] Norman Jewison is one of my heroes in this business. So we just decided to do this as a *pro bono* job."

C.O.R.E. would later be required to calculate the value of the visual effects they created for the film. That figure: C$400,000 (or more than half of *Cube*'s total C$750,000 budget).

Canadian Film Centre

Shortly after working on *Cube*, Robert Munroe joined the board of CFC where he has remained ever since. "In Canada we've always had this sense that we have to go out and find already existing stars or nobody will ever watch our movies," he says. "It felt insulated and isolated. The Canadian Film Centre is doing a pretty remarkable job of breaking down those cube walls."

175

Opposite: Munroe's work runs the gamut from Hollywood blockbusters to prestigious television series.

> '[Vincenzo] was never really a computer nerd or anything. I often laugh at how bad he is at technology, but for some reason he's managed to jump into that whole geek culture with *Cube*. It's like a classic nerd paranoid story.'
>
> ↘ **Hewlett**

Don't I Know You...?

Up until a few years ago Munroe always thought that Natali approached him out of the blue to work on *Cube*; this had certainly been how he put it to audiences whenever the pair appeared on discussion panels together. Finally, the director politely reminded him that they had actually worked together on a television pilot for CBS called *Shock Treatment* a couple years before *Cube*.

Recalls Munroe, "It was kind of a VFX-driven comedy with a young actor [Matthew Walker]—a kind of manic Robin Williams or Matt Frewer [aka "Max Headroom"] kind of guy. He lived as an avatar inside this boy's PC and he'd come out in different forms, whether it was as a superhero or sometimes he'd take on different shapes because he was a CG/visual effects creation."

Because the show was so VFX heavy, director Michael Schultz had wanted a storyboard artist, which is how Natali ended up getting involved.

"So Vincenzo would come to meetings with me and the director and sit quietly in the corner and take notes and draw storyboards," says Munroe. "I feel horrible because I should've recognized this talented artist sitting in the corner doing all this, but I was more focused on my interaction with the director; I really never paid this young man any heed. When he finally told me that was him [years later] I felt about as big as Ant Man."

Even if Munroe hadn't remembered Natali, the director remembered him and had been impressed by his work. However carefully he and Bijelic had crafted *Cube* to be a one-set story with a sharp focus on the actors' tensions, they both knew a certain amount of visual effects would be crucial to prevent it from having that stage play feel.

Cube's Titanic Challenge

"I'm sure if I looked at it today I would be embarrassed," says Munroe of the scenes he and his team put together of the glimpses we get outside the cube but inside the shell. But this is the admission of an artist who's seen his craft and its tools mature dramatically in sophistication over the 20 years since *Cube* made its debut.

Munroe started C.O.R.E. back in 1994 while acting as a visual effects supervisor on the TV movie adaptation of William Shatner's *TekWar* novels, he explains. "We were just a little department within the art department—an in-house video effects crew."

As the team tackled increasingly ambitious effects, they not only developed **sophisticated technological innovations**, but also learned how to make those effects better jell with the rest of the action on screen. *Cube* is a good example.

"The interior of the cube was pretty much the whole film—you were in a 14′ x14′ x14′ room and the actors were in a very intimate way," says Munroe. "The tension was very, very high, and then the claustrophobic quality was amplified. And *then* when we get to the part where we go outside the room—it was a challenge that it had to fit within the same film thematically, from an art direction standpoint, and even just a logical one."

Munroe got involved in the production early on, long before anything was shot, he remembers. "I'm typically the first person

Sophisticated technological innovations

Inspired by their work on *Mimic*, C.O.R.E. came up with a process to match the effect that specific gels would have on lighting—a system that got a real workout on *Cube*. "We created a very substantial supporting database that has photometric data for over 3,000 different lights used in the movie business, and over 500 different gels," says Munroe. "All you had to do was know what kind of light you had on set, input that, and the light was automatically calculated for you using this methodology. We used it extensively on *Cube*."

on a production prep and the last person off, or very close to it. You have to be there to help design the shots. It's critical that you're on very early because if you don't plan it out correctly, it's going to be shot incorrectly, it's going to be way more money in post. The most expensive shots are the ones that were unplanned, unexpected.

"It was pretty cool that in *this* little film we were using complete digital stunt doubles," say Munroe, "but that was the biggest challenge. We were doing stuff in some of those shots with completely digital doubles. The only other movie at the time that was doing that kind of thing was *Titanic*.

"This was before the time of really cheap and accessible cyber-scanning where you take an actor and put them on a turntable and there are a whole bunch of cameras that take pictures, giving you a 3D data set of that actor. You had to build it from scratch. Even if there was the technology at the time, we probably couldn't have afforded it for *Cube*."

In a detail that sounds a tad surreal if you don't know a lot about the early days of digital effects, C.O.R.E. ended up buying "a generic human being" 3D model from a company that specialized in them at the time.

"The challenge was we had to try to mold and form that generic body to look somewhat like (Maurice Dean Wint) and give him the same skin tone, the same hair color, the same wardrobe and all that," says Munroe. "And of course I told Vincenzo we just can't get that close [with the camera] because this is just a generic model. Vincenzo was happy about that because in his work

'[vincenzo] likes the stuff that's really, really micro or really, really wide. you can be up on somebody's eyeball and then the next shot is as wide as a city block.'

↘ **Munroe**

ZOOM IN TO RENNES EYE.

B:

he likes the stuff that's really, really micro or really, really wide. You can be up on somebody's eyeball and then the next shot is as wide as a city block. So he actually liked the fact that he had to stay wide. Those digital doubles had to be little performers and they were. Those shots had to be pretty much 100% CG."

Whatever the effects challenges *Cube* posed, Munroe says, "it's incredible how it still resonates with people 20 years later. There was nothing in that film that talked down to the audience—everything about it challenged you. I'm surprised at myself that I didn't realize what the trajectory would've been."

18: music without music

WHILE A ROUSING synth or orchestral piece can lend a film added dimension, such a score could've easily undercut the tension of *Cube*.

"Vince told me he didn't want anything that sounded like music," recalls *Cube* composer Mark Korven of Natali's direction. "He didn't want anything with melody or harmony or anything like that. It was a bit of a challenge because whenever I veered toward anything that sounded conventional as far as instrumentation, he didn't want to be able to recognize any instruments I was using. So I was really trying to dig deep to find new sounds."

What Korven came up with is something that initially feels like a gumbo containing a little *Alien* here, a smidgen of *Gremlins* there, but which quickly asserts itself as a wholly unique soundscape.

At the time of this writing he is enjoying some much-deserved acclaim for his moody soundtrack to Robert Eggers' slow-burn 2015 feature film debut, *The Witch*. To ratchet up the tension on that 17th century horror tale, he employed, among other instruments, a Swedish medieval bowed string instrument

Opposite: *Cube* composer Mark Korven shown here with the "Apprehension Engine," an instrument he co-created, that is used for scoring soundtracks.

called a nyckelharpa, a cello, an experimental bit of equipment called a megabass waterphone, and the improvisational talents of Toronto's choral ensemble The Element Choir.

"So now I'm getting all these calls from other people who want me to do horror stuff," he admits. "It's so easy to get pigeonholed in this business."

Korven began scoring films back in the late '80s with Patricia Rozema's (*Mansfield Park*) feature debut *I've Heard the Mermaids Singing*, and spent the next half-dozen years or so working in feature films before concentrating on documentaries and television series.

From what he recalls, his first interaction with the *Cube* team came from out of the blue with a call from producer Mehra Meh. "I don't really know how my name came up. There's really nothing in my reel that would indicate I could do something like that," he says.

The budget on offer was small: $1,000 and an additional $500 for expenses according to production records, though Korven remembers it more as "something like $3,500 which, for a feature film, was really more of an honorarium. But I knew it was going to be a great film and they put most of their money up on the screen.

"I said I'll do it but I need this and this and this in the contract," he explains. One of those riders gave him the right to release the soundtrack, which he did in 2008.

Little did the composer know that the creation of *Cube*'s soundtrack would require him to rethink what the purpose of a film score—and indeed music itself—actually is.

'In normal circumstances I would not have done the film but I knew Vince was really talented and that trumped everything.'

↘ **Mark Korven,**
Cube **composer**

Cube Soundtrack Production Notes

Like every other aspect of *Cube*, Natali and Bijelic gave a great deal of thought to the role music would play in creating the film's oppressive atmosphere. The following are excerpts from the production notes:

> ↘ "Sound and music more than anything are going to define [the cube's] personality."

> ↘ "Sound and music are a chance to really underline the stranger, existential and enigmatic parts of the story."

> ↘ "I wonder if there is something 'pretty' about the music that it might be more effective than a haunting score. Words that spring to mind: TIMELESS, ABSTRACT, PSYCHEDELIC, AMBIENT, ENIGMATIC, ETHEREAL. Films for reference: *Das Boot, Alien, Eraserhead, THX 1138, 2001: A Space Odyssey, The Shining, Koyaanisqatsi**.

* This last, Koyaanisqatsi, *is a 1982 experimental film by American director Godfrey Reggio that features a blend of time-lapsed and slow motion footage accompanied by a Philip Glass score.*

The Tension Between Words and Music

On its surface the *Cube* soundtrack consists of synthesizers with the occasional sampling—such as **vocals**—dropped in. Natali's insistence on leaving harmony and melody of any kind at the door pushed Korven to find new ways to work musically with what was on screen.

"I remember one hard sell I had with Vince," he says. "There's sort of a theme that goes din-din-din-din/din-din-din-din—if you can call it a theme. *That* was a really hard sell. It was too much like a conventional harmonic thing for him but I eventually sold him on it. I said, 'You've got to have *something* for people to hold on to, some kind of a recognizable theme.' So I managed to get that past the goalie. I got what he was going for—I thought that was totally cool that he wanted to do something different and didn't want anything conventional. He wanted the sound to be strictly a *Cube* sound." He chuckles. "Also, he's a total sweetheart too, so that helps a lot."

The density and importance of the dialogue to the plot in *Cube* posed another challenge—the score had to enhance the viewing experience without overpowering what is being said on screen. "You definitely have to craft things differently," Korven says. "The way a composer looks at a film score is that dialogue is the melody and what you're doing is backing up that melody, so you've got to stay clear of it. As they say in the business, dialogue is king."

It was dialogue, in fact, that led to his only real disagreement with the director.

"There were like two music montages in the film. After I'd

Vocals

The vocalizations you hear in the background were done by Korven's wife, Cathy Nosaty—a musician, composer, musical director and educator. Says Korven, "I had her improvise a whole bunch of sounds, sampled that, and used that in the score."

written the piece, over the second montage, Vince put in some ADR to help explain one of the character's motivations in the story. I really took exception to that because I thought, **'Hey, that was supposed to be music** —what's with all this dialogue going on over the top?' So I got a little upset by that.

"But on reflection—and Vince told me this at the time—he said, 'This may be the only chance I get to do a film exactly the way I want to do it.' Because as you move on through your career there are other powers that come in and they have influence over the creative choices that you're allowed to make. But when he said that, I kind of got it. Certainly years later I totally understand where he was coming from, that my role was really to help him to attain his creative vision for the film."

These creative differences aside, he remembers his experience on *Cube* being "very pleasurable, mostly because Vince would come over and we got along really great. He was very young and very positive and very enthusiastic and I really liked that."

His one regret? "I would've taken advantage of the popularity [of *Cube*]. It went to France and went through the roof there—it gained a real cult following. If I could rethink my course of action at the time, I would've connected up with a record company to [release the soundtrack]. I've had a lot of attention for the music and I feel like I didn't really take advantage of that. I threw something up on iTunes but it wasn't really a proper release—there's no *Cube* art or anything. I recently had an offer to do a real soundtrack for *Cube* but we've had some difficulty dealing with the artwork. You really need that artwork to properly ID the soundtrack."

'Hey, that was supposed to be music...'

'I dabble in filmmaking myself, just as an indie, low-budget guy," says Korven. "And once I started making my own films, I understood that perspective, that music is generally the tail end of the process. By the time someone has finished their film, music can be sort of an afterthought. Once I started working on my own short films, when someone came into my music studio and they'd finished their film, I just wanted to give them a big hug because they've done it. I have some idea of what they've gone through.'

EXT. CUBE - PROFILE ANGLE.

QUENTIN DROPS HOLLOWAY.

19: outside the cube

ONE OF THE reasons the original *Cube* movie works so well—and that the sequels for the most part do not—is that in Natali's universe, the world begins and ends inside that enormous mechanized hell. Except for a few crumbs of backstory from Worth, we are given no idea of what lies beyond the cube walls. While in hindsight it is precisely this tension that keeps our eyes glued to the screen for 90 minutes, it was also one more strike against it as far as the producers were concerned.

"They wanted a context," says Natali. "They wanted to know when this is taking place, where these people are from. A lot of people wanted us to cut outside the cube, to see who was behind the cube, who was pushing the buttons. It was a very scary thing for the producers—anyone who was behind financing the movie—to consider making a movie that doesn't answer those questions. I think a lot of people *watching* the movie are frustrated with the film because it doesn't offer those answers."

As we've seen, the earliest scripts not only peeked outside the cube but actually spent a reasonable amount of time there. It was only through the writing process that Natali and Bijelic dis-

Opposite: Natali's storyboard glimpse at the space between the outside of the cube and the shell.

'[The producers] wanted the Jigsaw guy [from *Saw*], they wanted the evil person pushing the buttons. And that was always the point where Andre and I would step away and say we can't do that because, for us, the power of the cube was that it was faceless. It had no human manipulator that we could see; the movie was entirely from the point of view of the rats trapped in the maze. For all of its flaws, I think it is absolutely an uncompromising version of that story.'

↘ **Natali**

covered that the less they showed beyond the prison, the more effective the story became.

Ironically, by the time *Cube* was being seriously considered for filming, The Feature Film Project was pushing the creators to show the audience exactly what they didn't want to show. Writer Graeme Manson and story editor Hugh Graham had joined the team at this point, tipping the argument further toward showing the world outside.

"At that time we considered showing Worth outside the cube," Natali admits. "I think we wrote something—we didn't shoot it—but he's in his office and you see him walk out into downtown Toronto—we couldn't have done anything else. The idea is that he walks into a very cube-like world. If you've ever been in downtown Toronto, it's full of very modern, grid-like structures. And all of this would be seen from a surveillance point of view, and that would be a prologue to the movie."

But they *did* shoot it.

William Phillips recalls it being pure guerrilla filmmaking. They grabbed Hewlett and said, "'OK David, in exactly 3 minutes we're going to roll the camera so you go through the other side of that building and just come out.' I think the security guards were all cheesed off. It was that classic young filmmaker thing of keep shooting until someone tells you you can't."

In the end, the footage wasn't used. But The Feature Film Project continued to push for something that would give the cube some context, however slight. At last Natali relented.

At the end of the final film, Andrew Miller's Kazan discovers

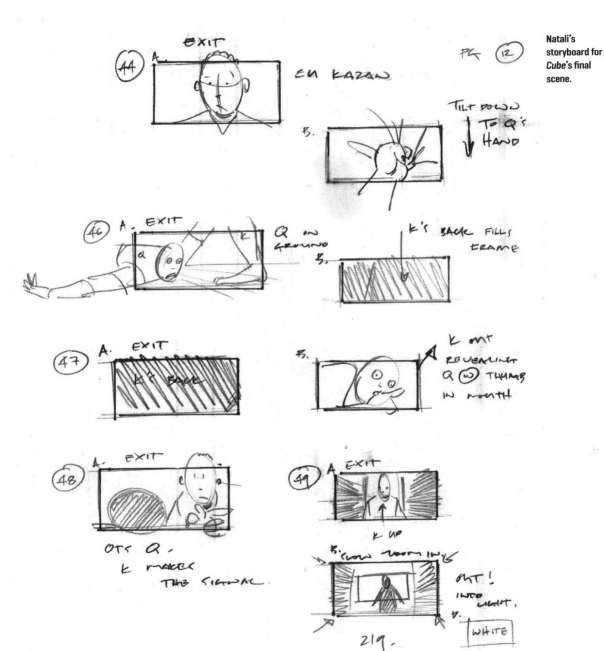

Natali's storyboard for *Cube*'s final scene.

189

Fri, Nov 15, 1996

PINK REVISED

SHOOTING SCHEDULE
THE CUBE

43

Script Dated: NOV 7th 1996

SC 130

EXT City — DAY - 4 — 2/8 Pages

Montage shots of busy city

SC 4

EXT Alley — DAY - -1 — 2/8 Pages

Worth is Captured

- CAST MEMBERS
  1. Worth
- ATMOSPHERE
  2 Thugs

- PROPS
  Worth's Briefcase

SC 129

EXT City — DAY - 4 — 2/8 Pages

Kazan is back in the city

- CAST MEMBERS
  5. Kazan

END OF DAY 20 - TOTAL PAGES - 4 4/8

To appease the Powers That Be, scenes outside the cube were shot but tossed during editing.

the exit and begins to walk into the light, the sole survivor of the carnage within.

While the main unit was wrapping up shooting, second-unit director Oscar Fenoglio shot an epilogue that picked up the action from that final scene. The big reveal? "It was Kazan out in the world wandering aimlessly among these cube-like buildings," says Natali.

"Vincenzo wasn't there [when it was shot] so we all knew that it would never be used," says Miller, who recalls the coda taking less than a day to shoot. "He's so hands on with everything. I think it probably was a producer's thing where he finally said, 'OK fine, go shoot something and we'll talk about it later.' "

Though it was cut into the movie, the team never showed it to anybody, Natali says. "It just became immediately clear that leaving the cube was a mistake. It also had the effect of shattering the reality we had created with our set. Once you juxtaposed the cube set with the real world, it started to make the cube set look phony. But when you see the movie without any external context, you believe it. Ultimately I think the real reason was that when we were looking at the end of the movie, that shot of Kazan walking into the light is so powerful, so iconic, that anything after that was going to be a letdown.

"So [the epilogue] was jettisoned and hopefully that footage has been lost and destroyed. It's no disrespect to Oscar, he did the best he could, but it was never going to work."

"There's a need in a lot of movies to wrap things up, to make things neat and comfortable and to give everybody an answer

'those scenes that producers or distributors are so desperate to add at the last minute are almost always the first scenes to be cut out.'

↘ **Phillips**

and a reason," says Hewlett. "I think the whole point of that film, which I loved, is that there is no big plan. It's almost like the banality of evil, all these tiny little betrayals that people do in their lives somehow leads to this massive evil."

"I don't know what the world was like when Kazan leaves the cube and I don't know what it was like when they entered it," says Miller. "There' s no question that ending is satisfying without answering the biggest question in the movie. That's such a rarity in movies and that's why Vincenzo is so protective of it ultimately. I think one of the lasting things about *Cube* is that ending because people do trick endings now, and people do surprise endings, and people do fakeout endings. But *Cube* is both satisfying and interesting at the same time, and that's just rare. Seeing him leave, it's a powerful thing and I think it sticks with you."

While the decision to retain that mystery might've been the right one storywise, the director believes it hobbled its performance in America. "There were overtures from [film distributor] Dimension when we first screened the movie in Toronto but they never made a real offer. There wasn't anybody of consequence out there at that time to release the film who could get behind it because it was just a little too weird.

"In fact, when Trimark picked it up initially—they were the company that released the film—they wanted me to shoot an ending, kind of an additional scene, not a big thing, but where you'd see Kazan walk out of the cube and you would see that he is walking into a space that is full of many other cubes. (And they also wanted to add an action sequence to the middle of the movie.) But thankfully because of the way we made the film and the deal we made with them, I didn't have to do anything. I refused. But that inclination was always there, and I think that's one of the reasons why the film was never allowed to get a big theatrical release. If you'll pardon the expression, it was just too outside the box."

'I think Andrew Miller and myself, I think we just kicked back all our checks [from *Cube*]. I think I have a check still somewhere that says 'zero dollars' because they had to do all the paperwork on it. So Andrew and I would get these checks with zero dollars on it. We talked about framing one and saying 'thanks for nothing.' But we had to be paid a certain amount of money because of whatever the rules and regulations were.'

↘**Hewlett**

incenzo Natali

OIS prix au festival de Gérardmer, dont le Grand, c'est le nombre d'or [de V]incenzo Natali, qui a trouvé avec son premier film, *Cube*, l'ad-équation [...] entre trouillomètre et SF intelligente. Un comble pour ce jeune [...] qui avoue son ignorance crasse des subtilités mathématiques ! Six per[son]- [...]s en quête de hauteur, coincés dans un cube aux proportions dan- [...], voilà la trame de ce trompe-l'œil claustro, filmé à la vitesse de la lumière [...]

n'avait succombé au côté obscur du 7e Art après le choc *Star wars* ! Ap[rès] [...]ryboarder, il intègre en 1996 une école de cinéma et subjugue ave[c son] métrage, *Elevated*, cloîtré (déjà !) dans un ascenceur possédé. Au [...] l'école se dit prête à financer son premier long : l'aventure de *Cube* [com]mencer. Le rêve aussi, puisqu'en dépit des péripéties (la pièce en plex[iglas] cauchemar pour l'ingénieur du son, les sas ne s'ouvrent pas), du bud[get] (350 000 dollars), le produit fini est exempt de concessions : "Je vou[...]

20: the slow punch of success

SHORTLY AFTER POST-PRODUCTION wrapped on *Cube*, Natali screened it for the two other Canadian directors arguably most responsible for the film: Canadian Film Centre Founder Norman Jewison and David Cronenberg.

"It was before *Cube* had been seen by anyone really," says Natali. "We screened it at Deluxe which is a lab—they have a very nice theater there. It might've been the first screening of the finished film, actually. Cronenberg is a very nice guy, just very supportive. It was a big thrill for me obviously."

After the screening, Natali called the director for a quote they could use for *Cube's* marketing. "After he gave it to me I think I sent him Alderson's head in a box as a thank you," Natali says. "And a *Cube* hat, if I remember correctly. It was a very beautiful sculpture."

Finally, *Cube* was submitted to what has become the launch pad for hundreds of successful films over the years: the Toronto International Film Festival (TIFF).

Since its founding in 1976, TIFF has grown into one of the most influential film festivals in the world, and not just in sci-

Opposite: A clipping from *Ciné Live* magazine's April 1999 issue. *Cube* found its most enthusiastic audience in France.

fi/horror circles, either. Works as diverse as *American Beauty*, *Black Swan* and *The King's Speech* have all enjoyed their world premieres there.

And *Cube*'s own hard-scrabble rise to cult status began there on Sept. 9, 1997—its world premiere.

In Canada 'They Tend to Eat Their Own'

Whatever success *Cube* ultimately enjoyed "happened in slow motion," says Natali with a laugh. "I describe it as a slow punch." Still reeling from the uphill battle to get the picture made in the first place, "I wasn't even aware it was a success until it had passed.

"Honestly there were moments when we were making *Cube* where I thought we wouldn't even be able to finish it because what we were trying to put on the screen was so far outside the budget and schedule we had. There are all kinds of issues that arose where there were serious concerns that the guarantor— the people who had put up the money—were going to step in and take over the film because, on paper, it was impossible to finish."

Certainly the director was not expecting much from *Cube*'s premiere at TIFF, at least not after he got his hands on a copy of Toronto's *Now Magazine*, a free alternative paper that also served that week as a guide to the film festival. As he told the author in 2009's *The New Horror Handbook*, "I think the first review for it was probably one of the worst reviews I've ever read for any movie ever. I thought 'This is going to be a disaster;

'When you make an independent film there are different levels of success. Certainly the first thing you realize when you've made a film is just finishing the movie is a form of success.'

↘**Natali**

FAX COVER

Message:

To Whom It May Concern:

This quote is from David Cronenberg and is for Vincenzo Natali.

Thanks.

D.C.

```
Cube is as ruthlessly beautiful and compelling as a
geometrical theorem. A significant debut for a gifted
writer/director.
```

197

To: Vincenzo Natali	From : David Cronenberg
Company :	Company : Toronto Antenna Ltd.
Fax Number :	Fax Number :
Pages including this cover page: 2	Subject : Cube Quote

A private screening for director David Cronenberg yielded a glowing blurb from the master.

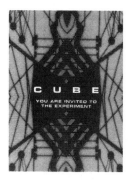

Welcome to the Experiment

"I think what's so much fun about *Cube* for me, but hopefully for the people watching the movie, is that it is a kind of experiment," says Natali. "When we first screened it, we handed out invitations to people and the tagline was 'You are invited to the experiment.' That had two meanings, of course. On one hand our characters are probably inside some kind of experiment—in my mind the cube has to be some kind of behavioral experiment, even if it's a long forgotten one or it's gone horribly awry. But for us, the people who made the movie, it was very much an experiment—we didn't know if it was going to work or not."

I'm never going to work again.' "

Recalls Andre Bijelic, "The reviews certainly weren't great around here; there were some pretty vicious ones locally, anyway."

"They never like you in Toronto," says Derek Rogers philosophically. "They never like you until you become known in France or the states."

"I think that's true," says Bijelic. "You have to become successful somewhere else to become successful in Canada—they tend to eat their own. Of course in Canada there's no real distribution system; it's so bad. Movies will play for a week or two to empty theaters and then they'll disappear."

In truth it was that fate that they all feared most for *Cube*. After all they had been through, the worst thing they could imagine was a few pissy reviews followed by waves upon waves of silent indifference. The *Now Magazine* piece had only increased that fear.

"It was a slow start for *Cube*," says Hewlett. "When it came out, nothing happened. We started working on *Nothing*, and the plan for that was that it was going to be an under-a-million-dollar movie because we assumed we weren't going to have any money. We thought that *Cube* had fizzled. But once it hit internationally, it took off. That made America take notice again."

"The cast met at a bar on Church Street," recalls Nicky Guadagni about the Toronto International Film Festival (TIFF) premiere. "We had a drink, then I was ushered into a waiting limo and it drove literally around the block to Yonge Street and we

The Festival Circuit

1: At Sundance, left to right: filmmaker Carol Clusiau, Natali, and producers Mehra Meh and Betty Orr **2:** Paris Film Festival. **3:** In Paris, left to right: Kelley Doris, Hewlett, Miller, Bijelic **4:** Natali celebrating at Sundance

...and starred Hewlett

"We're a pretty tight bunch," says David Hewlett. "I don't think we've really lost touch with many of the core *Cube* people. The [digital] effects guy, Robert Munroe, was at my wedding, and I met him from *Cube*. I think what happens with film, you get a bunch of people who you like and respect—I find they go hand in hand. When you find people who are hard workers and who are fellow nerds or geeks in this journey, you latch on and you don't let go because they understand what you're talking about and what you're excited about, and they want to be a part of it."

got out and there was this hyped-up, surreal walk along a red carpet—jeez like a *real* red carpet—and I left my body. When I came back into my body I was sitting watching the opening credits and eventually saw my face the size of a building, and I left my body again."

That weekend the film took home TIFF's Best Canadian First Feature Film award. Natali was awestruck.

David Hewlett recalls that the director turned around and gave the prize money to *Cube*'s "door doctor" and second-unit supervisor, William Phillips, to make his own film, *Milkman* (1999). The short was shot by *Cube*'s Derek Rogers with some second-unit work and storyboards by Natali**...and starred Hewlett.**

It also began a new, weird sort of existence for the filmmakers, Bijelic remembers. "Once it was done and it went around to festivals, that's when it was like a double life happening. I went to a film festival in Mexico City—it was like being a celebrity. We were put up in a nice hotel and we had a car and a translator doing press. Then I go back home and go back to bartending or whatever I was doing. It was this weird double life: half celebrity, half nobody." Natali is a bit more specific: "Maybe 70% nobody, 30% celebrity."

Trimark Pictures picked up *Cube* for a 1998 American theatrical release, with Cineplex-Odeon Films opening it in Canada a year earlier. Over time, it received DVD (and some theatrical) distribution in a number of countries, including Germany, the UK, Spain, Argentina and Sweden.

Natali gave the prize money *Cube* received at TIFF to the film's "door doctor," William Phillips, to use for his own short, *Milkman*.

'the french are fantastic at the nihilistic story...basically it's fall in love and throw yourself off a bridge. they have this fantastic curiosity to their filmmaking.'

"I was shocked that it even got sold internationally; that wasn't something I was expecting," says Bijelic. "I thought *maybe* it would get a video release in the US."

By 1999 the *Cube* contingent had settled into the empty-nest syndrome peculiar to the indie scene after a film's been set loose in the world. And that's when they started hearing certain rumblings coming from France.

"We went to this film festival in Paris," recalls Hewlett. "We had a screening there and people were really excited about it, we were signing things. That was the first time we'd had that experience. The weird thing was I was in Hungary years and years after *Cube* had come out everywhere else and there was this poster for it up because it had just been released there. It was doing well there as well."

Of that Paris festival Miller says, "I think collectively it was one of our happiest moments because we just couldn't believe that people liked it so much. We did a 2½ hour Q&A and they were so thrilled and supportive; we felt like rock stars. There's a picture of the four of us and we just look stunned, like little kids at Christmas."

"In truth when the movie was actually released in the United States and in Canada, it didn't perform very well," Natali admits. "It didn't make any money theatrically. It was a perceived success within the industry but it wasn't like the public at large even knew what the hell *Cube* was.

"However, nearly a year after its release in the states, it came out in France and it actually made a lot of money over there—it was a type of **Blair Witch success**. Maybe not quite on that scale, but it was a big box office hit in France. That was probably two years after I finished making the movie and I was in America, so I kind of heard it had done well but I didn't really know how well. If I had been aware of it at the time, I would've capitalized on it more, but I really didn't know."

And thus began the director's transition from the First-Time Canadian Film Director's cube to the larger, and infinitely more frustrating, cube called Hollywood.

But first, an intermission.

Blair Witch success

The Blair Witch Project was released in July 1999, three months after *Cube*. Of course nobody at the time could've predicted that the low-budget horror movie (made for an estimated $60,000) would go on to gross in excess of $240 million worldwide.

謎を解け。

21: sequels and imitators

LIKE ALL GREAT films (and quite a few rotten ones), *Cube* inspired sequels, as well as frequent—yet at the time of this writing, un-delivered upon—threats of a remake.

A lot of abuse has been heaped upon Andrzej Sekuła's *Cube 2: Hypercube* (2002) and rightfully so, especially as it commits the most unpardonable sin of all: making the viewer question the value of the first film. It belongs to that long, long list of hor-ror movie sequels that retell the story of the first movie, badly.

Summarizing the plot of *Hypercube* is nearly as challenging as watching it. That's saying something, chiefly because of a somnolent cast, poor direction, office-cubicle-like sets, and the movie's maddening habit of discarding ideas as quickly as it introduces them, only to scurry off in another direction. It feels not so much like a feature film as drama students reenacting the original *Cube* for YouTube.

It begins promisingly enough depicting people seemingly shrink-wrapped to gurneys, followed by one of these waking up in the cube. She enters another room and is promptly blown upward toward the ceiling. However, what follows is a virtual

Opposite: This promotional image for *Cube 2: Hypercube* is about as compelling as it gets for what proved to be a misguided sequel.

rehash of the cube characters meeting and getting to know (and suspect) each other, their personalities pretty close to the ones from the original.

In what turns out to be a truly catastrophic decision, the producers went with brightly lit cube rooms indistinguishable from one another, doubtless plunging the money saved into what ultimately turned out to be some pretty poor CG effects. And all in the cause of convoluting the original, straight-forward story into a nonsensical dive into alternate realities explained through frequent references to "the tesseract"—the geometric idea of the four-dimensional cube. When all that fails, they throw in a few seconds of jump-cut nudity guaranteed to please neither on a narrative nor an erotic level. (How do you fuck up nudity? Behold the master class.)

God bless the hearty soul who wrote up the detailed scene-by-scene synopsis on Wikipedia—it does an excellent job of reassuring you that you didn't miss anything regarding the plot, the writers did.

"I tried to watch a little bit of it but it drove me crazy," says David Hewlett. "No offense to everyone's hard work but I didn't see the point. If you're going to do a sequel, you either have to reinvent it like *Aliens* did or you've got to have some other question you want to answer."

While not unwatchable, *Hypercube* comes close. What we have is essentially a haunted house movie without the props, fear or imagination—check out the Season 4 *Buffy the Vampire Slayer* episode "Fear Itself" to see the concepts in *Hypercube*

Andrzej Sekuła's *Hypercube*

Sekuła, who photographed *Hypercube* as well as directing it, had just come off a fantastic decade of playing cinematographer for everything from Quentin Tarantino's *Reservoir Dogs* (1992) and *Pulp Fiction* (1994) to Mary Harron's horror/comedy classic *American Psycho* (2000). Presumably directing *Hypercube* was his reward.

played for maximum effect, complete with character development and everything. And the criminally underappreciated 2009 psychological thriller *Triangle* nails perfectly the "seeing other versions of yourself" idea that *Cube 2* squanders.

Cube Zero

Two years later, **Ernie Barbarash**, in his directorial debut, took another whack at what Lions Gate Entertainment by now seemed to be envisioning as a full-on franchise; the result was *Cube Zero*.

Your opinion of *Cube Zero* will be dictated largely by a) How ruined you were for sequels by *Hypercube*, and b) How interested you are in the world outside the giant torture device. These two movies couldn't be more different. From the very first minute of *Cube Zero* we find ourselves in a darker (literally), grittier cube more akin to the original. Rather than kicking things off with a victim who simply flies upward out of view of the camera, we get a proper, gory death by acid.

The first killing done, we switch scenes to the cube control room where a slightly-disturbed looking worker, Eric, saves the victim's demise on a DVD, writing the man's name on its shiny surface. The reason for his distaste becomes obvious as we find him sketching his co-worker as a superhero—our technician is apparently the sensitive type, if the eyeglasses hadn't already clued you in to that fact. (He also has a distracting resemblance to *Stargate SG-1*'s Michael Shanks.)

What follows is a pretty intriguing little sci-fi thriller that

Ernie Barbarash

A producer on *Cube 2: Hypercube*, Barbarash went on to direct a small raft of direct-to-video action films, including Jean-Claude Van Damme starrers *Pound of Flesh*, *Six Bullets* and *Assassination Games*. He also had the dubious distinction of directing Roger Moore's final film appearance in 2017's *The Saint*.

isn't satisfied with merely reproducing the first movie horribly (hello *Hypercube*), but actually brings something new to the table by asking the question: What effect would running the cube's day-to-day operations have on its operators?

"I thought they were very clever in changing the point of view of the film, I thought that was great," says Natali. "And they avoided what I always feared a *Cube* sequel would do, which is just remake the first one; that film has its own identity. I don't like it when it's simply a retread of the first one, which is invariably what most sequels are.

"It didn't jibe with my *Cube* personally because I felt that if there was someone pushing buttons outside the cube, I didn't see it as a Terry Gilliam *Brazil* type of world. I think the cube is too well designed for that. I didn't picture filing cabinets and maintenance overalls. I think that diminishes what the cube is. I think something that diabolical would run better than that, if indeed anyone were running it. But that's fine—it's very difficult. That's part of the reason why I didn't want to be involved with the *Cube* sequels—I just didn't know what I could do."

While the reason the original film works so well is precisely because we never see who's behind it, it also fails to be ultimately horrifying for the same reason. Yes, somebody dropped these poor people into the maze, but we never feel there's a real malevolence at work here—when the cube kills someone, it's never personal.

Part of what makes *Cube Zero* so effective is that we not only see a bit of the power structure, we also see it targeting specific

'I still go places with *Stargate* and people are always coming up with *Cube* covers to sign or asking me about that. It's become such a classic in its way.'

↘ **Hewlett**

people with real malice. None of the traps in any of the films quite compares in brutality to the virtual brain rape of cube inmate Cassandra in this installment, nor the lobotomizing of Eric at the end. (Apologies for spoiling a 15-year-old film.)

Getting to know the cube workers adds another level of horror to the situation, particularly as we quickly surmise that they're as likely to be dropped into the machine as anybody. This isn't Orwell's *1984*, the cube's similarities to that book's Room 101 notwithstanding; this is Stalinist Russia right down to the ill-fitting uniforms.

Cube Zero "had a really brilliant premise," says Natali. "I thought it was very clever." (Above: Martin Roach and Stephanie Moore.)

EVERY NIGHTMARE HAS A BEGINNING.

CUBE ZERO

Natali says *Cube* is like *Jaws* in that it 'never sequelized well because you're inevitably telling the same story.'

Cube Zero's greatest contribution to the *Cube* mythos has to be its ending in which a freshly brain-fried Eric is dumped into the cube behaving in a very Kazan-like manner. But is he supposed to *be* Kazan? It appears so as Andrew Miller, who played the original, was asked to appear in this film, too.

"That script was so great; it was so flattering and fun and it was really imaginative, and I thought it would've been really fun to do," he says. "Not that I regret not doing it. My issue at the time was it was almost impossible for me to imagine doing anything regarding *Cube* without Dave and Vincenzo, let alone everyone else. They were shooting in Winnipeg and I had this image of me in a cube in Winnipeg going, 'Where are my friends? Where are the other cube people?' That's the reason I didn't do it more than anything, because I thought it seemed like such a great idea. And I enjoyed the movie."

For his part, Natali is very philosophical about the sequels. "When we made *Cube* it seemed like a miracle that we actually squeezed an hour and a half out of that premise, let alone having to do multiple sequels. Honestly, kudos to them for actually doing something different with it. For me the power of *Cube* was in not giving you that point of view, but keeping the perspective with the rats that were trapped in the maze because that's what that movie's about."

Cube's Imitators

One of *Cube*'s enduring legacies is the spate of imitators that it has spawned, or at least gave the appearance of spawning. A complete list of people-driven-crazy-in-one-setting films that appeared after its premiere could easily take up a chapter in itself. This includes everything from the M. Night Shyamalan-plotted stuck-in-an-elevator flick *Devil* (2010) to the very-*Cube*-like 2009 British thriller *Exam*. Perhaps the very best of these one-set nail biters is another Canadian offering: Bruce McDonald's 2008 word-virus/zombie-invasion creepout *Pontypool*.

This in turn gave birth to an even more widespread subgenre: the captive-in-a-house flicks, which usually follow the boy meets girl, boy imprisons girl model. In one of those fascinating displays of zeitgeist, this **all came to a head in 2007-08** with a slew of such movies including *Captivity* (2007), *Frontier(s)* (2007), *Inside* (2007), *Martyrs* (2008), *The Strangers* (2008), *Funny Games* (2007), 2007's *An American Crime* and *The Girl Next Door* (both inspired by the same true crime event), and many, many more.

That is not to say the idea disappeared after that. One of the most anticipated horror flicks in recent years was *10 Cloverfield Lane* (2016), the (kind of) sequel to 2008's giant-monster fest *Cloverfield*, which dispensed with the kaiju in favor of locking

All came to a head in 2007/2008

A disturbing coda to this phenomenon came in April 2008 when Elisabeth Fritzl in Austria revealed that her father, Josef, had held her captive in his basement for 24 years where he beat and raped her, ultimately fathering seven children with her. Not only did this revelation come on the tail end of this cinematic craze, it actually reinvigorated it, inspiring fictionalized and nonfiction recreations of the now-notorious case.

This whole subgenre

There is even a whole sub-subgenre of buried-underground/ stuck-in-a-phone-booth/locked-in-the-trunk-of-a-car flicks that come along like clockwork, often used as relatively inexpensive calling cards for up-and-coming filmmakers. See *Phone Booth* (2002), *The Call* (2013), etc. This trend began way back in 1972 with the *The Longest Night*, a TV movie about a kidnapper who buries the daughter of a businessman in a sophisticated coffin that will keep her alive just long enough for him to collect the ransom. As if that wasn't horrible enough, this was actually based on the real-life 1968 abduction of Barbara Mackle.

Mary Elizabeth Winstead in John Goodman's underground bunker. Then there was 2015's *Room* based on the novel by Emma Donoghue. Even M. Night Shyamalan returned to the claustrophobic setting idea he'd explored in *Devil* with 2016's *Split*.

Arguably **this whole subgenre** was kicked off by the 2004 release of the first in what became an unsinkable franchise: *Saw*. Darren Lynn Bousman, director of *Saw II, III* and *IV*, acknowledged to the author that the series did indeed owe a debt, however small, to Natali's creation.

"*Saw* has *Cube* written all over it," says Hewlett. "It's very, very similar. My issue with *Saw* is that I'm not a big fan of torture porn stuff—it gets too much for me. It's not clever. Just because it's a twist doesn't make it clever. That's what drives me crazy about that stuff. Maybe I'm old." Still, he concedes, "those films do *look* cool. It's beautiful, but nobody has an excuse for making an ugly film these days; there are so many tricks you can use. If you have a bit of money then you should be able to make everything look gorgeous. The hardest part of filmmaking, I think, is getting a good script."

Of course *Cube* didn't invent the one-set feature film—*Das Boot, Rear Window, Glengarry Glen Ross* and *Persona* preceded it, to say nothing of one of Natali's chief influences: Hitchcock's *Lifeboat* (1944). Yet with very few exceptions, nearly all of the movies we recall being set in one location still include at least one scene elsewhere, making *Cube* truly unique.

'films that start cold and end cold—relatively abruptly—rely on audiences' imaginations to fill in the backstory and epilogue. in low-budget filmmaking, this is a great resource because imagination can take you much further than film.'

↘ **William Phillips**

22: in the wake of *cube*

ABOUT A YEAR after his first feature film debuted, Vincenzo Natali exited the world of *Cube* to enter one recognizable to all first-time directors: Hollywood limbo.

"I would drive into Los Angeles whenever I needed to take meetings," he remembers. "After the film came out, I got an agent in the states and I started to do the Hollywood shuffle. I met a lot of people and entered that whole circle of hell. And that's a whole other kind of adventure that has very little to do with actually making movies. I can't even count how many meetings I must've done, and really not a single one of them led to any kind of substantial, measurable result. That's another form of torture, but the kind of torture every young filmmaker dreams of. It was a very frustrating process for me, to be honest."

Yet he knew that to the extent there's anything approaching a career path for directors, this was it.

"I did some TV episodic work just to pay the bills, but I moved to Los Angeles and started meeting with studios and pitching ideas," he remembers. Directing a few episodes of *Star Trek* creator Gene Roddenberry's *Earth: Final Conflict*, he

Opposite: Natali and Miller (Kazan) on the set of *Tremors* in 2018.

'There are three different models of me now. There's a little 'pewter troll' as I call it that doesn't look anything like me, then there's a couple of actual *Stargate* collectibles. I've got the Battle McKay and I've got the Nerd McKay. My son actually sleeps with it. My son goes to bed with his 'daddy doll' he calls it.'

↘ **Hewlett on his *Stargate* action figures**

continued to approach studios with ideas for more boundary pushing features, to no avail. Although *Cube*'s modest success had given him a certain amount of "traction" in the industry, that industry just wanted more of what was already in theaters.

"I think if you look at a lot of filmmakers, their careers follow that trajectory—they start out doing really interesting stuff and then progressively move into more conventional material," he says. "That's just because of the way the system works, it's very backward looking. That was my frustration when I came to Hollywood to try to make movies here. I still wanted to do original things, I wanted to push the boundaries a bit, and what I realized over a period of several years is that the industry isn't interested in that. It just wanted a repackaged version of past successes, and that remains the case.

"The challenge that every director has is how do you work in this very expensive, high-risk medium where everyone is terrified because they all know their jobs hang by a thread, and one failure can mean the end of their careers, or certainly can freeze their careers. There's just a tendency to play it safe, and more so now than ever because movies cost more than they ever have. How do you assuage those fears and still do something that's new? That's why something like *District 9* [2009] is so extraordinary, because it got out into the mainstream—it was a real success but it defied any sort of existing model."

Today, *Cube* co-writer Andre Bijelic works as a television editor in Toronto.

↘Bijelic, shown here with "Oliver" (as in "Oliver Twist.")

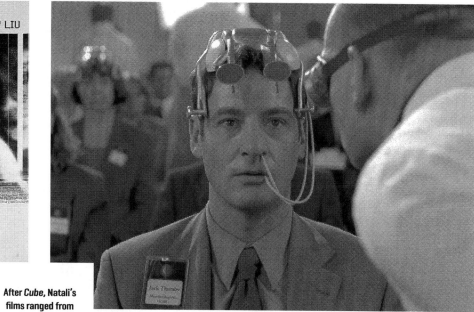

After *Cube*, Natali's films ranged from *Cypher* (above) to *Splice* (right), as well as *Nothing* (below).

From *Cypher* to *Splice*

Natali's next feature film project was another science-fiction epic. Written by friend Brian King, 2002's *Cypher* starred Jeremy Northam and Lucy Liu in a convoluted tale about corporate espionage with a distinctly Philip K. Dick flavor—a sort of *A Scanner Darkly* for the corporate world.

Shot by *Cube*'s Derek Rogers and featuring a David Hewlett now more trusting of his own acting abilities, *Cypher* is a taut little thriller with some creepy scenes that will stay with you long after the movie has ended. (A double-bill alongside John Carpenter's 1988 classic *They Live* will leave you cowering in the corner beneath your tin foil hat in no time.)

A writer-director at heart, Natali returned the following year with the David Hewlett/Andrew Miller two-hander *Nothing*—a whimsical contemplation on **the nature of consensus reality**. Written by Miller and his then-writing-partner Andrew Lowery, and based on an idea by Natali, it tells the tale of two roommates who open their front door to discover the world has disappeared, replaced by an all-white void.

"There was a time when he was trying to figure out how to do an incredibly inexpensive movie with me and Dave [Hewlett] and he had a bunch of these two-man movies," Miller explains. "I don't know if *Cube* was in that same pile of ideas or came before, but there was another alien abduction movie that I still want to do at some point, and then *Nothing*. All the ideas had something to do with either our world disappearing or their world disappearing or feeling incredibly isolated."

The nature of consensus reality...

Natali actually envisioned *Nothing* and *Cube* as being part of a loose thematic trilogy; the third movie was to be called *Echo Beach*. Says the director, "I think the binding element is characters finding themselves in an inexplicable metaphysical situation, or trapped in a metaphysical conundrum. Each film has been successively more minimalist. It was going to have one actor in it, that was the whole concept. *Lost* is a show that touches on certain things I wanted to do with *Echo Beach*; it's just such a huge part of the popular consciousness now, I'm not sure it's where I want to go. Occasionally *Echo Beach* pops up on my computer desktop and I toy with it, but I have certain reservations so I don't know that it'll ever be a movie. We'll see."

Let's get the old gang together

At his mother's prompting, a 17-year-old Andrew Miller enrolled at Leah Posluns Theatre in North York, Ont., where he met Hewlett. "I was in the younger group and Keanu Reeves was in the older group," he remembers. "Everyone else in the play who were all our age and younger were these kids from theater school, and they were incredibly pretentious and annoying—I couldn't get far enough away from them. Then I turn around and see this other guy who also can't get far enough away from them and it's Dave, and we're like 'Hey, how ya doin'?' That's how we bonded. I met Vincenzo at the play, too — he came to see us."

Again photographed by Derek Rogers, *Nothing* even features narration by *Cube*'s psychotic Quentin, Maurice Dean Wint. It was also produced by Steve Hoban, who had performed similar duties on his short ur-*Cube* film *Elevated*, and by this time had beloved cult horror flick *Ginger Snaps* (for which Natali created storyboards) under his belt. Where *Nothing* had been an apparent **"let's get the old gang together"** romp with all the earmarks of something cooked up over beers, Hoban and Natali's next major collaboration, 2009's *Splice*, was the director's real follow-up to *Cube*.

With a budget of about $25 million U.S. (compared with *Cube*'s $600,000+ U.S.) and directing a story of his own writing (with Antoinette Terry Bryant and Doug Taylor), Natali was again able to indulge his love of science fiction and horror, while also depicting one of the most moving love stories ever seen in either genre.

Adrien Brody and Sarah Polley are the Bonnie and Clyde of the genetic engineering world, creating a human-animal hybrid they call Dren (Delphine Chanéac) for the scientific hell of it. The emotional and visual shit storm that follows has early David Cronenberg written all over it, with one crucial difference—while you might not like the characters necessarily, you can't help but care about them, including the primal Dren. (David Hewlett, incidentally, shows up just long enough to be killed, continuing a pattern of appearances in Natali films that remains unbroken to this day.)

Like *Cube*, *Splice*'s ending could just as easily be viewed as

'i dread [my son] seeing some of the stuff i've done because it's going to be like 'let me explain that to ya: mortgage payments.''

↘ Hewlett on some of his film and television work

a beginning—certainly fodder for a sequel, anyway. Despite positive response from genre audiences and winning some awards, its earnings were modest at best. This could hardly be attributed to script, direction or production values—all were better than they had any right to be.

"Even though *Splice* was a $25 million film, in terms of what I had to put on the screen, it was just as hard getting that movie finished as it was getting *Cube* finished," says Natali. "The real issue isn't necessarily the unions or even the cost of the movie, it's about who you're making the movie with and what their agenda is. And I've been fortunate in that all my films have been made independently of a studio. I haven't found myself in a position yet where I've had to change anything in one of my movies to satisfy the producers or the distributor. So you can blame me for everything, it's all my fault. No one made me do this," he says with a laugh.

"The not-so-good side of it is you're not guaranteed distribution in the same way you might be if you were working with a major film studio. That's sort of been my albatross. My movies haven't been distributed well in North America until *Splice*. The others were hardly even released theatrically at all there."

Ultimately *Splice*'s fate came down to the changing face of movie distribution, especially in North America. Up until the late '90s *Splice* would've leapt off shelves in video stores, and in the mid- to late-2010s it would've been snapped up by Netflix and streamed in perpetuity.

Add to that the stiff competition it faced in the horror sector—2009 was a bumper year for horror: *The Human Centipede*, *Triangle*, *Drag Me to Hell*, *Orphan*, *The House of the Devil*, *Zombieland* and the *Friday the 13th* reboot all came out to name just a few.

"It's such a different industry now," says Hewlett. "When Vincenzo sold *Splice* to Dark Castle, I think they went in and re-edited it. People forget it is a business. You can fight to be an auteur that exerts complete control over your films but then you're making films for 50 bucks because nobody's going to give you any money."

Whatever the reason for *Splice*'s modest takings, it failed to give its director the momentum necessary to escape the cube labeled "journeyman director."

Prior to *Splice*'s release, Natali was hoping to direct the cinematic adaptation of J.G. Ballard's class-war dystopian novel **High Rise**, and was even rumored to be ready to tackle William Gibson's cyberpunk classic *Neuromancer*. But *High-Rise* ultimately went to Ben Wheatley (*Kill List*) in 2015, and *Neuromancer* remains untouched by celluloid...unless you count *The Matrix* franchise.

He returned to genre cinema in 2013 with *Haunter* starring Abigail Breslin, a taut but tame horror flick whose only real accomplishment was to remind us just how well 2009's *Triangle* pulled off the stuck-in-a-time-loop story. At times creepy direction and the always-memorable David Hewlett (as the main character's father) were the only two highlights in an otherwise plot-by-numbers script by *Cypher* writer Brian King.

"Vincenzo's a visionary," says Hewlett. "He's got such an original mind and a different perspective on things that some people love, some people hate, whatever. It's so rare these days to see a movie with a personality on it. It always feels a bit like a bureaucracy, like a company made this as opposed to a person. The Kubricks of the world are few and missed if you ask me. It's such a huge industry now that unless you're James Cameron, you're not gonna be able to exert that kind of control over a film."

Moving from Cube to Cube

Unable to gain a foothold in feature films in the 2000s, Natali moved back to Toronto and found himself highly in-demand as a television director. Yet what would've seemed like something of

High-Rise

This was probably a lucky escape for Natali as the book, like nearly all of Ballard's novels, is too cold and punishing for the mainstream and art house crowds, and not punishing enough for the burn-it-to-the-ground gore hounds. Wheatley's adaptation was extremely faithful to the book and suffered for it. For a real ice-bullet-to-the-heart experience, check out David Cronenberg's 1996 adaptation of Ballard's car-wrecks-turn-me-on extravaganza *Crash*. [*Cube's* Nicky Guadagni appears briefly as a tattooist.]

'I spent a few days on *Splice*, four days or something like that. It's come in, be a slimy arrogant asshole, leave again. They pay a big chunk of money, it's great. It's a good way to earn a living.'

↘ **Hewlett**

a career tailspin 20 years ago today is arguably a step up. As *Cube* so ably demonstrated, Natali is a visionary. And by 2015—when he finally hit his stride on the small screen—the only place to find groundbreaking visionary storytelling was on television.

In case you've forgotten, your top 10 high-grossing 2015 choices in the cinema were: *Star Wars: The Force Awakens*, *Jurassic World*, [*Fast and*] *Furious 7*, *Avengers: Age of Ultron*, *Minions*, *Spectre*, *Inside Out*, *Mission Impossible: Rogue Nation*, *The Hunger Games: Mockingjay—Part 2* and *The Martian*. For those keeping score, there are only three original films on that list, and one of those is based on a comic series that's more than 50 years old.

However that same year on television you could watch *Game of Thrones*, *Mr. Robot*, *Better Call Saul* (aka *Breaking Bad*-lite), *Orphan Black*, *The Walking Dead*, *Wayward Pines*, *True Detective* (though not the good one) and *Downton Abbey* to name but a few shows. By 2015 television had become *the* place to tell a story.

Natali hit the ground running. Right off he directed episodes of the aforementioned Canadian sci-fi series *Orphan Black* (co-created by *Cube* co-writer Graeme Manson), as well as the American remake of the French masterpiece *The Returned*. But it was with his substantial contributions to the TV series *Hannibal* that the director showed visionary show runners just what he could do. From there he would direct episodes of *Westworld*, *The Strain* and Neil Gaiman's *American Gods*. Most recently he landed a TV remake of *Tremors*, written and executive produced by Andrew Miller (Kazan) and starring Kevin Bacon.

This isn't so strange in hindsight as the director who could

One of Natali's storyboards for the *American Gods* episode "Lemon Scented You" (S1/E5). [Note the exquisite detail in the final shot.]

No matter where their work takes them, the core group of Natali, Hewlett and Miller remains as strong as it was before *Cube*.

never imagine creating a successful sequel to *Cube* the movie once toyed with the idea of turning it into a television series.

"It actually would've been very much like *Lost*," Natali admits. "This was years before *Lost*, of course, which would make it not worth while to do right now. In that TV concept the cube was like a bridge between these artificial environments, but they would mimic real-world ones. It was to follow one character as he traversed these various worlds and, in the process, slowly learned more and more about himself, and ultimately realized that he was the architect of the cube.

"In fact the Sci-Fi Channel [presumably before it was Syfy] wanted to do it but said first you have to make a *Cube* TV movie, and I started to get the feeling they weren't willing to commit to the series. They wanted a 2-hour pilot and I started thinking this is smelling a lot like *Cube 4*. They would've paid me and everything, but I was worried that it would end up being the Sci-Fi Channel movie of the week—they weren't going to guarantee any kind of series. I stepped away from it. I'm very careful with *Cube*; I've never wanted to tarnish what that original movie was for me, so it always had to be done in the right way."

With a *Cube* reboot reportedly under development as recently as 2015 with Jon Spaihts (*Prometheus, Passengers*) and Saman Kesh (*Controller*), there's every chance that we will, sooner or later, return to the Kafkaesque world we know so well. Whether it will be "done in the right way" isn't as certain. But then nothing ever is in the world of *Cube*.

'We always make sure that we stay in touch because we were friends long before *Cube*, and remain friends long after. It's still the film I have the fondest feelings for because I think it was all of our first experience with a success that was truly ours; we all had some part to play in it.'

↘ **Hewlett**

227

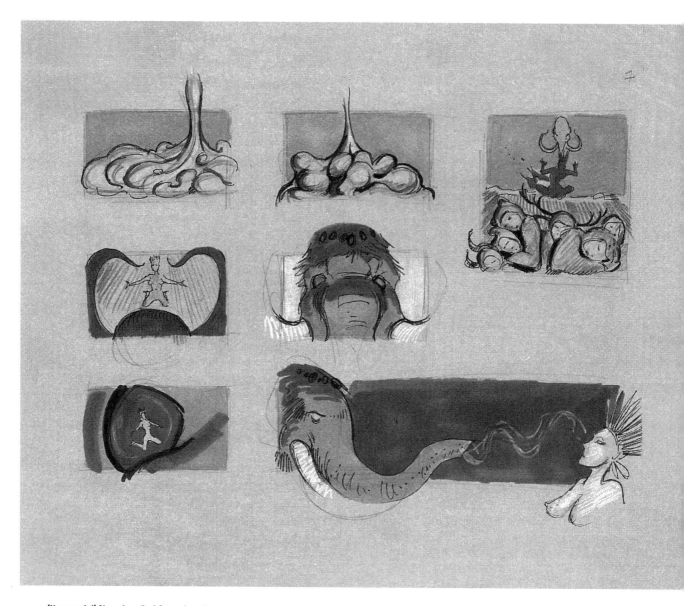

'Nunyunnini' *[American Gods]* storyboard
excerpts 7 and 11 for CG short that opens the
Natali-directed "Lemon Scented You" (S1/E5).

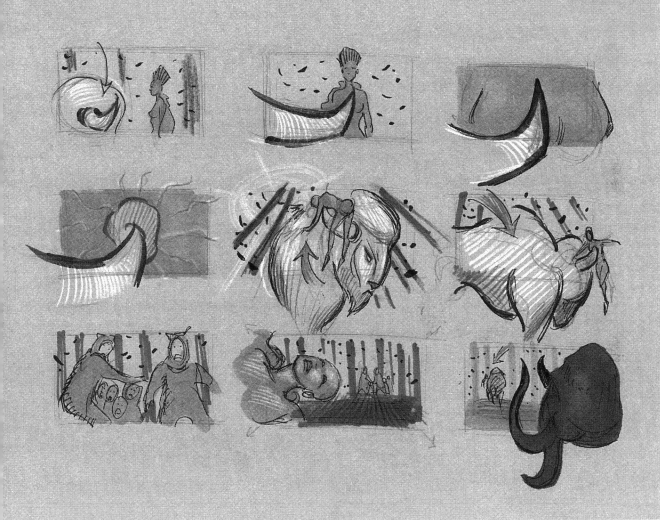

23: the *cube* archive

Director Vincenzo Natali kept a startling amount of paperwork, images and illustrations documenting the making of *Cube*, which all appear here with his kind permission.

The first page of the very first draft of the *Cube* script, written by Natali.

FADE IN:

1   INT. THE CUBE

The interior of a PERFECTLY SQUARE ROOM. All six walls are identical: ten feet in height and length, a square door in the centre of each one.

VARIOUS SHOTS exploring the details of the room: CORRODED METAL that composes the walls, WIRE ENCASED LIGHTS emitting dim illumination, WATER trickling down from the ceiling, MOSS growing in it's damp corners.

The silence is broken by the OS sound of PANTING and FOOTSTEPS. Someone is approaching the room.

One of the doors opens violently and THE SPIDERY FIGURE OF A MAN topples to the floor. He is clothed in the FRAYED REMAINS OF A BUSINESS SUIT. His gaunt, unwashed face speaks volumes about fear and suffering.

The man skitters around the room with the desperation of a hunted animal. He is searching for something.

CLOSE ON a moss encrusted portion of wall. The man's hands enter FRAME and claw at the moss revealing an engraving in the metal underneath: the digits, 9216.

He has found what he was looking for.

Hands trembling, the man takes out a PENCIL and scribbles some calculations in a TATTERED NOTEBOOK.

His activity is interrupted by an INHUMAN ROAR that sounds from outside the room. SOMETHING MONSTROUS IS COMING.

The man returns to his calculations with increased fervour. He makes an error and erases a portion of the calculation.

ANOTHER ROAR. This time closer.

The man is at the brink of total panic. His pencil tears into the paper. Sweat drips on the page.

ANOTHER ROAR. Even closer.

The man completes the calculation. Next, he removes a SMALL CUBE SHAPED OBJECT from a pouch at his waist. It appears to be some kind of map of the room. The sides are divided into four squares with a number printed inside each one. He rotates the sides like a Rubik's Cube, realigning the numbers.

Watching the characters swap personalities, merge and form through the various script revisions is akin to watching a patch of cells grow into a child. (Very *Splice*.)

Opposite: Here we have the rare opportunity to compare the action in a script with Natali's own sketches.

[handwritten:] Ryker's Blackjourn

28

                         FORD
     If you can control him.

Quentin turns to the others.

                    QUENTIN
          Okay. It's clear.

Quentin retrieves the boot.

[handwritten:] ✱ MAYBE WE GO TO RYKER HERE - WATCHING THEM TALK ABOUT HIM.

[handwritten:] ✱ MAYBE ARNOLD DOES HIS "I'LL UP EACH OTHER SPEECH" HERE

                    ARNOLD
     Don't worry about it. I know his type. Leave
     it to me.

[handwritten:] RYKER: "DON'T WORRY - THE ONLY MAN WHO HAS TO FEAR ME IS + ONE WHO PUT ME IN HERE!"

Arnold steps through the doorway. *[handwritten:]* TOUCH OF IRONY SINCE RYKER DESTROYS MOST OF THEM.

INT. CUBE 22

Arnold traverses the room, signals for the others to follow.

Quentin, Ford, Worth and Ryker enter. Quentin moves to the floor
door. He slides it open.

                    QUENTIN
          Arnold! Look at this.

Arnold kneels beside him, looks inside.

INT. CUBE 23

An unconscious PRISONER lies face down on the floor.

Arnold jumps into the room. He moves to the prisoner, turns him
over. He is older than the others, about sixty. The man has a large
bruise on his skull.

Arnold looks to the ceiling.

                    ARNOLD
          Ford! Get down here...

Ford pokes his head through the door, leaps in. He joins Arnold,
checks the man's breathing.

                    ARNOLD
          Is he dead?

                    FORD
          No. He's breathing. His pulse is faint, but
          steady.

Quentin and Worth jump in the room.

                         ARNOLD
          Look, all I know is that you can't lose hope.
          This place is designed to drive you insane.
          You have to fight it. You have to stay calm
          and keep your mind clear...I don't know if
          we'll make it out of here alive, but I do know
          we won't make it out of here alive if we give
          up. We have to keep a positive attitude...Come
          on, let's move...

Quentin casts the boot. He nods to Arnold.

INT. CUBE 26

Arnold enters, takes a few steps inside. The others are huddled by
the doorway.

Arnold stops, gestures for the others to follow.

Suddenly, a large, metal disc launches out from one of the walls
and slices right through Arnold's neck.

Arnold's head rolls off his shoulders, bounces on the ground. His
body collapses to the floor.

Terrific

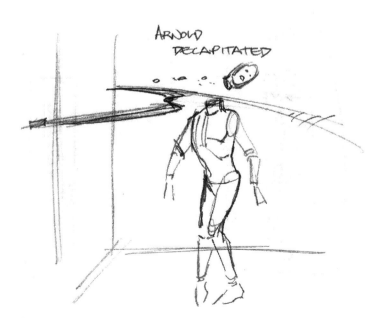

ARNOLD DECAPITATED

Early Plot Synopsis

Written at the time Natali and Bijelic were being courted by Norstar, the following pages show the writers attempting to compromise over what to show outside the cube. However, Norstar insisted on revealing a villain behind it all—something the pair refused to do.

CUBE

Welcome to the cube...

The latest advance in technological terror: eight thousand rooms, all perfectly identical, some perfectly lethal.

Seven convicts are dropped into the structure, armed only with the clothes on their backs.

Purpose of the experiment: unknown.

The way out: unknown.

They have only three days to escape before they die of thirst.

Each prisoner holds a piece of the puzzle.

If they work together, they might just make it. But first, they must overcome the greatest obstacle...

Each other.

CUBE IPGA . CDR   A

CUBE
Synopsis

The year: 2069.

The world has changed. Not for the better. Governments have fallen. Multi-national corporations have taken their place, creating a capitalist, totalitarian state.

Competing corporations are racing to create **A.I.** *[Artificial Intelligence]* - a super-brain, a computer that thinks independently of its user. The first company to develop **A.I.** will control the most profitable invention since the automobile.

This new society is based on buying power. If you are not a consumer, you are considered worthless...

FADE IN:

A perfectly square room, ten feet in length and width. The walls are metallic, emblazoned with strange, textured patterns. There are hatch-like doors in the centre of the walls, floor and ceiling. And above the doors are engravings of a nine-digit number.

A man is dropped into the room. He slowly regains consciousness. He has no idea where he is. He notices that he's dressed in a prison uniform.

The man discovers that all doors lead to identical rooms. He moves through the structure, slowly and cautiously.

Suddenly, he freezes. His body is sliced into hundreds of little cubes by a razor-sharp, wire grid.

TITLE OVER: **CUBE**

Seven more prisoners are placed in this maze:

- McNeil, a tough, arrogant mercenary.
- Rennes, a philosophical escape artist.
- Holloway, a female terrorist.
- Quentin, a silent, ruthless assassin.
- Worth, an enigmatic character with a big secret.
- Leaven, a brilliant, egocentric, female mathematician.
- Kazan, a trusting, mentally retarded man.

Early Plot Synopsis

(continued)

The idea of the victims being criminals is still present, with Worth having a greater hand in the cube's workings than he has in the actual film.

They are all hardened criminals, with the exception of Kazan, whose only 'crime' is that he serves no function in the capitalist system.

They quickly realize that some of the rooms conceal lethal boobytraps and that they are on their own - armed with nothing but the clothes on their backs. There is no food. No water. They have only three days to escape before they die of thirst.

The prisoners don't get along, but they need one another. There's no way they can make it out alone, so they form a tenuous alliance.

McNeil becomes their leader, despite strong competition from Holloway and Quentin. McNeil guides the others from room to room, using boots from their uniforms to identify and trigger boobytraps.

McNeil's reign is suddenly cut short when the boot method fails. He walks right into a trap and is ripped to shreds.

McNeil's demise leaves the others despondent. The odds against them seem insurmountable. Tension rises as Holloway and Quentin fight to fill the void left by McNeil's death.

Just when things are at their darkest, a ray of light emerges. Leaven uncovers a formula for spotting boobytraps by using the numbers engraved above the doors. This information re-energizes the group. They still have a chance. They just might make it out.

Now led by Holloway, the group continues to move through the maze - but they don't get very far. Leaven's formula is dramatically disproved when Rennes sets off a trap and is brutally killed by a spray of acid.

In the ensuing chaos, Worth inadvertently reveals his true identity. He is a guard. He had orders to kill anyone who managed to escape, but accidentally trapped himself in the cube. An enraged Holloway and Quentin threaten to kill Worth unless he shows them the way out, but Worth swears he knows nothing that could help them. All he knows about the design of the maze is that it is made up of eight thousand rooms and is surrounded by an outer shell.

Worth explains that the cube is part of a project to create artificial intelligence. It is a massive behavioral experiment to study the intricate workings of the human mind. The prisoners have implants which monitor their brain and physiological functions. They have been placed in the most extreme conditions imaginable to tax their abilities to the limit. The information gathered from this collection of minds will be used to create one super-mind.

In the midst of Worth's confession, Leaven suddenly screams in delight. She has just discovered that the engraved number in every room is a co-ordinate - a point on an imaginary map that marks where you are in the maze. As it turns out, they are only a few rooms from the edge.

En route to the edge, Holloway forms a bond with Kazan. He fills her with a sense of purpose, which she lost when her son was accidentally killed by a bomb she built for a terrorist campaign.

The group reaches the edge. They open the last door to reveal...blackness. Nothing but blackness as far as the eye can see. The outer shell is beyond reach.

Using a rope made of knotted shirts, Worth tries swinging across to the outer shell, but it's just too far. Quentin, clearly becoming unstable, seizes this opportunity to get rid of the treacherous Worth. He lets go of the rope, sending Worth tumbling down into the dark abyss.

Quentin is sick of taking orders from Holloway. He takes control by force. Quentin makes the others move along the edge of the maze, hoping to find an exit.

In one of the rooms, they discover the body of Rennes. Leaven bursts into insane laughter when she realizes that they have been moving in circles. Quentin explodes with rage, then collapses in despair. This is the end of the line. They're finished. Doomed.

Or are they? An idea forms in Holloway's mind. They weren't at the edge when Rennes was killed. And if they haven't moved to Rennes, then Rennes must have moved to them. So the rooms are moving.

Leaven suspects Holloway is right. She recalls a room they passed through earlier - a room with unusual co-ordinates. She surmises that, at a certain point, this room acts as a bridge between the cube and the outer shell. They must get to the bridge-room before it moves out of the escape position. Time is running out.

Armed with this knowledge, Leaven is also able to calculate a new formula to identify boobytrapped rooms. There's just one problem - the calculation is too complex to do mentally.

That's when Kazan speaks up. It turns out that he's not mentally-retarded, as previously thought, but is actually an autistic-savant, capable of solving complex mathematical problems.

Quentin becomes desperate to get out. He is now completely out of control. Quentin pressures Kazan to speed up, but succeeds only in confusing him. Kazan can't be rushed.

Holloway and Leaven realize Quentin's behaviour is jeopardizing their chances of escape, so they trap him and knock him unconscious.

Early Plot Synopsis
(continued)

Here the ending is a happier one with Holloway and Leaven joining Kazan in escape, the cube destroyed. In short, it is a typical Hollywood ending.

Holloway, Leaven and Kazan race to the bridge. Just as Leaven steps into the bridge-room, Quentin re-appears and attacks her.

Holloway rushes to Leaven's defense. Together, they overpower Quentin.

The room starts to move out of position.

Leaven exits the cube. Holloway tries to get Kazan to step out, but he's too frightened to leave, so she steps out first and takes him by the hand. Before Kazan makes it, he is pushed out of the way by Quentin.

Quentin leaps up to the door. It's too late. He is sliced in half as the bridge-room continues to move downward.

Kazan is still trapped inside. Holloway tells Kazan not to move from the room. She will get him out.

Holloway and Leaven leave the underground structure. They find themselves in a remote, desert-like location, surrounded by several concrete buildings and protected by an electrical fence. Using information given to them earlier by Worth, they succeed in eluding and overpowering the guards posted by the exit.

Holloway and Leaven arm themselves and break into the command centre. They try to shut down the generator that powers the cube, but accidentally initiate an overload. They only have an hour before the cube and surrounding area are vapourized by a nuclear explosion.

Holloway, using her terrorist skills, constructs an explosive device and blows a hole through the outer shell of the cube.

Holloway lowers herself into the structure. Leaven guides her from the command centre, via radio link.

After some near-fatal encounters with boobytraps, Holloway finds Kazan. They start towards the exit, but the growing power surge cuts off the link to Leaven. Only minutes remain before the reactor explodes.

Holloway, realizing that they are close to the edge, leads Kazan in a daredevil escape, scaling the exterior of the cube.

Holloway and Kazan rejoin Leaven. Their happy reunion is short-lived, however, as they realize that it is impossible to reach a safe distance before the entire complex is incinerated.

Just then, they hear the sound of an approaching helicopter. A team of scientists and company officials arrive. They have lost contact with the command centre and have come to investigate. They rush to the breach in the cube's shell.

Holloway, Leaven and Kazan remove the pilot and hijack the helicopter.

The team members look up in surprise as their transport takes off. Their attention is then drawn to a colossal rumble, emanating from the subterranean structure.

The helicopter rockets away at top speed. It is suddenly silhouetted by the intense flash of a nuclear blast. Nothing remains of the cube site, except for a massive, smouldering crater.

Holloway, Leaven and Kazan fly off into an uncertain, but hopeful, future.

THE END

Morris = N/A.
Arnold = Arnold Schwarzenegger
Quentin = Woody Allen
Ford = Harrison Ford
Worth = Humphrey Bogart (Casablanca)
Riles = Michael Biehn (The Abyss)
Ellis = Jeremy Irons (Reversal of Fortune)
Leaven = Robin Williams (Awakenings)
Egon = Dustin Hoffman (Rainman)

Dreaming Big

239

With so many characters, it's only natural that Bijelic and Natali would try to assign familiar faces to the cast. That said, let's all picture Woody Allen as Quentin for a moment...

CUBE Script Notes

To: The Advisory Committee
From: Vincenzo Natali and Andre Bijelic

CUBE is a project that we have been working on for some time now. We have progressed from draft to draft with the steady, methodical pace of our characters passing from room to room. Fortunately, our journey has not been fraught with as many traps and dead ends. Each new draft of CUBE has improved on its predecessor and we are confident that we are nearing our final destination. What follows is an outline of what we believe are the strengths and weaknesses of the current draft, as well as the direction the story needs to take to become fully realized.

From the start, CUBE struck us as a great concept. The idea of throwing a bunch of people into a diabolical maze and having them fight for their lives seemed inherently dramatic and compelling. We spent a great deal of time devising a story that was worthy of the premise. On a basic level, we feel we have succeeded. The mechanics of the story - how the characters meet, what happens to them, how they solve the mystery of the puzzle - seem to work quite well.

What the script lacks, however, is a *soul* - a human dimension to offset its cold, sterile environment. Discovering what the characters are about needs to be as interesting as discovering what the cube is about.

With this in mind, here is how we intend to shape the next draft:

The conflict between the prisoners will come to the fore. As it is, there are two dramatic threads at work. The first is the story of how the prisoners manage to solve the puzzle of the cube, the second is the story of how they grow divided over helping KAZAN. In the current draft, the characters' relationship to the cube overshadows their relationship to each other. We would like to focus more on the human drama and, in turn, make the film less of a mathematical exercise and more of a psychological exploration.

To do this, the characters must have more weight and the forces that ally and divide them need to be strengthened. Although the characters are intriguing, they are sketchy and play little more than functional roles. There is little context or background information about them. As a result, much of the dialogue lacks the flavour and personality of real speech. The characters seem emotionally disconnected from their pasts and from one another. We hope to define and clarify who they are and weave their histories into the fabric of the story.

One possible route is to make them all hardened criminals who have committed reprehensible crimes. Previously, most were victims of an intolerant, fascistic government. By our standards, they were anything but criminals. In the new version, they will be guilty of acts that we - the audience - also condemn. They will be people with a history of violence and exploitation, their morality twisted, ambiguous or non-existent. And yet, we must sense that they have the potential for change, that there is a glimmer of compassion, goodness, maybe even regret for what they have done. They are not evil, merely human, with contradictions, foibles and imperfections that we can understand and relate to.

The cube becomes an instrument of redemption, a second chance at a life they assumed ended in prison. Their survival is dependent on their willingness to help each other. They must learn to trust and compromise. They form a bond that grows out of necessity, but eventually becomes much more profound and meaningful. They become friends and, together, begin to recover their humanity. Thus, their journey through the maze is also an emotional and psychological passage. Like Dante's "Inferno", they begin as wretched souls cast beneath the earth and then, slowly, painfully, rise toward the light.

The obstacles the prisoners must overcome are both physical and mental. The immediate threat is the cube - its traps and the impenetrability of its design. The other, more insidious threat, is their own volatile natures. The heart of the story lies in their struggle with the inner forces that threaten to tear them apart.

Ultimately, we want to show that the prisoners give in to fear and mistrust. They have the means and knowledge to survive, but are incapable of working as a unified whole. By the end of the film, QUENTIN and WORTH should become so wrapped up in hatred that they would rather destroy each other than escape. KAZAN is the sole exception. He is the only one who is not caught up in the insanity and, as a result, is able to leave the cube.

The theme of the film, therefore, is that no outside threat to our

Script Notes

(continued)

Though undated, these notes suggest that they were made just prior to story editor Hugh Graham, and possibly Graeme Manson, coming on board.

survival is as great as the one that exists inside us. Or to paraphrase Shakespeare: "The real fault lies not within our <u>cubes</u> but within ourselves." It raises questions about fate and character. Were the prisoners ever really capable of change? Could they have worked together if events had unfolded slightly differently? Or were they doomed from the start?

The challenge we face is to make this dramatically plausible and not just an intellectual conceit. What we need is a believable source of conflict. Fortunately, the cube is fertile ground for fear and paranoia. It may simply be a matter of developing one of the story's existing conflicts, such as the debate over KAZAN, or the possibility that WORTH is a spy. Perhaps it is the culmination of a number of little things that lead to an indelible rift in the group - a disagreement about the direction they should be taking, the issue of who should risk life and limb by being the first to enter a room... or any number of things.

Once the story has the thematic clarity and power that we hope it will, the question of what the cube is will no longer be an issue. As it stands, we feel it is dissatisfying that the purpose of this terrible place is never explained. But if the focus of the film is on the tragic failure of the prisoners to work together, then a simple explanation of the cube would be a disappointment. The mystery and impenetrability of the cube heightens the allegorical and metaphorical quality of the story. It keeps the action within the framework of a terrifying and incomprehensible world whose occupants are capable only of understanding its basic mechanics, never its ultimate meaning or purpose.

Likewise, the issue of what awaits KAZAN outside is entirely dependent on how much emphasis is placed on the *act* of leaving. If the point of the film is that he is the only one capable of leaving the cube because the others are too caught up in some private hell, then it is his *action* that is significant, rather than his destination.

We would like to show the characters trying to grasp their situation and give them more opportunity to conjecture and hypothesize what the cube might be. How do they deal with the absurdity and cruelty of this world? And how does the apparent indifference of their universe affect their relationships? These are the questions that we want to answer.

We would also like to provide a clearer sense of time and place.

The world that the characters come from is a cruel and bleak one. It is a society that is cold and repressive enough to consider KAZAN's disability a crime. When the prisoners arrive, they are not especially surprised by the diabolical nature of their punishment. In this context, their behavior and criminal past becomes more understandable and the characters, in turn, become more sympathetic. It also isolates them from the hope of ever being saved by anyone other than themselves. They are alone in the universe, free to make what they will of their lives.

One final issue we would like to address is the question of repetition in the story. The key to avoiding that problem, we believe, rests in our ability to make the human drama build and progress, so that we are not just repeating the same events. The story will continue to evolve as long the relationships continue to evolve. If anything, the maddening claustrophobia of the cube will serve to fuel the drama. As Hitchcock proved in LIFEBOAT, ROPE and REAR WINDOW - and more recent suspense films such as RESERVOIR DOGS, DAS BOOT and ALIEN serve to remind us - limited space doesn't result in a limited story.

Our approach to the rewrite will involve several stages. The first will be to choose a story editor to help plan our strategy in detail. Specifically, we are looking for someone who can contribute many years of experience in dealing with classical story structure, someone who likes and can relate to the material but who will be tough, methodical and uncompromising. Together, we will map out a detailed revision plan incorporating the approach we have mentioned. The second step will be for us to lock ourselves in our own little cube and bash out the next draft. Finally, if the script still needs work, we would consider bringing in an outside writer for a polish. We don't expect that the script would require anything beyond that.

The feedback on CUBE has been remarkably consistent; the issues that concern us are the ones that everyone else points to. CUBE, like all great fantasy, from Kafka to Kubrick, should illustrate some aspect of the human condition. Right now, the script has those elements in it, but they aren't refined enough to reach their full thematic clarity and power. The script that we have now is already a tightly structured, involving page turner. All we need to do is to add depth to its human dilemmas to mine its full potential.

In these undated notes we find Natali honing the film's "elevator pitch," perhaps for the Canadian Film Centre, but also for the media interest the filmmakers knew would be vital to its success.

CUBE

Recent interview with VINCENZO NATALI

① What was the original GOAL?

→ "To make a movie that could take place in one entirely enclosed set/space!"

A. Problem: Entire film crew would be confined in the small space.

Solution: Use a light-weight, hand-held 35mm camera with its own sound boom.

Result: Looks like a documentary.

B. Problem: Wanted the impression of many different rooms.

Solution: Change walls and colours. All shots with one type of wall have to be performed at the same time.

Result: With good editing and acting, continuity and the impression of many rooms is assured.

the MATHEMATICS OF
CUBE

Basics:
① Large cube with many rooms.
② People awaken in a room in the **CUBE**.
③ Can move between rooms through doors.
④ Some rooms are dangerous.

Goal:
① Find the edge/side wall of **CUBE**.
② Need to know location.
③ Need to know orientation.
④ Need to know which rooms are dangerous.

Solution: Use numbers to encode all the needed information.

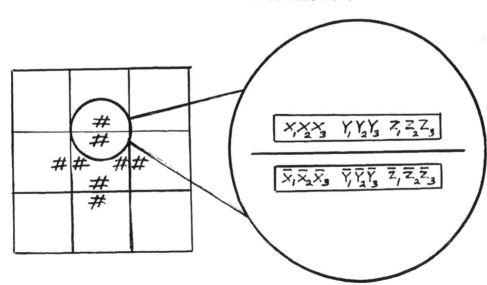

$$X_1 X_2 X_3 \quad Y_1 Y_2 Y_3 \quad Z_1 Z_2 Z_3$$

$$\overline{X}_1 \overline{X}_2 \overline{X}_3 \quad \overline{Y}_1 \overline{Y}_2 \overline{Y}_3 \quad \overline{Z}_1 \overline{Z}_2 \overline{Z}_3$$

Concept Sketches

There are five distinct types of illustrations Natali used for *Cube*:
1: Simple storyboards;
2: Slightly more complex scene sketches;
3: Character sketches;
4: Detailed character renderings (some in color); **5:** Detailed storyboards (see p. 248)

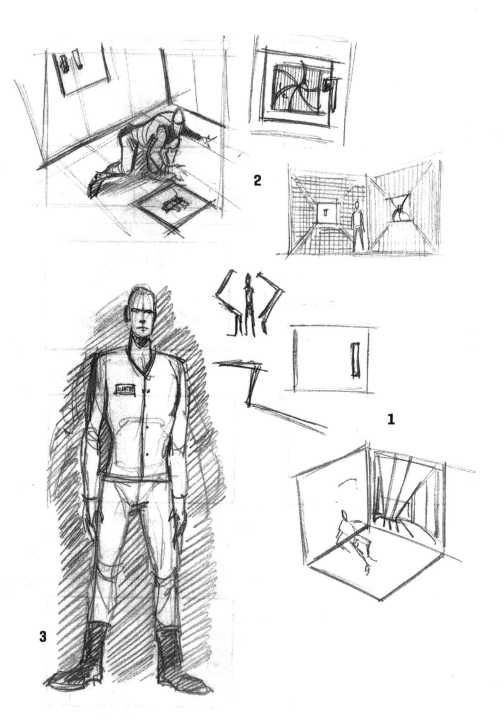

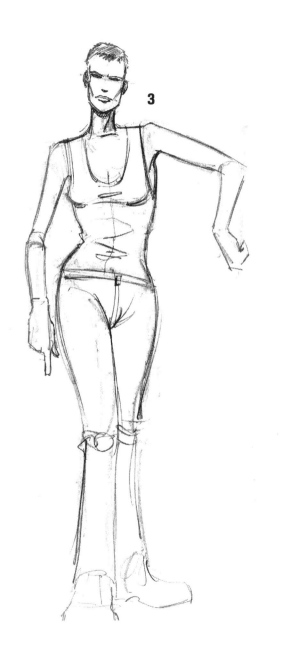

3

4

Early Storyboards

The level of detail in Natali's storyboards is such that, if they were laid end to end, you could probably create an animated film from them.

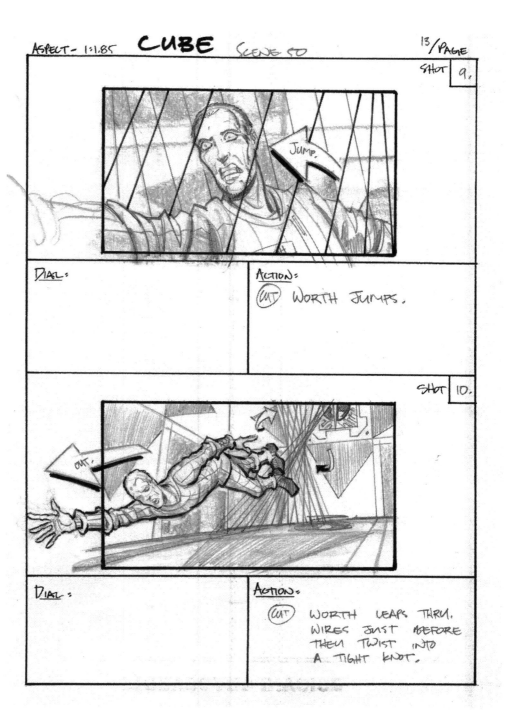

CUBE SCENE 58

SHOT 1.

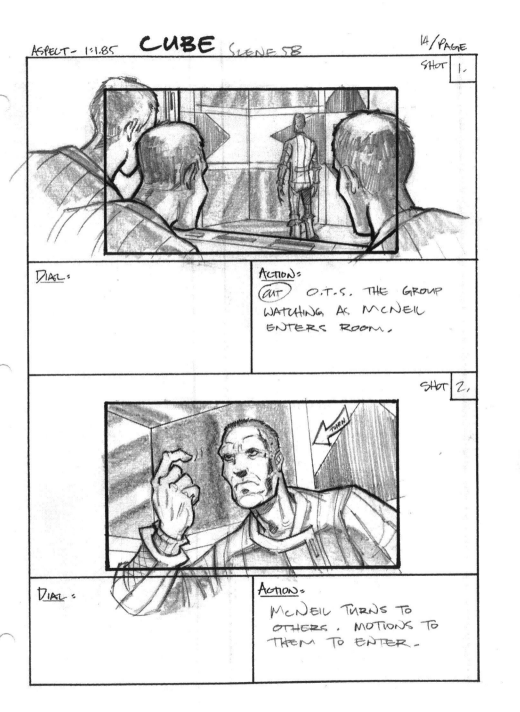

DIAL:

ACTION:
(CUT) O.T.S. THE GROUP
WATCHING AS MCNEIL
ENTERS ROOM.

SHOT 2.

DIAL:

ACTION:
MCNEIL TURNS TO
OTHERS. MOTIONS TO
THEM TO ENTER.

Hellraiser Walls

(continued)

The *Hellraiser* influence glimpsed in the very first script [see p. 58] appears to creep into Natali's conception of the cube walls—it's hard not to think of that film's infamous puzzle box (below).

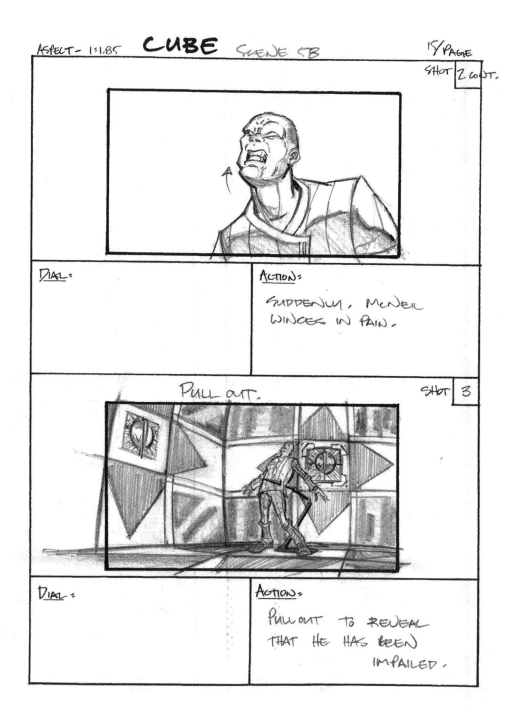

ASPECT - 1:1.85 **CUBE** SCENE 5B   1⁵/₈ PAGE

SHOT 2 CONT.

DIAL:

ACTION:
SUDDENLY, MCNEIL
WINCES IN PAIN.

PULL OUT.   SHOT 3

DIAL:

ACTION:
PULL OUT TO REVEAL
THAT HE HAS BEEN
IMPAILED.

SHOT | 4.

DIAL:

ACTION:
(CUT) TO THE GROUP
REACTING.

SHOT | 5.

DIAL:

ACTION:
(CUT) MCNEIL STRUGGLES
TO FREE HIMSELF.

ASPECT - 1:1.85   CUBE SCENE 5B   17/PAGE

SHOT 6.

DIAL:

PAGE ② TRIANGLES RISE.

ACTION:
CUT DOWNSHOT ON MCNEIL STRUGGLING. TRIANGLES START TO RISE.

SHOT 7.

DIAL:

ACTION:
CUT KAZAN & RIKER HOLD BACK HOLLOWAY.

SHOT | 8.

DIAL:

ACTION:
(CUT) McNEIL INCHES HIMSELF OFF POLE.
TRIANGULAR PANELS RISE IN FG.

SHOT | 9.

DIAL:

ACTION:
(CUT) OTHERS LOOK ON HELPLESS.

ASPECT - 1:1.85   CUBE   SCENE CB   19/PAGE

                                                      SHOT 10.

DIAL:

ACTION: (CUT)
C.U. OF MCNEIL'S
SIDE AS HE FREES
HIMSELF FROM THE
POLE.

                                                      SHOT 11.

DIAL:

ACTION:
(CUT) WIDE. MCNEIL
FREE.

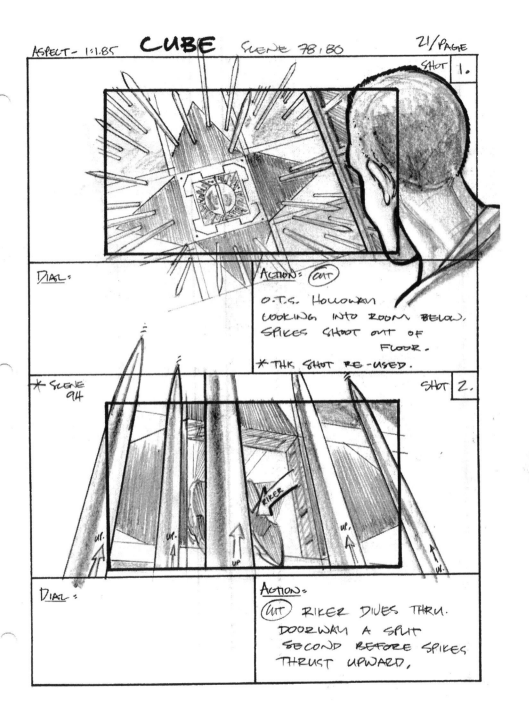

SHOT 1.

DIAL=

ACTION= (CUT)

O.T.S. HOLLOWAY
LOOKING INTO ROOM BELOW.
SPIKES SHOOT OUT OF
                    FLOOR.
* THIS SHOT RE-USED.

255

* SCENE
  94

SHOT 2.

DIAL=

ACTION=
(CUT) RIKER DIVES THRU.
DOORWAY A SPLIT
SECOND BEFORE SPIKES
THRUST UPWARD,

From the Beginning

From as early as October 1994, Natali had a clear
idea of the size and basic look of the cube.

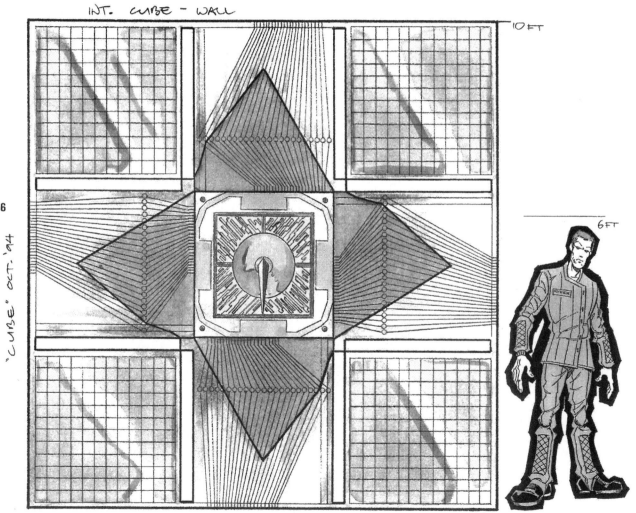

EXTERIOR CUBE SHOTS.

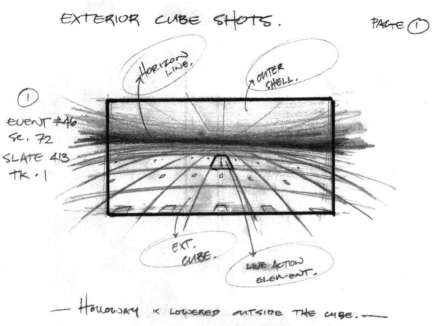

① HORIZON LINE.

OUTER SHELL.

① EVENT #46
Sc. 72
SLATE 413
TK · 1

EXT. CUBE.

LIVE ACTION ELEMENT.

Exterior Cube Sketches

A to-the-point sketch of Holloway's perilous exploration of the space between the cube and its outer shell.

257

—— HOLLOWAY IS LOWERED OUTSIDE THE CUBE. ——

- VERY WIDE TO CLEARLY ESTABLISH SCALE.
  & TO GIVE THE SPACIAL RELATIONSHIP
  BETWEEN THE EXT. OF THE CUBE AND
  THE OUTER SHELL.

* ADD SOME CURVATURE TO IMAGE
  TO SUGGEST LENS DISTORTION.

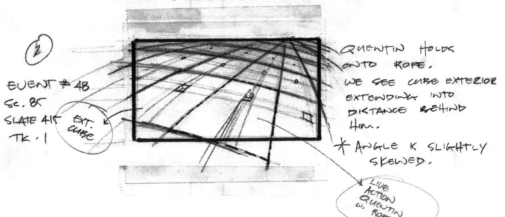

② EVENT #48
Sc. 85
SLATE 415
TK · 1

EXT. CUBE

QUENTIN HOLDS
ONTO ROPE.
WE SEE CUBE EXTERIOR
EXTENDING INTO
DISTANCE BEHIND
HIM.

* ANGLE IS SLIGHTLY
  SKEWED.

LIVE ACTION
QUENTIN
W. ROPE

Death by Cube

The death of Quentin in all its fiendishly technical detail.

VIEW LOOKING UP AT BRIDGE CUBE.

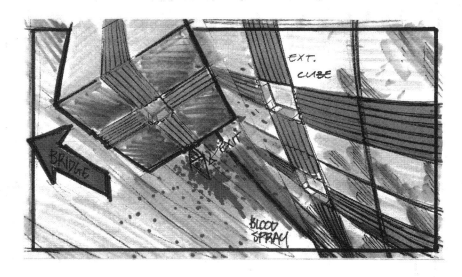

BRIDGE CUBE SEPARATES FROM THE EXIT ON A HORIZONTAL PATH, SEVERING QUENTIN.

BRIDGE CHANGES DIRECTION, DROPPING PAST CAMERA.

The Bridge Descends

Natali's command of perspective here, as well as his ability to tackle complex action, hint at the talent the comic book world lost when he chose to pursue filmmaking instead.

TILT DOWN TO FOLLOW BRIDGE CURE AS IT DESCENDS INTO THE ABYSS, DISAPPEARING FROM VIEW.

ANGLE LOOKING UP SHAFT.

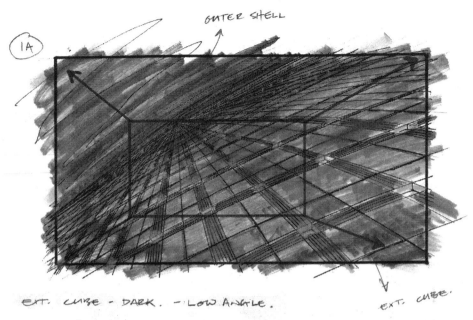

(1A)

OUTER SHELL

EXT. CUBE - DARK. — LOW ANGLE.

SLOW ZOOM·OUT

EXT. CUBE.

✳ THIS DRAWING DOESN'T
ACCURATELY DEPICT THE
SPACE BETWEEN THE OUTER
SHELL AND THE CUBE EXTERIOR

(1B)

HOLD ZOOM·OUT AS WORTH (OFF CAMERA)
OPENS DOOR ILLUMINATING EXT. CUBE.

Only What's Necessary

With an animator's eye Natali brings entire scenes to life with the absolute minimum of detail.

CUBE: THE ARRIVALS   PG ①

① A 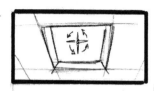   ANGLE ON
                                      CEILING
                                          DOOR

⑤    DOOR
                                      OPENS

② 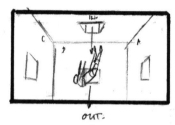   W. DROPS IN

                                      - THUD -

                           OUT.

③    EXTREME DOWNSHOT:
                                      W. ON FLOOR

                                      - HE ROLLS OVER.

④    W.   B.
                                      WAKES   ...THEN PASSES
                                                 OUT AGAIN.

                                      FADE OUT

⑤ A 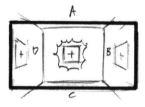 H.H. : W.'S POV
                                      OF CEILING
                                      DOOR SLAMS SHUT!

                           B.
                              RACK OUT OF
                                                  FOCUS.

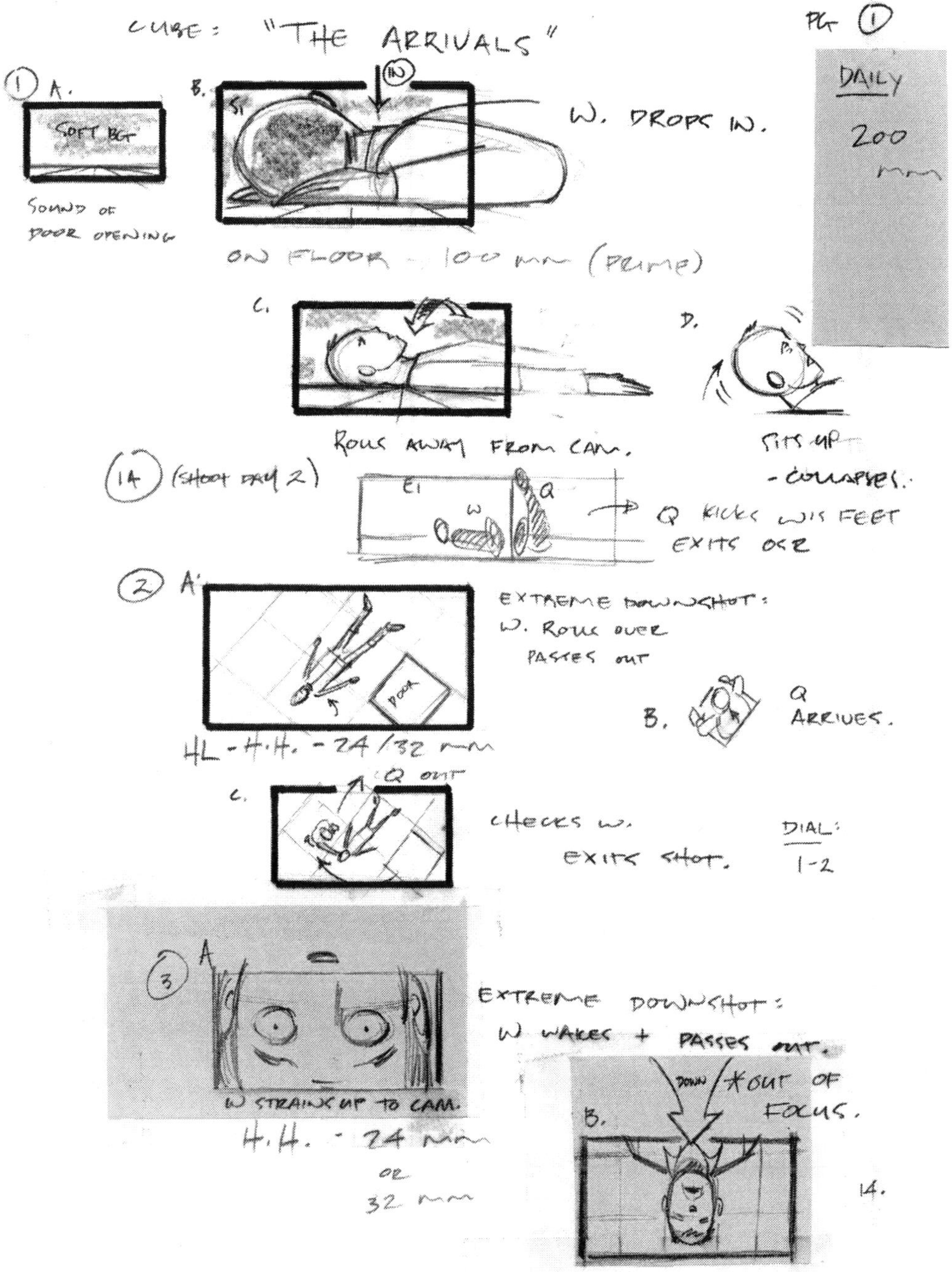

CUBE: "THE ARRIVALS"

① A.

SOFT BG

SOUND OF
DOOR OPENING

B.

S1

IN

W. DROPS IN.

ON FLOOR - 100 mm (PRIME)

DAILY

200
mm

C.

ROLLS AWAY FROM CAM.

D.

SITS UP
- COLLAPSES.

(1A) (SHOOT DAY 2)

E1

W   Q

Q KICKS W'S FEET
EXITS OSR

② A.

EXTREME DOWNSHOT:
W. ROLLS OVER
PASSES OUT

DOOR

HL - H.H. - 24/32 mm

B.

Q ARRIVES.

C.

Q OUT

CHECKS W.
EXITS SHOT.

DIAL:
1-2

③ A.

W STRAINS UP TO CAM.
H.H. - 24 mm
OR
32 mm

EXTREME DOWNSHOT:
W WAKES + PASSES OUT.

B.

DOWN / OUT OF
FOCUS.

14.

Breaking Out

Particularly fascinating is the way the director sketches the scene first, then decides where to draw in the camera's view. Note how body parts appear to exceed the limits of the camera, obscuring parts of the box.

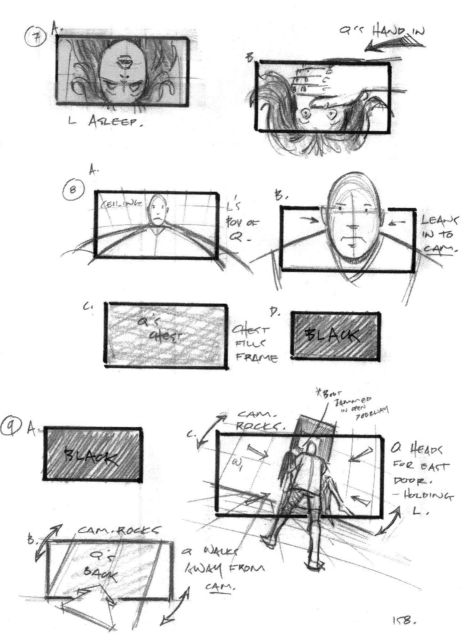

⑦ A.

L ASLEEP.

Q'S HAND IN

③

⑧ A.

CEILING   L'S
POV OF
Q.

B.

LEANS
IN TO
CAM.

C.

Q'S CHEST

D.

CHEST
FILLS
FRAME

BLACK

⑨ A.

BLACK

CAM.
ROCKS.

C.

*BOOT
JAMMED
IN OPEN
DOORWAY

Q HEADS
FOR EAST
DOOR.
— HOLDING
L.

B.

CAM. ROCKS

Q'S
BACK

Q WALKS
AWAY FROM
CAM.

158.

10 · A · CUBE 20 · EXTREME UPSHOT

E-2

CEILING

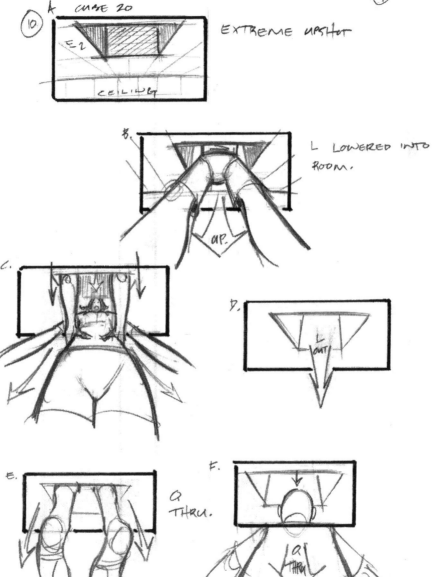

B. · L LOWERED INTO ROOM.

UP.

C.

D. · L OUT

E. · Q THRU.

F. · Q THRU.

159.

Shady Characters

At times the director in Natali wrestles with the would-be comics artist, particularly when it comes to the level of shading he uses for his characters.

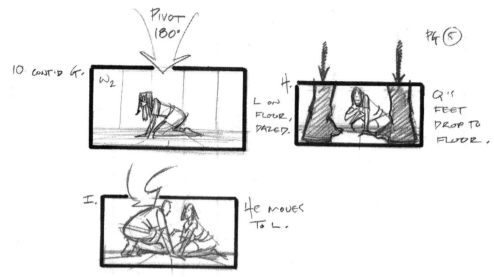

PIVOT 180°

10. CONT'D G.

W₂

PG ⑤

H.

L ON FLOOR, DAZED.

Q'S FEET DROP TO FLOOR.

I.

HE MOVES TO L.

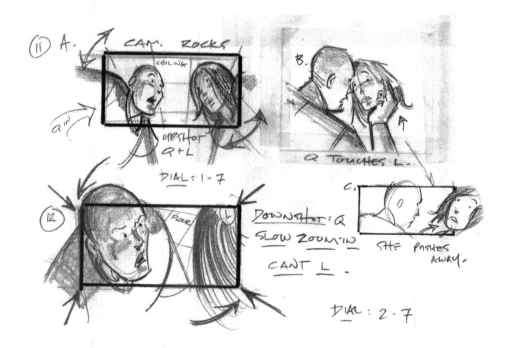

⑪ A.

CAM. ROCKS

CEILING

Q'S

UPSHOT Q+L

DIAL : 1-7

B.

Q TOUCHES L.

C.

SHE PUSHES AWAY.

⑫

FLOOR

L

DOWNSHOT: Q
SLOW ZOOM IN
CAN'T L.

DIAL : 2·7

160.

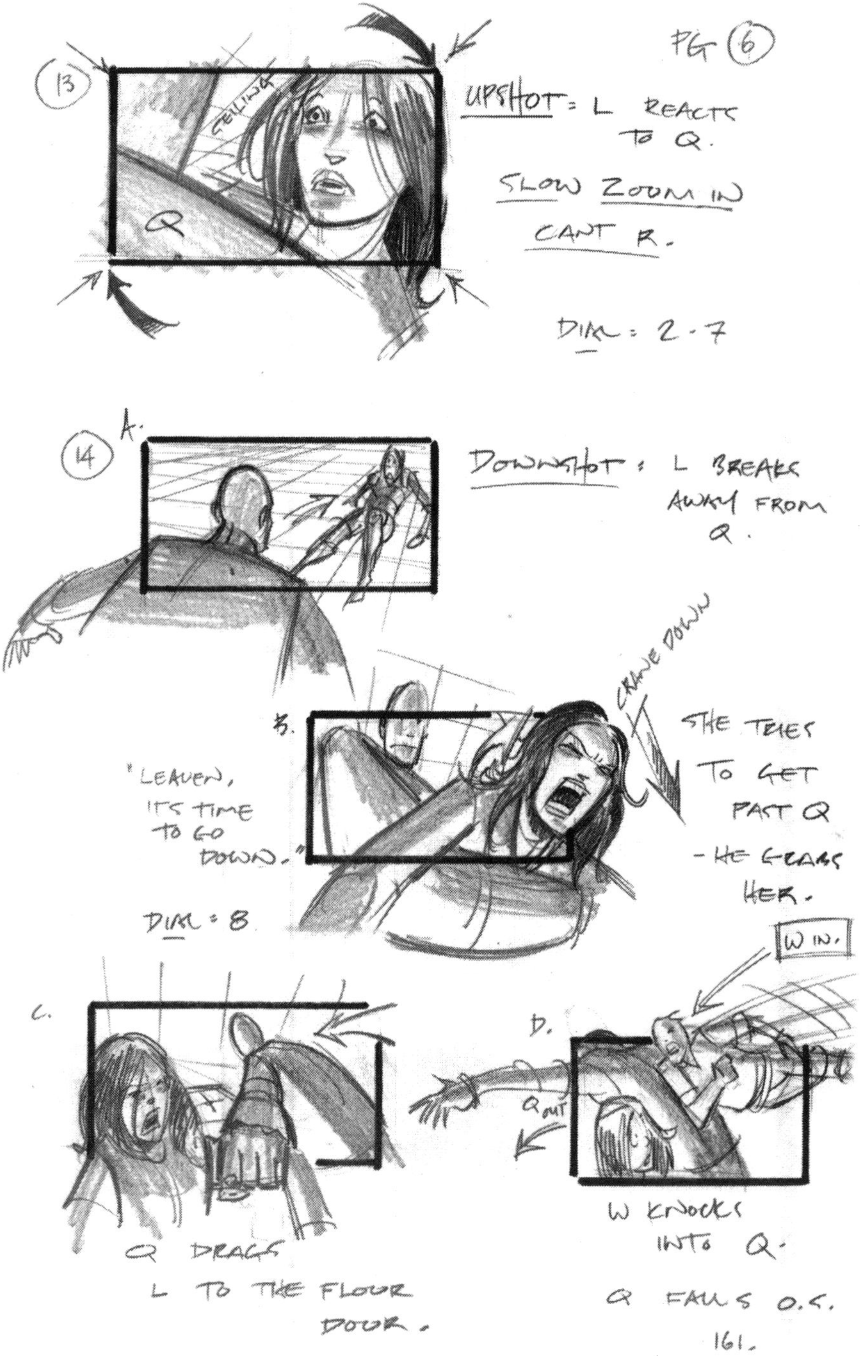

13

UPSHOT = L REACTS TO Q.

SLOW ZOOM IN

CANT R.

DIAL = 2 · 7

14 A.

DOWNSHOT = L BREAKS AWAY FROM Q.

267

CRANE DOWN

SHE TRIES TO GET PAST Q — HE GRABS HER.

B.

"LEAVEN, IT'S TIME TO GO DOWN."

DIAL = 8.

WIN.

C.

Q DRAGS L TO THE FLOOR DOOR.

D.

Q OUT

W KNOCKS INTO Q.

Q FALLS O.S.

161.

Raging Quentin

Scenes that made the jump from storyboard to screen are often as interesting to discover as those that did not.

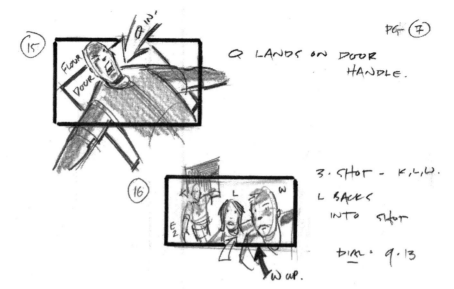

PG ⑦

Q LANDS ON DOOR HANDLE.

3. SHOT - K,L,W.
L BACKS
INTO SHOT

DIAL: 9.13

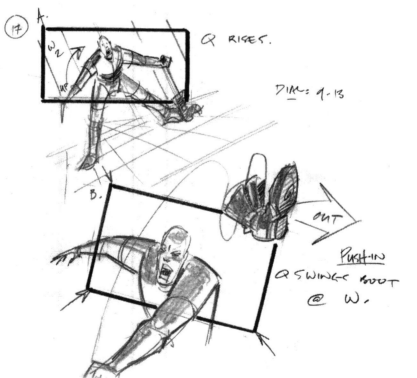

Q RISES.

DIAL: 9.13

OUT

PUSH-IN

Q SWINGS BOOT @ W.

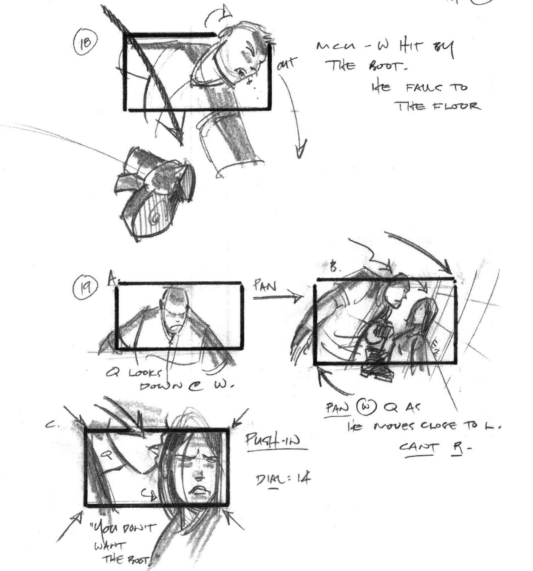

⑱

out

MCU - W HIT BY
THE BOOT.
HE FALLS TO
THE FLOOR

⑲ A

PAN →

B.

Q LOOKS
DOWN @ W.

PAN Ⓦ Q AS
HE MOVES CLOSE TO L.
CANT R.

C.

Q

PUSH-IN

DIAL = 14

"YOU DON'T
WANT
THE BOOT!"

PG (9)

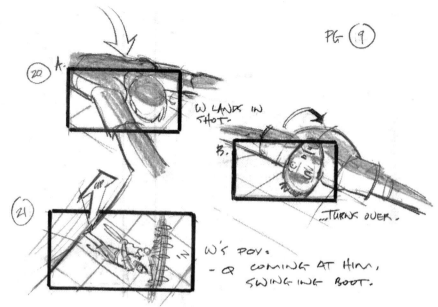

20 A.

W LANDS IN
SHOT.

B.

...TURN OVER.

21

W'S POV.
- Q COMING AT HIM,
SWINGING BOOT.

SLOW ZOOM IN

22 N₁

K SCREAMS.

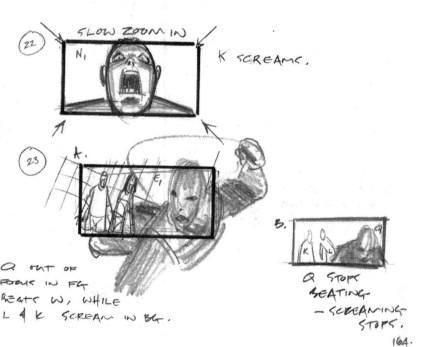

23 K.

E₁

Q OUT OF
FOCUS IN FG
BEATS W, WHILE
L & K SCREAM IN BG.

B.

K   L

Q STOPS
BEATING.
- SCREAMING
STOPS.

164.

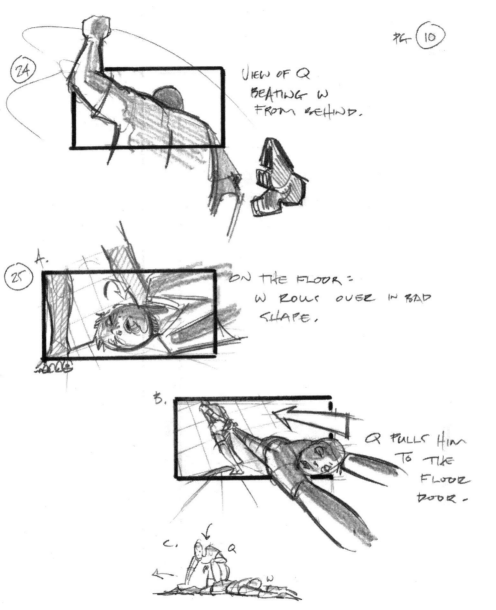

(24) VIEW OF Q
BEATING W
FROM BEHIND.

(25) A.

ON THE FLOOR =
W ROLLS OVER IN BAD
SHAPE.

271

B.

Q PULLS HIM
TO THE
FLOOR
DOOR.

C.

OPENS FLOOR DOOR.

@#$! Button...

One of the lighter moments in *Cube* in storyboard form.

* THIS SCENE CONT'D FROM OVERHEAD MAP. PG ①

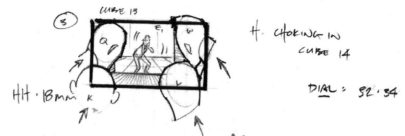

③ CUBE 13

HH · 18mm

H. CHOKING IN CUBE 14

DIAL = 32·34

④ A. CUBE 14

HH · 18mm

* FLOP AXIS ON ENTIRE SEQ

Q, K, L, W PEER THRU DOORWAY IN SHOCK.

DIAL = 32·35

B.

... DEFLATE,

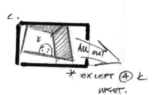

C.

All out

* EX LEFT ④ L UNSEEN.

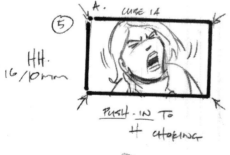

⑤ A. CUBE 14

HH · 16/10mm

PUSH · IN TO H CHOKING

B.

C. TURNS TO OTHERS,

DIAL = 35

... COUGHS UP BUTTON.

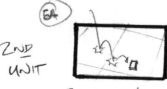

⑤A

2ND UNIT

ZOOM · WHATEVER.

PLINK PLINK

INSERT: BUTTON FALLS TO GB. FLOOR.

272

(11) A.

CUBE 2

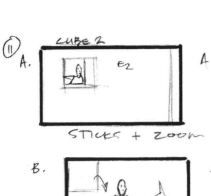

E2

A. PEERS IN

STICKS + ZOOM (25mm)

B.

UP

CLIMBS INTO ROOM.

C.

SOMETHING STRIKES
HIM FROM BEHIND.

SSHREK!

ADJUST →

(12)

CUBE 2

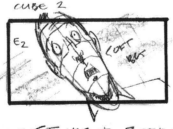

E2

LOFT

C.U. A - BLOOD LINES
APPEAR.

(CANT L) *REPLICA

STICKS + ZOOM (150 mm)

(13)

CUBE 2

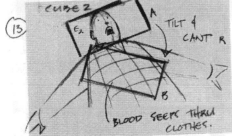

E2

A

TILT ↑
CANT R

BLOOD SOAKS THRU SHIRT.

B

(CANT R.)

BLOOD SEEPS THRU
CLOTHES.

STICKS + ZOOM

Cubing of Alderson Rough

While Natali put a great deal of thought into camera angles and coverage for other scenes, it is easy to imagine him looking forward to sketching out the traps most of all.

Cubing of Alderson Rough

(continued)

The trap that kicks off the film is given the "dissection" it deserves.

⑭ CUBE 2

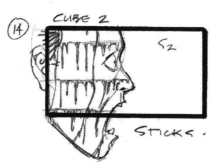

S_2

ECU: PROFILE A

BLOOD SEEPS OUT.

✳ REPLICA

STICKS · ZOOM (150 MM)

⑮ A. CUBE 2

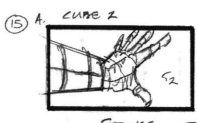

S_2

A'S HAND FALLS TO PIECES.

✳ REPLICA

STICKS - ZOOM (150MM)

B.

C.

CUBE 2

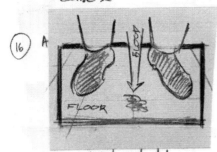

16 A

...BLOOD... THEN
PIECES
   OF A. FALL ONTO
      THE FLOOR.

STICKS - ZOOM

B

CUBE 2

17

REST OF HIS BODY
SPLASHES DOWN
   * REPLICA LEGS.
STICKS - ZOOM

275

CUBE 2

18
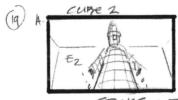

E.C.U.
   A'S EYES
      * ACTOR

STICKS - 16 mm

19 A   CUBE 2

E_2

B.   cut.

* REPLICA

STICKS - ZOOM (90 mm) - ?
HIS ENTIRE BODY COLLAPSES.

⑳

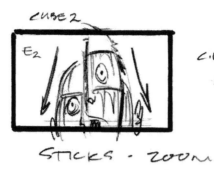

CUBE 2

E₂

C.U.
A.'S HEAD
COLLAPSES.
✗ REPLICA

STICKS - ZOOM

㉑

CUBE 2

E₂

MESH
DOWN   ✗ FOREGROUND
(S/A 19.)   MINITURE

HOLD A BEAT to
REVEAL BLOOD SILHOUETTE.

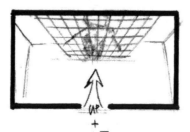

UP & OUT
OF SHOT

UP
+
OUT.

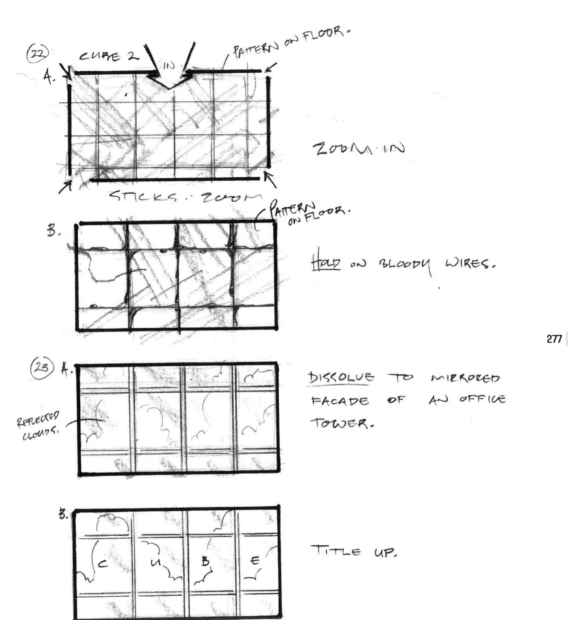

(22)

CUBE 2   IN   PATTERN ON FLOOR.

A.

ZOOM·IN

STICKS · ZOOM

B.

PATTERN ON FLOOR.

HOLD ON BLOODY WIRES.

(23) A.

REFLECTED CLOUDS.

DISSOLVE TO MIRRORED FACADE OF AN OFFICE TOWER.

B.

C U B E

TITLE UP.

Cubing of Alderson Rough

(continued)

Some scenes were revised using nothing more sophisticated than Post-It Notes (see the last two illustrations below).

"ALDERSON CUBED"

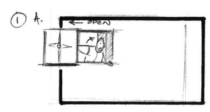

① A.

DOOR OPENS.

   A. POKES HIS HEAD IN.

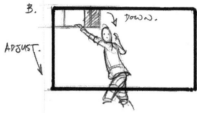

B.

ADJUST.

... STEPS INTO ROOM.

C.

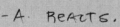

... STEPS FORWARD.

BRIGHT WALL.

PAN.

D.

SLASHING SOUND
- A. REACTS.

②

RED GRID PATTERN APPEARS ON A.'s FACE.

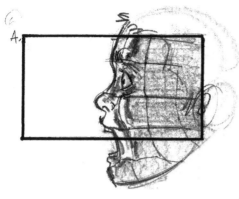

A.

E.C.U. PROFILE A. (SILHOUETTE) IMPRESSIONS CAN BE SEEN IN HIS FACE.

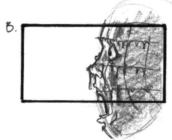

B.

BLOOD SEEPS OUT.

⑦

C.U. A.'S SHIRT BLOOD SOAKS INTO THE FABRIC.

⑨

A.

C.U. A'S HAND.

B.

FALLS TO PIECES.

C.

⑩

E.C.U. A.

SHAKING.

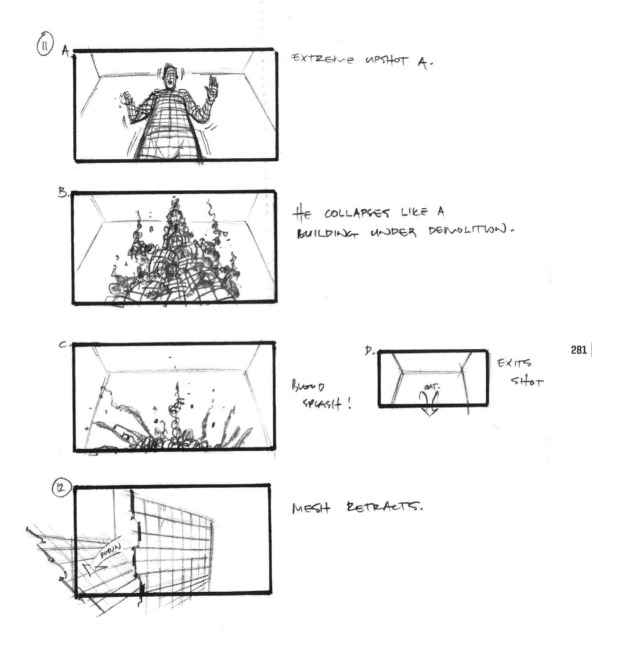

11 A. EXTREME UPSHOT A.

B. HE COLLAPSES LIKE A
BUILDING UNDER DEMOLITION.

C. BLOOD
SPLASH!

D. EXITS
SHOT

ait.

281

12 MESH RETRACTS.

DOWN

The Little Things

Sometimes it's the tiny details that jump out at you from these renderings. Here we see that Natali's vision of how the doors open made it to the film.

R. IN EXTREME FG.
L, Q & H DISCUSS HIM
IN BG.

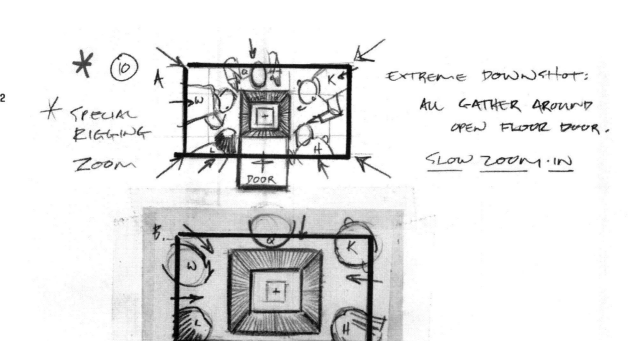

✶ SPECIAL
RIGGING
ZOOM

EXTREME DOWNSHOT:
ALL GATHER AROUND
OPEN FLOOR DOOR.

SLOW ZOOM·IN

HOLD

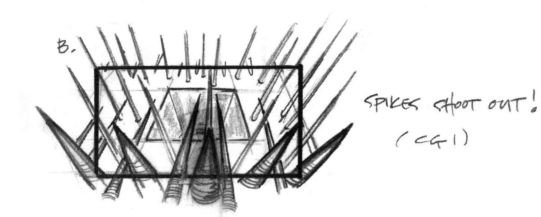

B.

SPIKES SHOOT OUT!

(CG)

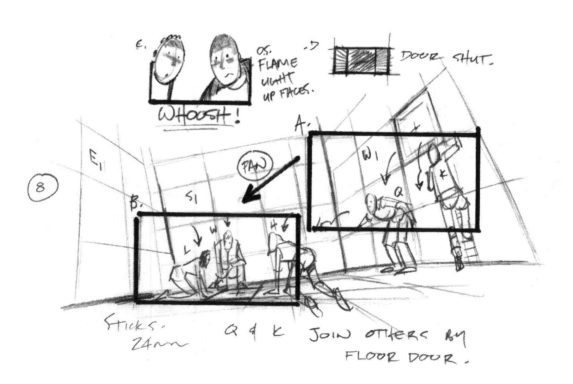

E.

OS.
FLAME
LIGHT
UP FACES.

DOOR SHUT.

WHOOSH!

A.

8

E₁

B.

S₁

W₁

Q

PAN

L   W   H

STICKS.
24mm

Q & K   JOIN OTHERS BY
FLOOR DOOR.

Room to Room

Storyboards go beyond just framing the action. Here Natali is keeping track of which room a given action is taking place in—Cube 19, in this case.

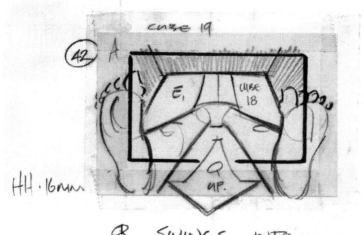

Q SWINGS INTO
THE PASSAGEWAY
TO CUBE 19.

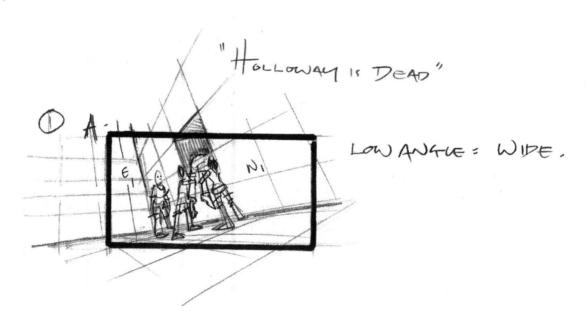

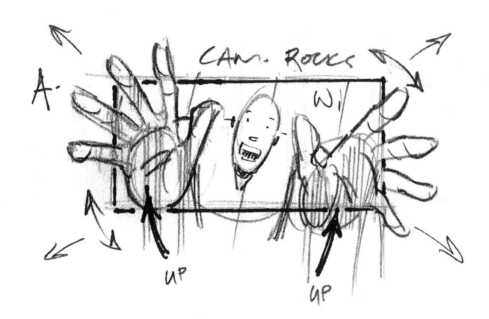

CAM. ROCKS

A.

W.

UP

UP

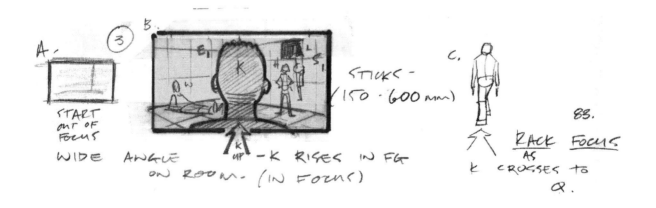

A.

③

B.

START
OUT OF
FOCUS

WIDE ANGLE
ON ROOM. (IN FOCUS)

K UP — K RISES IN FG

STICKS —
(150 · 600 mm)

C.

83.

RACK FOCUS
AS
K CROSSES TO
Q.

Pencil as Camera

Some visual nuances that one might assume were the creation of the cinematographer (below) were actually laid out by Natali in his storyboards.

MASSIVE CAMERA SHAKE!

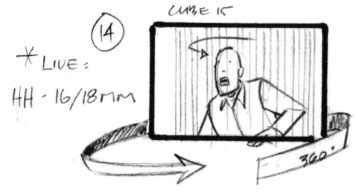

CUBE 15

14

✳ LIVE: HH · 16/18mm

360°

Q ROTATES CLOCKWISE WHILE CAM. ROTATES 360° COUNTER CLOCKWISE.

(22) A. CUBE 29

B.

FITS IT INTO
HER BROKEN
LENS.
- CLICK -

L BRINGS
BLOODY SHARD OF
GLASS UP.

(30) A.

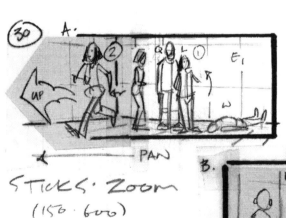

L UP.
PAN W. HER AS
SHE PACES.

287

STICKS· ZOOM
(150·600)

B. HOLD

C.

MOVES
K OUT
OF THE
WAY.

53 — ANGLE ON L
THRU. R'S LEGS.

LEGS

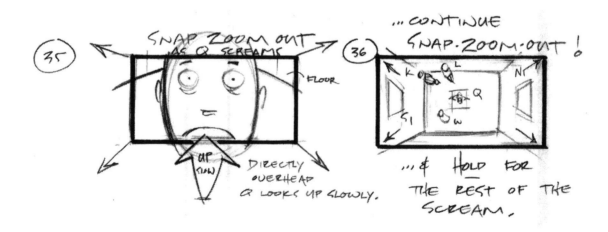

35 — SNAP ZOOM OUT
AS Q SCREAMS
FLOOR
UP
(UP)
DIRECTLY
OVERHEAD
Q LOOKS UP SLOWLY.

36 — ...CONTINUE
SNAP.ZOOM.OUT!
...& HOLD FOR
THE REST OF THE
SCREAM.

(13) ANGLE THRU CEILING HATCH.
GROUP COME INTO VIEW.
 — EA SPEAKS.
 " TRAP."   DIAL = 12·14

STICKS - 24/32

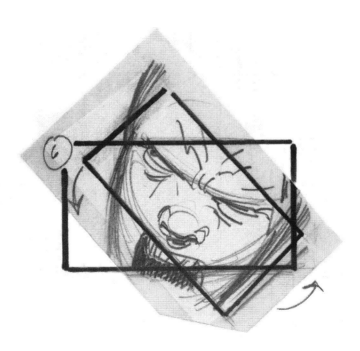

The Traps We Did Not See

Throughout the director's notes we find sketches of traps that never made it to screen. Some, like "banzai," can intrigue with their names alone.

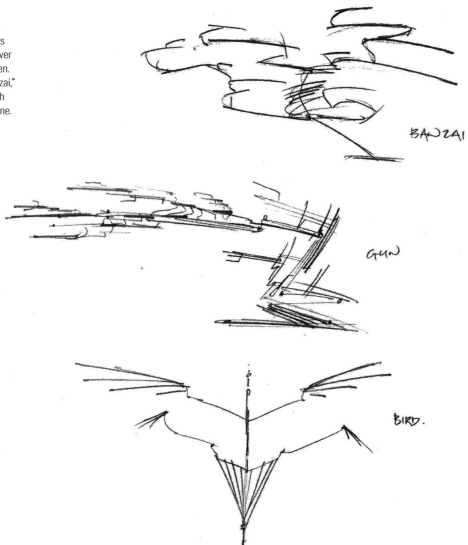

SOME TRAP CONCEPT IDEAS...

BANZAI

GUN

BIRD.

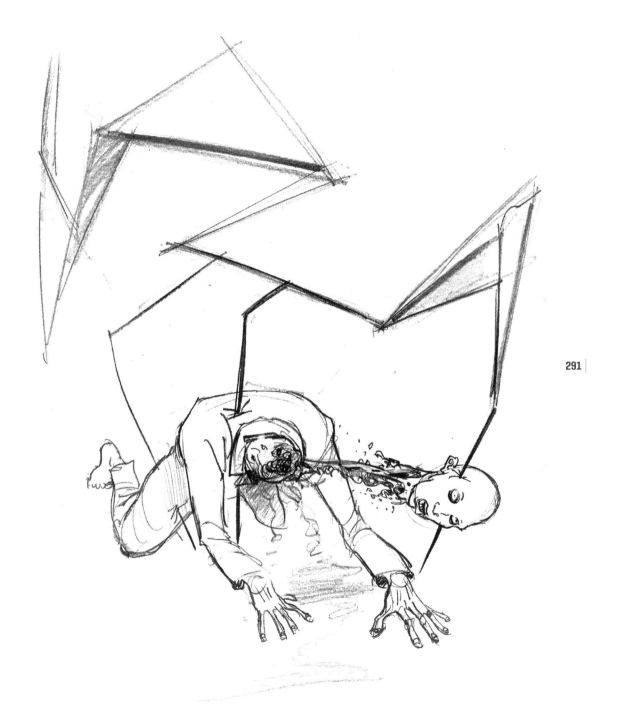

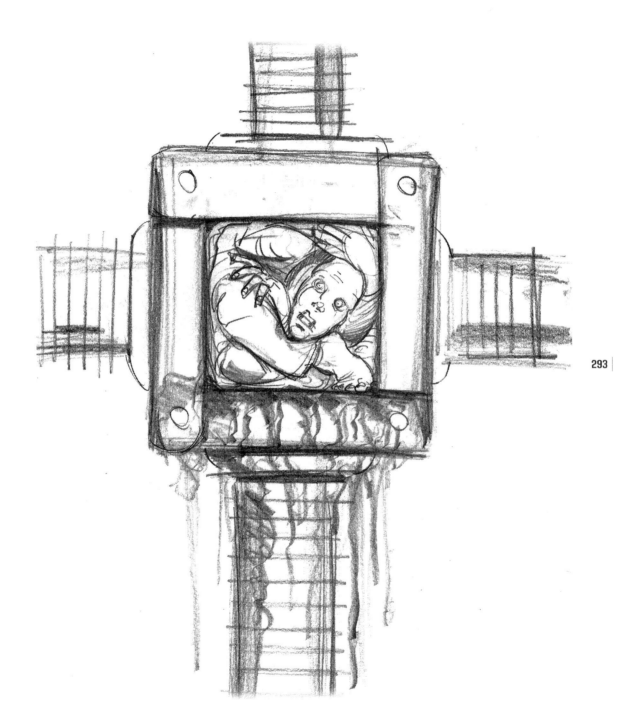

The Traps We Did Not See

(continued)

Over time the traps that Natali envisioned grew increasingly more elaborate.

The Traps We Did Not See

(continued)

At last we find a trap that did, in fact, make it into the final film (sort of)—the mesh screen that cubes Alderson in the opening sequence (see opposite page).

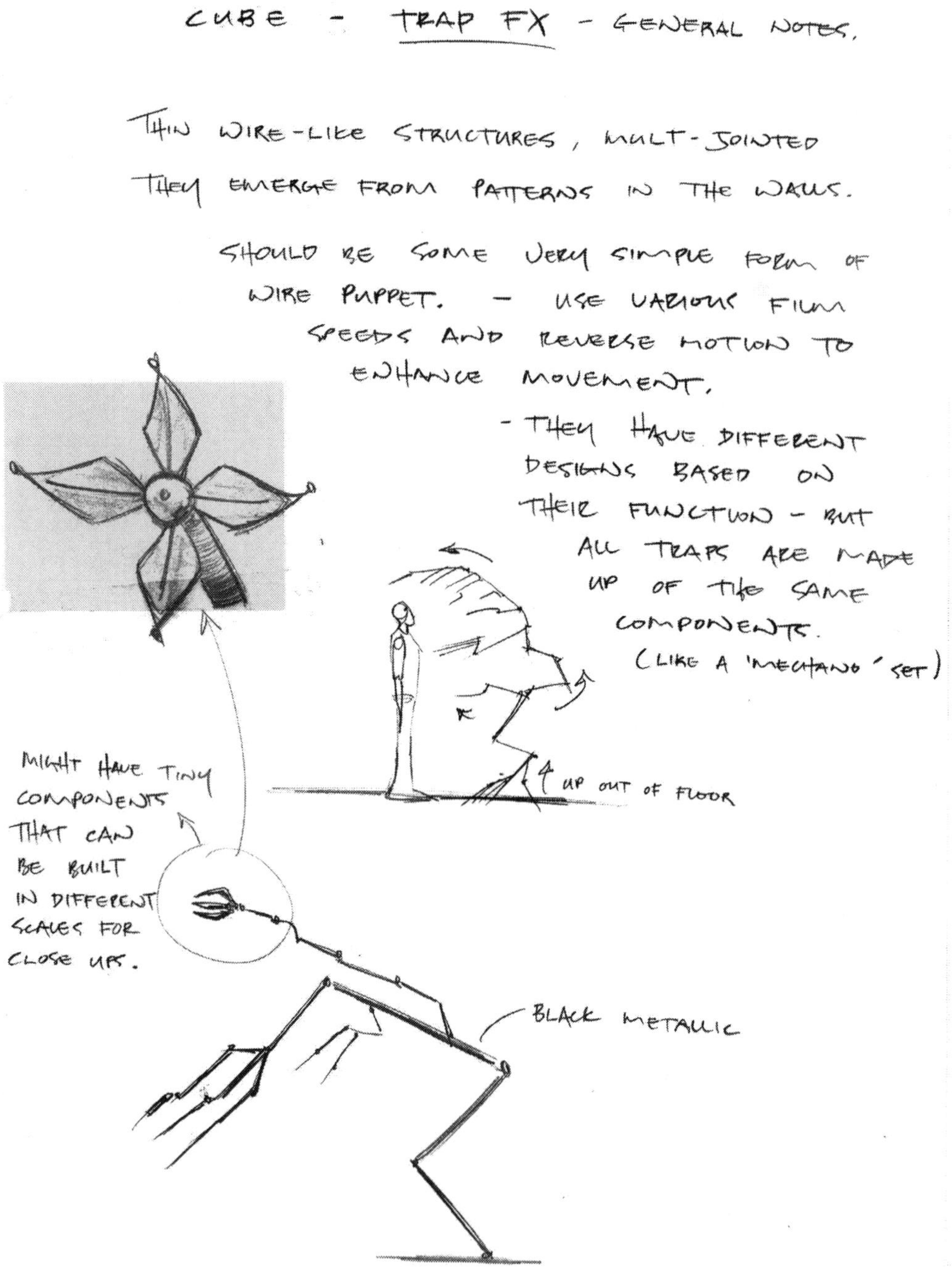

CUBE — TRAP FX — GENERAL NOTES.

THIN WIRE-LIKE STRUCTURES, MULT-JOINTED THEY EMERGE FROM PATTERNS IN THE WALLS.

SHOULD BE SOME VERY SIMPLE FORM OF WIRE PUPPET. — USE VARIOUS FILM SPEEDS AND REVERSE MOTION TO ENHANCE MOVEMENT.

— THEY HAVE DIFFERENT DESIGNS BASED ON THEIR FUNCTION — BUT ALL TRAPS ARE MADE UP OF THE SAME COMPONENTS.

(LIKE A 'MECHANO' SET)

UP OUT OF FLOOR

MIGHT HAVE TINY COMPONENTS THAT CAN BE BUILT IN DIFFERENT SCALES FOR CLOSE UPS.

BLACK METALLIC

"THE MESH"

PROFILE:
MESH SLICES
ALDERSON.

C.

A.

B.

SCALE OF MESH
TO ALDERSON.

297

BRACE ④ MESH
LOOKS LIKE WALL PATTERN.

BLOODY OUTLINE
OF ALDERSON

MESH
"ACCORDIONS"
BACK UP
TO CEILING.

At times Natali's sketches of the cube and its death chambers resemble action figure playsets (see opposite page).

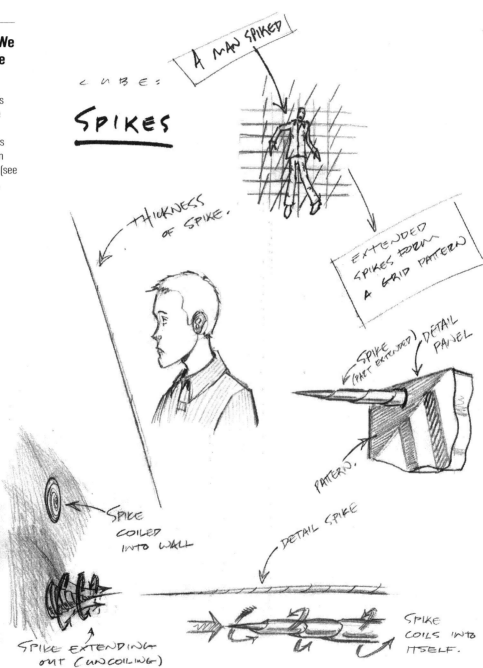

CUBE:

SPIKES

A MAN SPIKED

THICKNESS OF SPIKE.

EXTENDED SPIKES FORM A GRID PATTERN

SPIKE (PART EXTENDED) DETAIL PANEL

PATTERN.

DETAIL SPIKE

SPIKE COILED INTO WALL

SPIKE EXTENDING OUT (UNCOILING)

SPIKE COILS INTO ITSELF.

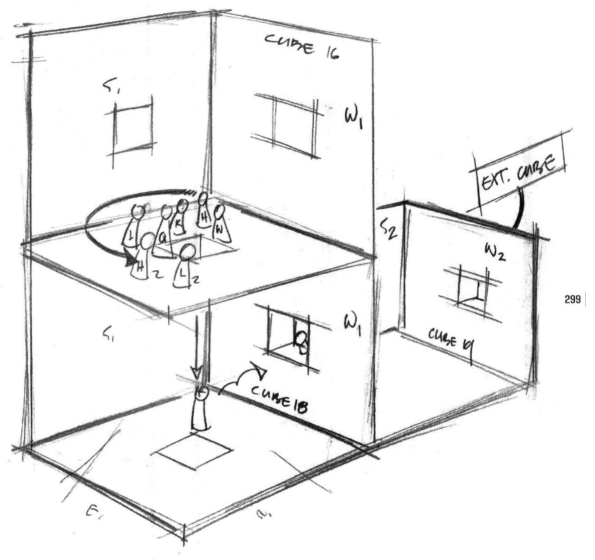

CUBE 1G

S_1

W_1

S_2

EXT. CUBE

W_2

299

CUBE 1J

S_1

W_1

CUBE 1B

E_1

W_1

"THE SPIKE ROOM"

The Traps We Did Not See

(continued)

Some of the killing devices not realized on screen reveal Natali's Japanese influence in terms of their symmetry and nature themes, such as the 'Venus flytrap.'

MCNEIL DEATH

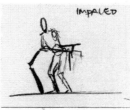

IMPALED

MOVE IN

PETALS UP

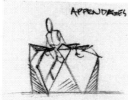

APPENDAGES

SPIN

- SCREAMS WE DON'T KNOW WHY.
- STRANGE TEARING SOUND
- BLOODY GRID FORMS ON HIS SKIN

GEOMETRIC. MOVE INCREDIBLY FAST.

LIKE MOUSETRAP

CUBE

FLOWER PETALS

OREGAMI / VENUS FLYTRAP DEATH

⑪ A. CUBE 18

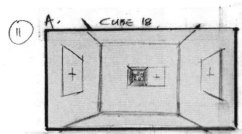

ANGLE ON CEILING DOOR.
- THE GROUP PEER IN.
- KAZAN SPEAKS -

B. STICKS · 16/18mm

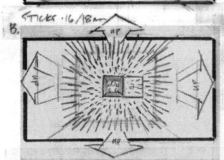

"... CAUSING THOUSANDS
OF THIN METAL SPIKES
TO SHOOT OUT FROM
THE WALLS IN A
'WAVE' PATTERN.

C.

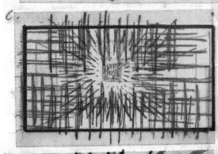

D.

"... ENDING WITH SPIKES
COMING UP IN FG.

E.

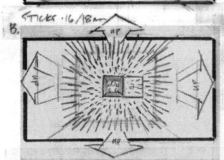

SLOWLY
SPIKES
RECEDE INTO
WALLS.

101.

SPACE ROOM & ACID DEATH   PG ①

— CUBES 7 & 8 —

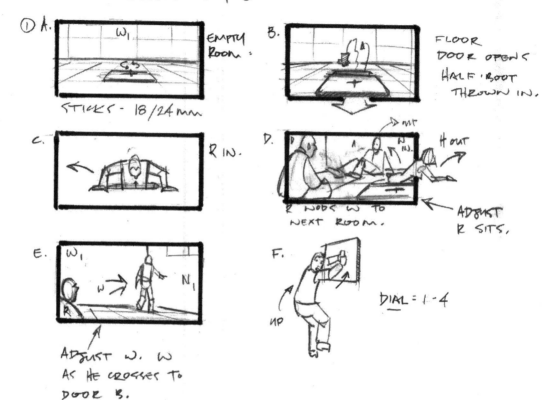

① A.
W_1

STICKS - 18/24 mm

EMPTY
ROOM:

B.

FLOOR
DOOR OPENS
HALF · BOOT
THROWN IN.

C.

R IN.

D.   H OUT

R NODS W TO
NEXT ROOM.

ADJUST
R SITS,

E. W_1 N_1
W

R

ADJUST W. W
AS HE CROSSES TO
DOOR B.

F.

UP

DIAL = 1-4

② A.   FLOOR
L
IN.   Q IN

L & Q COLLAPSE ON
FLOOR.

DIAL = 1-5

B.

L & Q
OUT.

STICKS · 24 MM

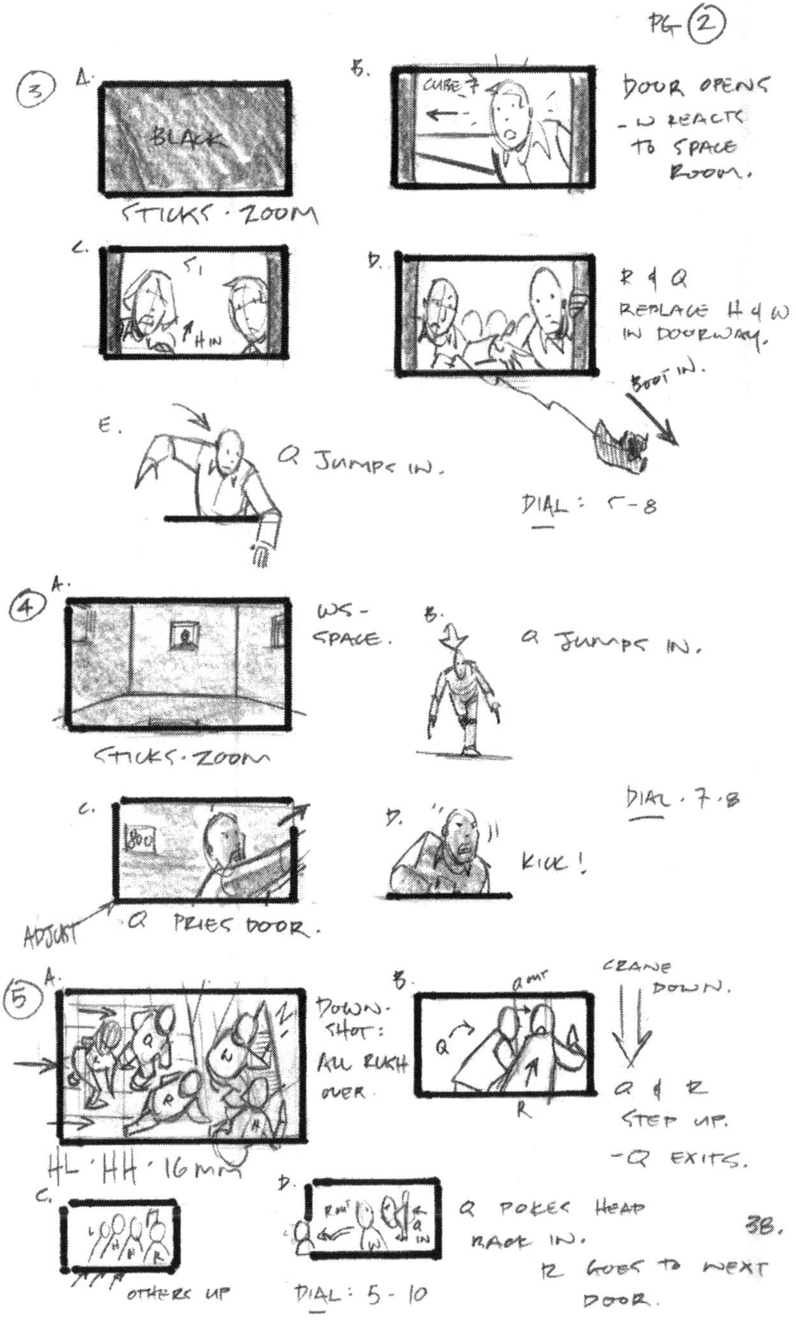

③ A.

BLACK

STICKS · ZOOM

B.

CUBE 7

DOOR OPENS
— W REACTS
TO SPACE
ROOM.

C.

S₁
H·W

D.

R & Q
REPLACE H & W
IN DOORWAY.

BOOT IN.

E.

Q JUMPS IN.

DIAL : 5-8

④ A.

STICKS · ZOOM

WS -
SPACE.

B.

Q JUMPS IN.

DIAL · 7·8

C.

YOU

ADJUST   Q PRIES DOOR.

D.

KICK!

⑤ A.

HL · HH · 16mm

DOWN·
SHOT:
ALL RUSH
OVER.

B.

Q→   Q OUT

R

CRANE
DOWN.

Q & R
STEP UP.
—Q EXITS.

C.

OTHERS UP

D.

DIAL: 5-10

Q POKES HEAD
BACK IN.

R GOES TO NEXT
DOOR.

38.

303

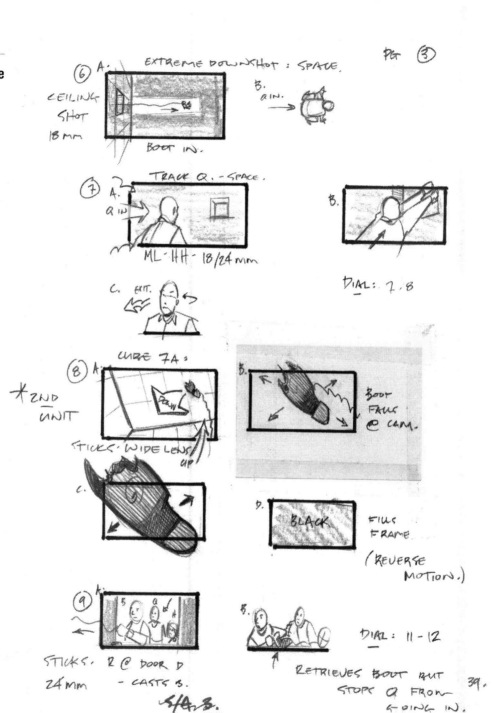

PG ③

⑥ A. EXTREME DOWNSHOT : SPACE.
CEILING SHOT 18mm
BOOT IN.
B. Q IN. →

⑦ TRACK Q. - SPACE.
A. Q IN →
ML · HH · 18/24 mm
B.
DIAL: 7.8

C. EXIT.

⑧ A. CLOSE 7A :
*2ND UNIT
STICKS · WIDE LENS · UP
B. BOOT FALLS @ CAM.
C.
D. BLACK
FILLS FRAME
(REVERSE MOTION.)

⑨ A.
STICKS. 2 @ DOOR D
24mm - CASTS B.
B.
DIAL: 11 - 12
RETRIEVES BOOT BUT STOPS Q FROM GOING IN.
39.

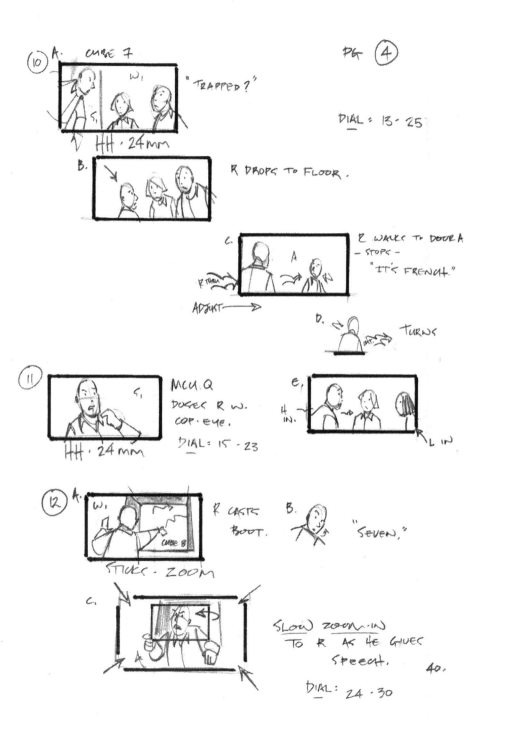

10 A. CUBE 7   PG ④

"TRAPPED?"

DIAL = 13 - 25

HH · 24mm

B.   R DROPS TO FLOOR.

C.   R WALKS TO DOOR A
            — STOPS —
R THRU   "IT'S FRENCH."
ADJUST →

D.   TURNS

305

11 MCU Q
    DODGES R W.
    COP · EYE.
    DIAL = 15 - 23
    HH · 24 mm

E. H IN.
    L IN

12 A. W₁   R CASTS   B.   "SEVEN,"
        CUBE 8   BOOT.
    STICKS · ZOOM

C.   SLOW ZOOM · IN
            TO R AS HE GIVES
            SPEECH.   40.
            DIAL : 24 · 30

Acid Trap

We finally see the rough storyboards for a trap we *are* familiar with...

✳ ⑬

A

HH · 16mm

R. IN EXTREME FG.
L, Q & H DISCUSS HIM
IN BG.

B.

L & H COME UP TO HIM.

TURN.

⑭ A. CUBE 8

E₂

ANGLE INSIDE CUBE B.

JUMP

R. JUMPS IN - SENSES
SOMETHING AMISS.

STICKS · 24mm TILT

"MERDE"
DIAL: 30·31

✳ 150·600
DAILY: ZOOM

HH · 24mm ⑮ B. CUBE 8

A.

W₂

B.

R BACK TO CAM.

REVERSE ANGLE:
R TURNS TO CAM.

HE IS SPRAYED
IN THE FACE W. ACID.

✳ CUBE 8

STICKS. ZOOM

WIDE - R TURNS
SNAP ZOOM·IN

⑮B

✳ CUBE 8

SNAP ZOOM INTO EYE.   4).
12F· 250

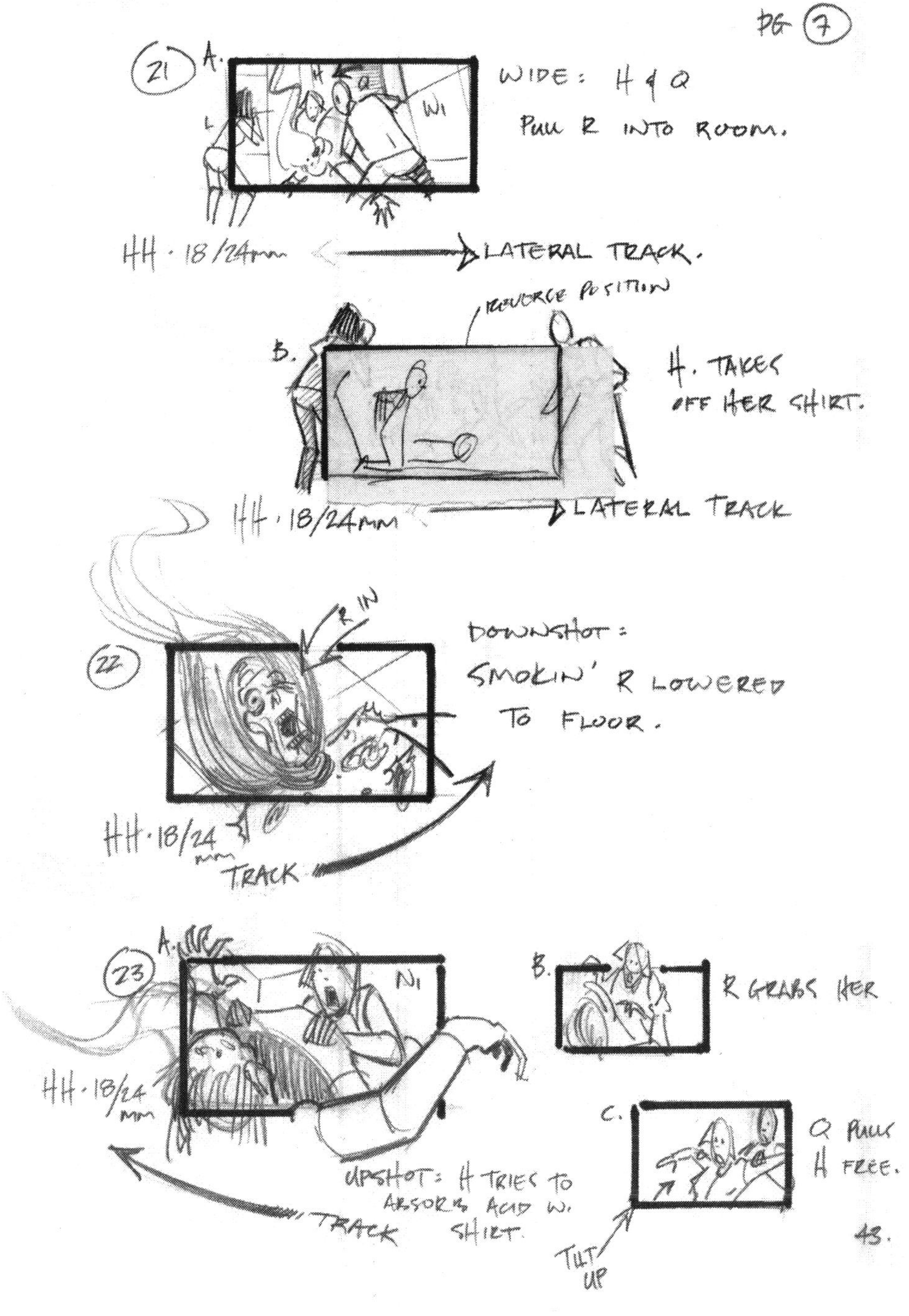

21 A. WIDE: H & Q
PULL R INTO ROOM.

HH · 18/24mm ←————→ LATERAL TRACK.

B. REVERSE POSITION

H. TAKES
OFF HER SHIRT.

HH · 18/24mm ————→ LATERAL TRACK

22 R IN

DOWNSHOT:
SMOKIN' R LOWERED
TO FLOOR.

HH · 18/24 mm TRACK

23 A. N₁

B. R GRABS HER

HH · 18/24 mm

UPSHOT: H TRIES TO
ABSORB ACID W.
SHIRT.

TRACK

C. Q PULLS
H FREE.

TILT
UP

43.

Acid Trap
[continued]

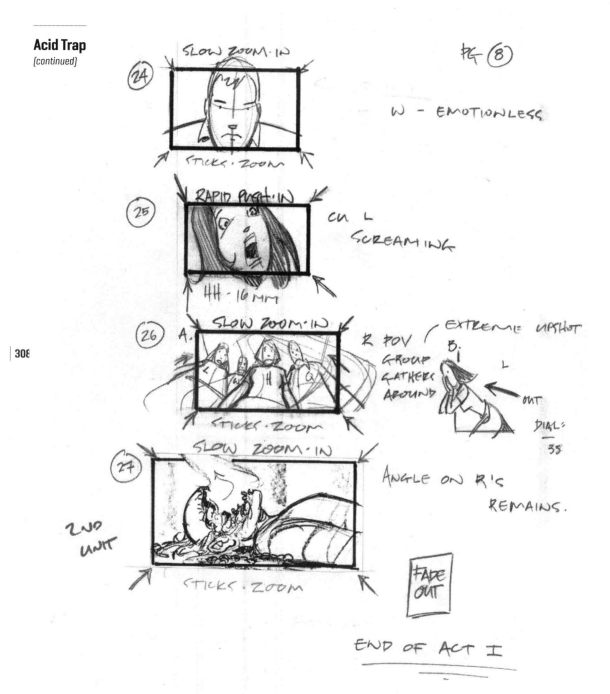

SLOW ZOOM·IN

PG (8)

(24)

STICKS·ZOOM

W - EMOTIONLESS

(25) RAPID PUSH·IN

CU L
SCREAMING

HH · 16 MM

(26) A. SLOW ZOOM·IN

STICKS·ZOOM

R POV
GROUP
GATHERS
AROUND

EXTREME UPSHOT
B.
L
OUT
DIAL·
38

(27) SLOW ZOOM·IN

2ND UNIT

STICKS·ZOOM

ANGLE ON R'S
REMAINS.

FADE OUT

END OF ACT I

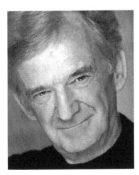

'I always liked Wayne Robson [escape artist Rennes pictured here on *Cube* set with Wint and Guadagni following the acid trap]. He was a buddy from before. But he got killed off pretty quick. He's gone now—dear Wayne. He finally made it to Stratford a few years ago—he was over the moon to be working there—then died of a heart attack while they were still in rehearsal.'

↘ **Guadagni**

Shell Games

In this sketch we get some sense of the rooms in relation to the outer shell.

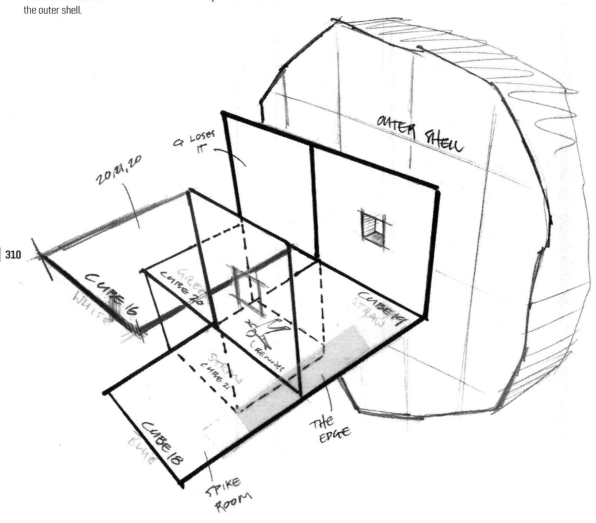

3·D MAP OF THE EDGE

OUTER SHELL

Q LOSES IT

20,19,20

CUBE 16
WHITE

GREE
CUBE 20

CUBE 19
STRAW

STRING
CUBE 21

CUBE 18
BLUE

THE EDGE

SPIKE ROOM

Mapping Out the Cube

The Post-It Note edit here gets an assist
from a couple of strips of masking tape
which themselves are written upon.

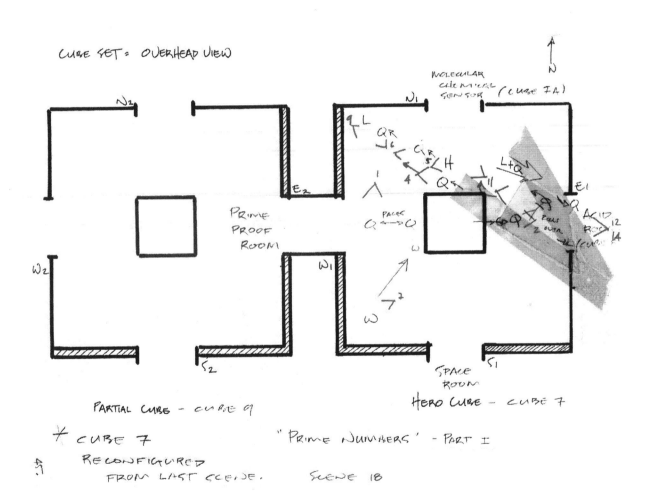

CUBE SET: OVERHEAD VIEW

PARTIAL CUBE - CUBE 9

HERO CUBE - CUBE 7

✗ CUBE 7
♪ RECONFIGURED
FROM LAST SCENE.

"PRIME NUMBERS" - PART I

SCENE 18

Cube Plus

One of *Cube's* most brilliant innovations was the use of a set that actually included a half-cube attached to a full one.

Opposite: The scissors lift hinted at in the sketch opposite is used here while shooting Holloway's death.

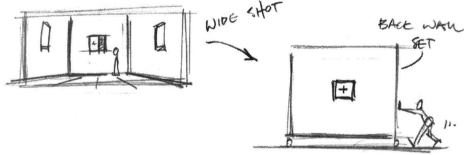

SECTION OF WALL

SET

SCISSOR → - LIFT

C.U. SHOT

Row

WIDE SHOT

BACK WALL SET

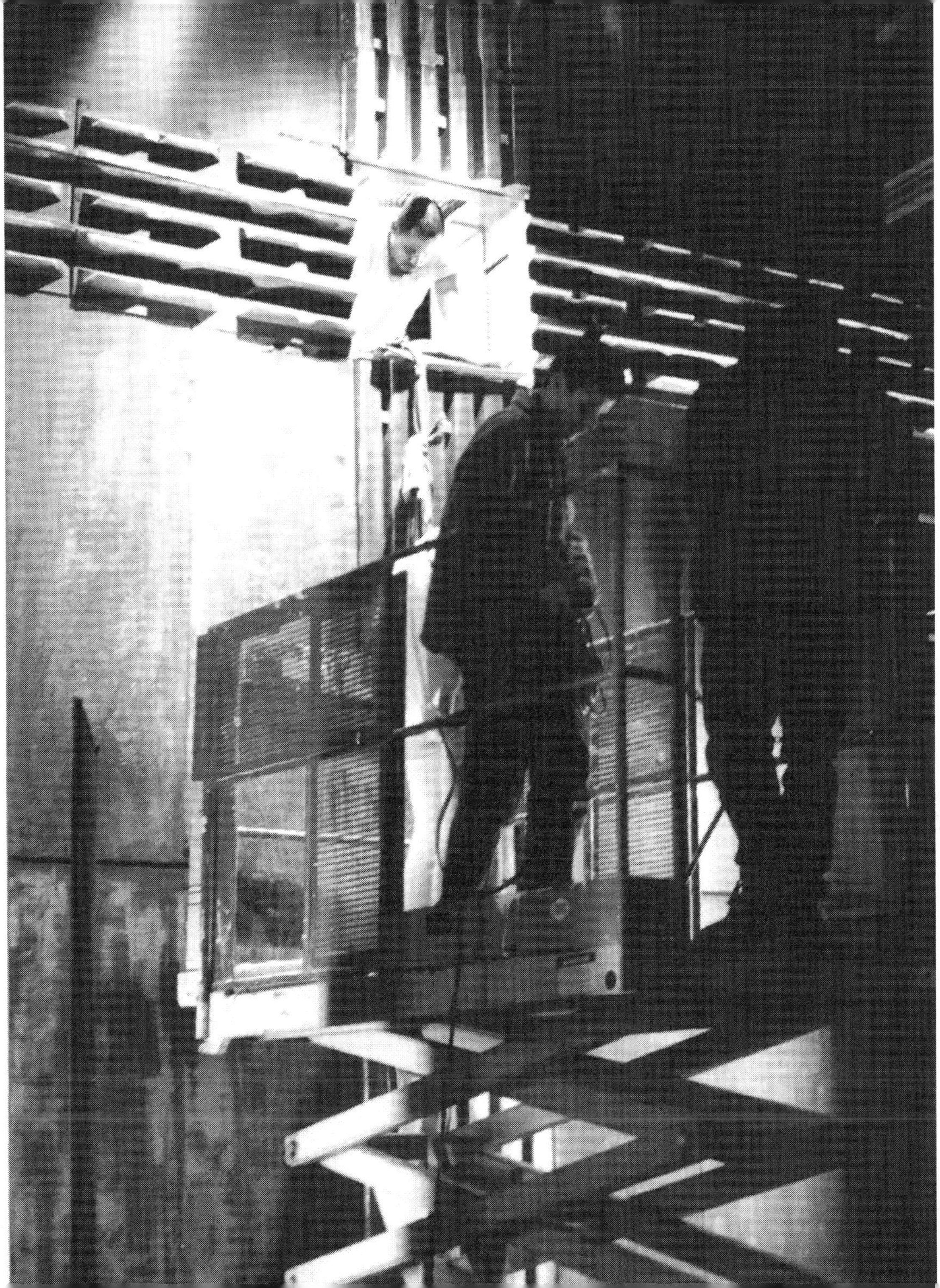

Post-It Note Paste-up

One of the virtues of sticky notes was their ability to be repositioned at will, the better to alter the order of actions in a scene.

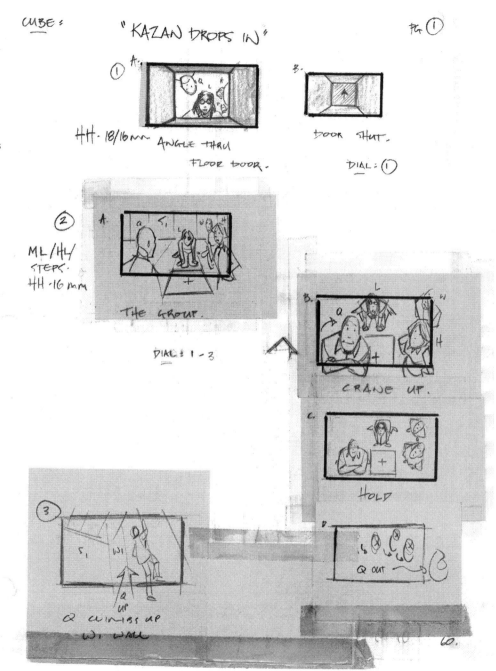

CUBE:

"KAZAN DROPS IN"

PG ①

① A.

HH. 18/16mm ANGLE THRU FLOOR DOOR.

B.

DOOR SHUT.

DIAL: ①

② A.

ML/HH/ STEPS. HH. 16mm

THE GROUP.

DIAL ‡ 1 - 3

B. CRANE UP.

C. HOLD

D. Q OUT

③ Q CLIMBS UP W. WALL

60.

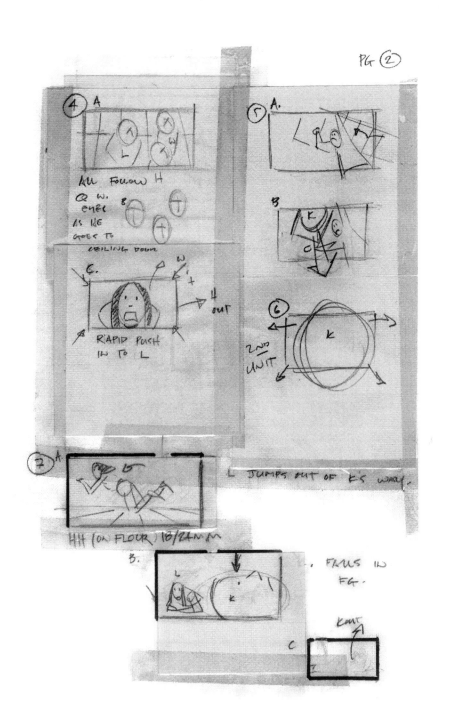

④ A

All Follow H
as W.
eyes 8
as he
goes to
ceiling door

C.
H out
RAPID PUSH
IN TO L

⑤ A.

B

⑥
2ND
UNIT
K

⑦ A
HH (ON FLOOR) 18/24 M M

L JUMPS OUT OF K'S WAY.

B.
L
K

. FALLS IN
FG.

K out

C

Prime Inserts

The director's ability to render the room-code montage in storyboard form is a testament to Natali's ability to see beyond the edges of the paper when bringing everything together.

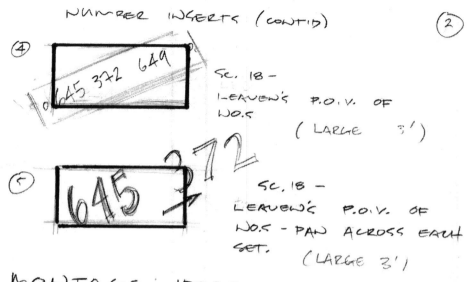

NUMBER INSERTS (CONT'D)   ②

④

645 372 649

SC. 18 —
LEAVEN'S P.O.V. OF
NO.5
(LARGE   3')

645 372

SC. 18 —
LEAVEN'S P.O.V. OF
NO.5 - PAN ACROSS EACH
SET.   (LARGE 3')

MONTAGE IDEAS

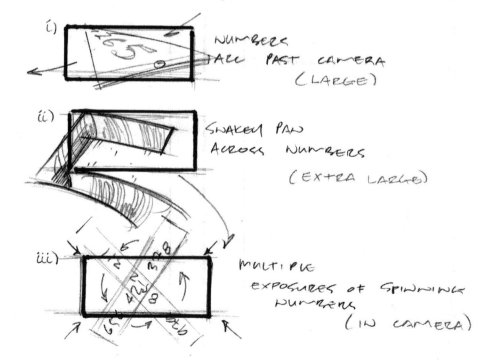

i)

NUMBERS
FALL PAST CAMERA
(LARGE)

ii)

SNAKEY PAN
ACROSS NUMBERS
(EXTRA LARGE)

iii)

MULTIPLE
EXPOSURES OF SPINNING
NUMBERS
(IN CAMERA)

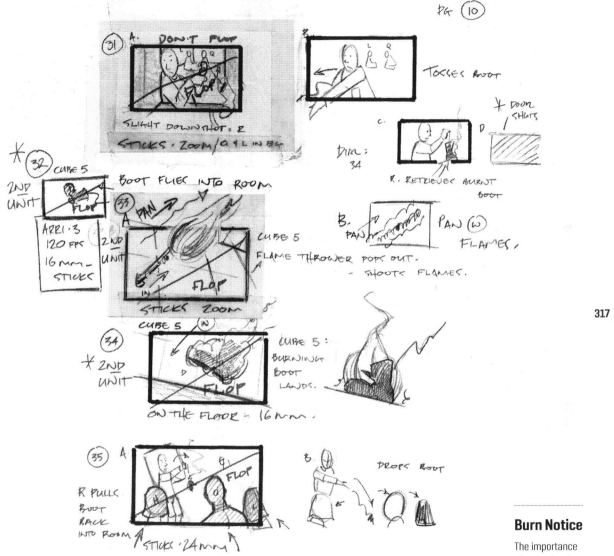

317

Burn Notice

The importance
of second-unit
filming is glimpsed
in the familiar
boot-flambé scene
sketched out here.

Wrap Party

1: Hewlett with girlfriend at the time Jill Riley **2:** Bijelic. **3:** Left: *Cube* second camera operator Dany Chiasson (wife of filmmaker Bruce McDonald) **4:** Script supervisor Lisa Burling **5:** Hewlett with "door doctor" William Phillips **6:** Co-writer Graeme Manson **7:** Natali and Hewlett, sleep deprived and ready to party **8:** Nicky Guadagni and Andrew Miller

Trailer Storyboards

The film trailer envisioned here is one of mature restraint, focusing as much on the characters as it does on the traps.

CUBE TRAILER.

PAGE ①

①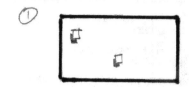

BLOCKS FORM AGAINST WHITE BG.

②

DISSOLVE TO QUENTIN TURNING IN SLOW MOTION (STEP PRINTED).

③

GRAPHIC : "YOU"

④

QUICK DISSOLVE TO NEGATIVE IMAGE.

⑤ A.

LEAVEN SCREAMS

B.

QUENTIN CAUGHT IN WIRES

QUENTIN PUNCHES WORTH

BUNCH OF ACTION SHOTS CUT TOGETHER EXTREMELY FAST.

⑥

MORE BLOCKS FORM
AGAINST WHITE BG.

⑦

DISSOLVE TO LEAVEN
TURNING IN SLOW MOTION.
(STEP PRINTED)

⑧

GRAPHIC: "ARE"

⑨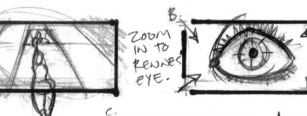

QUICK DISSOLVE
TO NEGATIVE IMAGE.

⑩

HOLLOWAY
CLIMBS
UP TO
QUENTIN
OUTSIDE
CUBE.

A.

B.
ZOOM
IN TO
RENNES
EYE.

C.

DOOR
SHUTS.

ANOTHER
SERIES OF
ACTION SHOTS.

Trailer Storyboards
[continued]

The trailer wording is similar in spirit to the invitations that were handed out for the very first screenings, which read 'You are invited to the experiment.'

⑪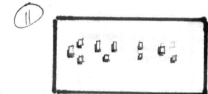

MORE BLOCKS FORM AGAINST WHITE BG.

⑫

DISSOLVE TO RENNES LOOKING UP IN SLOW MOTION (STEP PRINTED)

⑬

GRAPHIC = "INVITED"

INVITED

⑭

QUICK DISSOLVE TO NEGATIVE IMAGE

⑮ A.  B.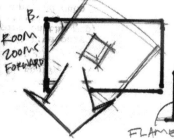

RENNES BURNING FACE REVEALED

ROOM ZOOMS FORWARD

C.

FLAME THROWER

ANOTHER SERIES OF ACTION SHOTS.

⑯ 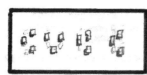 MORE BLOCKS.

⑰  DISSOLVE TO
HOLLOWAY LOOKING DOWN.
(STEP PRINTED)

⑱ 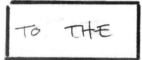 GRAPHIC = "TO THE"

TO THE

323

⑲  QUICK DISSOLVE TO
NEGATIVE IMAGE

A.

⑳  B. BLOODY ALDERSON
CAMERA SHAKE

SPIKES

ANOTHER SERIES OF
ACTION SHOTS.

'CUBE' TRAILER CONT.

㉖

BLOCKS FORM
"CUBE"

㉗

QUICK DISSOLVE
TO NEGATIVE
IMAGE. — FADE OUT

㉘

HARD CUT TO WORTH
AS HE SCREAMS,
"THERE IS NO WAY
OUT OF HERE!"

FADE OUT

FINI

CREDIT
BLOCKS

Ads, Posters & Promotions

Print promotion of *Cube* was pretty consistent from country to country.

Ads, Posters & Promotions

(continued)

When in doubt, stick Hewlett in a room and have him look crazy (from an early printed promo).

Opposite: More treasures from the *Cube* archive.

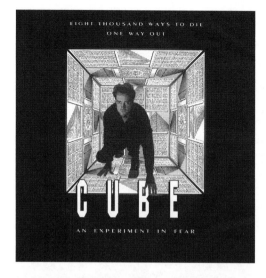

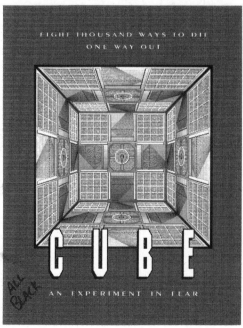

Ads, Posters & Promotions
[continued]

Excerpts from
Japanese and
French press books.

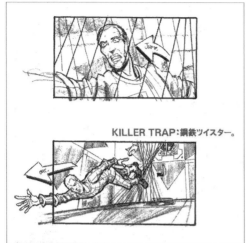

KILLER TRAP：鋼鉄ツイスター。

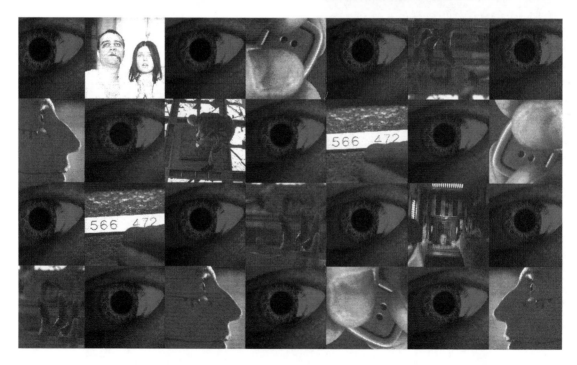

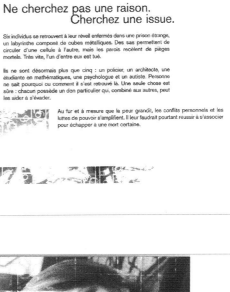

SYNOPSIS

Ne cherchez pas une raison.
Cherchez une issue.

Six individus se retrouvent à leur réveil enfermés dans une prison étrange, un labyrinthe composé de cubes métalliques. Des sas permettent de circuler d'une cellule à l'autre, mais les parois recèlent de pièges mortels. Très vite, l'un d'entre eux est tué.

Ils ne sont désormais plus que cinq : un policier, un architecte, une étudiante en mathématiques, une psychologue et un autiste. Personne ne sait pourquoi ou comment il s'est retrouvé là. Une seule chose est sûre : chacun possède un don particulier qui, combiné aux autres, peut les aider à s'évader.

Au fur et à mesure que la peur grandit, les conflits personnels et les luttes de pouvoir s'amplifient. Il leur faudrait pourtant réussir à s'associer pour échapper à une mort certaine.

FICHE TECHNIQUE

Réalisateur	Vincenzo Natali	Chef décoratrice	Jasna Stefanovic
Producteurs	Mehra Meh	Directrice artistique	Diana Magnus
	Betty Orr	Monteur	John Sanders
Producteur exécutif	Colin Brunton	Musique	Mark Korven
Scénaristes	Andre Bijelic	Effets digitaux et Animation	C.O.R.E.
	Vincenzo Natali		Digital Pictures
	Graeme Manson		Bob Munroe
Supervision du scénario	Hugh Graham		John Mariella
Directrice pour le		Effets prosthétiques	
Feature Film Project	Justine White	et visuels	Caligari Studios
Directeur de production	Norah Wakula	Réalisateur 2ᵉ équipe &	
Directeur de la photographie	Derek Rogers	superviseur post-production	William Phillips

INTERPRETATIONS

Quentin	Maurice Dean Wint	Worth	David Hewlett
Leaven	Nicole DeBoer	Kazan	Andrew Miller
Holloway	Nicky Guadagni	Rennes	Wayne Robson

Couleur - Année : 1999 - Durée : 1 h 26 - Format : 185 - Son : Dolby SR, DTS

www.metrofilms.com

A Global Phenomenon

This thoroughly Canadian film nevertheless struck
a deep chord in audiences around the world.

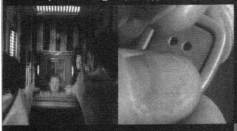

Cube the Mini-Comic

One of the most curious *Cube* promotions is this 4-x-4 inch comic, which features a 12-page story written by *30 Days of Night* comic writer Steve Niles, with art by Paul Lee. Structured as a "Choose Your Own Adventure"-style story, the characters die horribly in all but one instance, this last bringing them back to the beginning to start again.

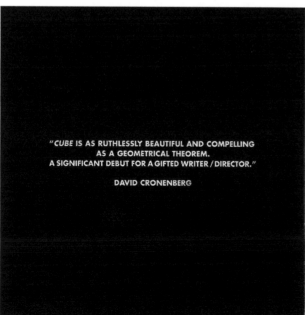

Reviews

While they didn't always get the details right (*Richard* Natali?) reviews, on the whole, were positive.

Recently out

CUBE ★★★★½

What a relief it is to stumble across a sci-fi film that's not filled with expensive eye-candy effects and flimsy one-dimensional characters. On a near-non-existent budget, writer-director Richard Natali has crafted one of the most thought-provoking and visually dazzling sci-films since 2001: A Space Odyssey, a stark drama about six characters who wake up and find themselves inside a series of interlocking cubes. So good is this Canadian-made film I wouldn't be surprised to see a Hollywood remake starring Bruce Willis or Kurt Russell — without the originality, of course. Rated M (Alistair Moffat)

"The West Australian" 8th March '99

Cube squares up against the big guns

FILM

CUBE (M)
Nicole Deboer, Nicky Guadagini
Directed by Vincenzo Natali
Reviewed by Alistair Moffat
★ ★ ★ ★ ½

THESE days sci-fi normally means big budget blockbusters, filled with expensive 'eye candy' effects and flimsy one-dimensional characters.

What a relief to stumble across Cube, the feature film debut for Canadian writer/director Vincenzo Natali.

On a nearly non-existent budget, director Natali — with help from cinematographer Derek Rogers and production designer Jasna Stefanovic — has crafted one of the most thought-provoking and visually dazzling sci-fi films since 2001: A Space Odyssey.

And they have done it without star players, layers of visual effects and the marketing hype normally associated with this sort of film. Let's hope that someone in Hollywood may have taken notice of this tiny Canadian film, and realised that all the special effects in the world can't make up for a lack of plot or believable characters.

After an extremely gruesome prelude we are introduced to the six characters of the film.

They wake to find themselves imprisoned in a strange cell — a cube with interconnecting doors. Eventually the characters meet up and discover that although they are free to move from cell to cell, some are booby-trapped and it is impossible to tell which.

This is where the film's characters are suddenly forced to cooperate and trust each other and things get interesting. Perhaps Cube works best as a kind of psychological drama, even though it is dressed up as a sci-fi film.

The characters are vastly different, yet they are presented as normal 'anybodies': a cop, a thief, a doctor, a student, an architect and an autistic adult.

There are so many questions thrown up by the film. Who built the cube? Who is controlling it? Is it aliens or is it the government?

But the film-makers don't try to make it easy for you. In fact there are no answers, only more questions.

And in the end that is what a really good sci-fi film should do, get you thinking.

X-Press Magazine (street press)
4th March '99

CUBE Square Dancing

Directed by Vincenzo Natali
Starring Nicole de Boer, Maurice Dean Wint, Nicky Guadagni, David Hewlett, Andrew Miller

Imagine waking up in a dark room. You don't know where you are, how you got there, or why you're there. The room you're in is cubic with doors at the centre of each wall. There are identical rooms, differentiated only by colour, on the other side of every door. What would you do if you knew that some of these rooms were equipped with the most elaborate and deadly booby traps ever invented? Would you stay put, hoping to be rescued?

That's exactly what an unrelated group of six face in *Cube*. There's Quentin (Wint), an easily agitated cop, Holloway (Guadagni), a nervous doctor, Worth (Hewlett), an architect with something to hide, Kazan (Miller), an autistic man with a hidden gift, Leaven (de Boer), a closet maths genius, and Rennes (Robson), a professional escape artist. The group must unite to figure a way out by using the seemingly unrelated numbers. The only thing within the Escher-like maze to give the prisoners a clue to escape is a cryptic series of numbers between the doors of each cube.

Filmed tightly in 21 days on a $600,000 budget in a warehouse in director Natali's hometown of Toronto, *Cube* is an impressive sci-fi horror debut. It stings the repetitive Hollywood blockbusters with the best of cinematic tension and innovation and proves the spirit of low budget, envelope-pushing filmmaking is alive and kicking.

Speaking from California, Natali reveals that his passion for film began with a 'religious experience' when seeing *Star Wars* as a kid. "There really hadn't been anything quite like it before, and it was the realisation of all the stuff that I loved in comic books. Frankly I've never had an experience in a movie theatre quite equal to that one."

Cube shares *Star Wars'* spirit of innovative, ground breaking science fiction filmmaking. Despite some eye-popping visuals, *Cube* reveals that psychological play can be more deadly than special effects.

"The gamble we took was putting our biggest effect in the first five minutes of the movie. The thinking behind that was, 'well, once we've shown it, we'll never have to show it again.' What's really important is the threat of a trap rather than there being a trap. We had trap sequences which had to be cut from the film because we couldn't afford to do it. Ultimately, the film really benefited because where we couldn't have an effect, we would replace it with a character piece or plot twist. We were forced to be more creative and intelligent than we might have been."

Designed to overtake the tensions of the physical dangers, at times *Cube* falters on the level of a weak psycho-dialogue, where perhaps one or two more trap sequences would have satisfied.

"What we really aspired to do with *Cube* is to take you to a world that you've never been to before. We were extremely lucky because we

Holloway (Guadagni), Quentin (Wint), Worth (Hewlett), Leaven (DeBoer)

had really great people working on it, and all the effects were donated, with terrific world-class artists working on the movie. It's really extraordinary to me to think that this movie is opening in Australia," he chuckles.

"I never would have imagined that it would travel that far. So many Australian filmmakers influenced me, like George Miller or Peter Weir. That whole crowd — they're just extraordinary. *The Road Warrior* (*Mad Max*) is one of the great science fiction films of all time. Probably one of the most imitated too."

Seldom does a film surface which breathes life into the dreary routine of formula, repetition, re-invention and stereotype. When it does, it lifts the spirits and restores faith in this often uninspired artform.

— SHANNON J HARVEY.

335

Natali's good looks ensured that his own face was depicted nearly as often as those of the *Cube* cast in print pieces.

Suspect #1:
Vincenzo Natali

First Time
OFFENDERS

What really changes when a young filmmaker's first big feature is a huge success? You'd be surprised...

Vincenzo Natali is a self-described film geek who began making Super 8 films in his early teens. After working as a storyboard artist for the animation studio Nelvana, Natali attended the Canadian Film Centre. It was through the Centre's Feature Film Project that he was able to make *Cube*, an imaginative film that placed six people in a maze, forcing them to find a way out. A festival winner (Toronto, 1997) *Cube* became a popular success in France.

"I doubted that *Cube* would even get into the Toronto International Film Festival. I was afraid that, because it was a science fiction film, it wouldn't be taken seriously. But the opposite happened. Because it wasn't typical indie film fare, it stood out. The reception was really positive. We actually walked away with an award [for the Best First Canadian Feature]. For me, because Toronto is home and I've gone to the festival for so many years, it was one of the best things that ever happened.

"I've been so lucky with *Cube*. It didn't open spectacularly and it didn't make a lot of money in North America, but it slowly disseminated itself through the world festival circuit. I've been fortunate in that I've been able to go all over the place with it.

"What's funny about travelling around with a film like *Cube* is that it invariably gets invited to all the sci-fi horror film festivals, which I love because I'm a sci-fi horror geek.

"One of the best festivals I went to was in a small French town called Gerardmer. It's a lovely provincial town that, for one week of the year when the festival arrives, turns into Tim Burton-ville. There are severed heads in the windows of all the stores and body

parts littering the streets and people dressed like ghouls. It's an odd experience. And people like [the Italian cult film director] Dario Argento, who is rather ghoulish in his own way, are walking around.

"After *Cube* did well at that festival, Samuel Hadida, of Metropolitan Filmexport, the French film distributor, became interested and enthusiastic about the film. He spent a million dollars promoting it. Hadida was very clever. He aimed it directly at the hard-core sci-fi audience, which is the crowd the film is meant for. Then he released it at a really good time, when there wasn't anything major around. It did quite well.

"The French are so respectful of filmmakers and the art of film. They have a completely different mentality than the Americans. It was a film geek's dream: I was completely feted and treated lavishly while I was there promoting the film. It was fantastic! I love Paris.

"After I made *Cube* you could say that I was considered marketable. I actually got an agent and did the whole Hollywood shuffle. I took a lot of meetings down south. People will return my calls now. But it's still a struggle to get original material made, at least for me. I'm really fortunate that I have my new project, a science fiction film called *Splice*, set up here in Canada, with Robert Lantos' company, Serendipity Point, involved in producing it.

"I didn't make any money doing *Cube*. But it has completely changed how people perceive me. Now I am taken seriously as a director."

TIME OF DAY 1:37 AM

SUSPECT Vincenzo Natali

DISTINGUISHING FEATURES Cube

The Men's Look

I LOVE PARIS

Like the other 18 directors whose short films make up the long one called *Paris, je t'aime*, all Vincenzo Natali had to do was come up with five minutes set in Paris, based on the theme of love. The only Canadian among the contributors, who include Gus Van Sant, Walter Salles and the Coen brothers, Natali (best known for *Cube*, 1997) helmed a "vampire love story," shot in the Rue de Madeleine. "It's every filmmaker's dream," he says over the phone from Los Angeles, about the freedom granted by the project and his month-long stay in Paris. The city's style captured his imagination, while the films of Cocteau informed it, but "I tried not to be too self-conscious. I didn't want to force the Frenchness of it."

About his own style, Natali is self-deprecating. "I don't like to be flashy. I have a certain affection for minimalism, both cinematically and in clothes," though he does admit to a predilection for colourful socks. "Outwardly I'm very simple, but if you were to look below the ankle..." Clothes matter more in his films. The next is *High Rise*, which Natali will adapt from the J.G. Ballard novel and will also direct. "You can count on haute couture, and lots of blood." For him, "they go together like peanut butter and chocolate." LAURA deCARUFEL

VINCENZO NATALI. LOS ANGELES, JULY 21, 2006. PHOTOGRAPHED BY SARAH WILMER.

Reviews

(continued)

Coverage of *Cube* ran the gamut from prestigious publications to the genre press.

Production Slate

compiled by Andrew O. Thompson

American Cinematographer

MARCH 1998

INVENTIVE PLOT SPARKS
THE SPANISH PRISONER

FREDDIE FRANCIS, BSC
EARNS CAREER KUDOS

SPECIAL FOCUS:
INDIE FILMS

Visit Us Online at www.cinematographer.com

bove: le de s on s her fellow captors contemplate their bizarre predicament in *Cube*. Right: Aldersen (Julian Richings) gazes in awe at the kaleidoscopic, cubic prison.

Gleaming the *Cube*
by Mark Dillon

Picture, if you will, six total strangers awakening to find themselves confined within a seemingly endless series of interconnected rooms, each of which is, in fact, a cube — one of thousands comprising a single massive cube. A mathematical formula seems to hold the key to the captives' escape from this mysterious, M.C. Escher-like nightmare, provided they can survive a succession of fatal booby traps, and one another.

This is the premise of the Canadian independent film *Cube*, a sort of *Ten Little Indians in the Twilight Zone* which signals the 35mm feature debut of director Vincenzo Natali and cinematographer Derek Rogers.

Recently featured as a midnight movie at the Sundance Film Festival, *Cube* was produced with the financial backing of the Canadian Film Centre's Feature Film Project. The Toronto-based CFC was founded in 1986 by hometown director Norman Jewison as a training ground for Canada's emerging film and television writers, producers, and directors; the Feature Film Project was estab-

lished six years later, offering some of the Centre's graduates the opportunity to make a feature film with a $350,000 cash grant (approximately $250,000 American) matched with the equivalent monetary value in services donated from the local film industry. What makes *Cube* stand out from the CFC-FFP's previous output is its science-fiction scenario and ambitious visuals; the film features a deft combination of old-fashioned cinematic ingenuity and digital effects work which belies its $1 million budget (Canadian).

Natali had previously done a stint at Toronto's Ryerson Polytechnic University film program, followed by work as a storyboard artist at the Nelvana animation studio. On the strength of several short films, Natali became a director-in-residence at the CFC, where he saw several shorts shot by Rogers, a fellow Ryerson alumnus. Rogers had left film school as an aspiring director, but later accepted cinematographic duties on a documentary that was shooting in Zimbabwe. Eventually, Rogers veered into dramatic work, but he found his documentary experiences to be invaluable, noting, "That work taught me to assess real-life situations, set up and light fast, and be fluid with a handheld camera."

Natali found these abilities to be a boon as he prepared his 30-minute CFC short *Elevated*, in which three people become trapped in an elevator, with one of the trio convinced that aliens have taken over the building. Both the director and cinematographer considered the

short to be a warmup for *Cube*, according to Natali, *Elevated* allowed them "to show that we could make a box — in this case the elevator set — visually interesting, which was one of the reservations people had about making *Cube*." (*Elevated* was later nominated for Best Short Film at the Genies, the Canadian equivalent of the Academy Awards.)

Cube, however, entailed six characters journeying through more than 50 identical yet visually diverse cubes. Inspired by Stanley Kubrick's *2001*, Natali envisioned a "symmetry and mathematical design to the sets," which would create the sense of a "pristine future." But Rogers dissuaded him from going with entirely white cubes, expressing the concern that they would appear to be too similar. "I pushed the idea of multiple colors, similar to a Rubik's Cube," he recalls. With the main cube set standing in for 50, the filmmakers differentiated each with one of five colors — white, green, straw, red, and blue. The budget allowed for the construction of only 1 1/2 actual cubes — one full-standing set and a hatchway that offered a view of two

other walls. Production designer Jasna Stefanovic constructed the cube out of white frosted Plexiglas walls decorated with black patterns and diagrams; in total, the structure measured 15' x 15' with a hatch on each of the six sides

Photos by Sophie Giraud.

16 March 1998

CUBE

IM LABYRINTH DES TODES

Stellen Sie sich einmal vor, Sie wachen morgens auf; Sie sind jedoch nicht in Ihrem Schlafzimmer, sondern im Innern eines großen Würfels. Sie haben keine Ahnung, wie Sie hierhergekommen sind und warum Sie diese merkwürdige Gefängniskluft anhaben. Sie untersuchen den Raum und stellen fest, daß alle sechs Seiten des Würfels – d. h. alle vier Wände plus Decke und Boden – völlig identisch sind. Alle haben genau in der Mitte eine kleine Schleuse, durch die Sie gerade so hindurchpassen.

Die Schleusen lassen sich glücklicherweise ganz leicht öffnen, und so können Sie auf Entdeckungsreise gehen. Was Sie sehen werden, wenn Sie eine der Schleusen öffnen, ist auf den ersten Blick vielleicht nicht sehr aufregend: Hinter der Schleuse verbirgt sich ein Raum, der genauso aufgebaut ist wie der, in dem Sie sich gerade befinden; er hat lediglich eine andere Farbe. Aber immerhin: Es ist ein Anfang. Suchen Sie nach einem Ausgang. Aber seien Sie vorsichtig. In einigen Räumen sind unsichtbare Mechanismen versteckt, die mit Ihrem Körper sehr brutale Veränderungen vornehmen können. Veränderungen, die Sie nicht überleben ...

Insgesamt sechs Menschen befinden sich in der gerade beschriebenen Situation: ein Polizist, eine Ärztin, ein aus Ausbrecherkönig berüchtigter Krimineller, eine College-Studentin, ein Autist und ein kaufmännischer Angestellter. Als erstes versucht die ungleiche Notgemeinschaft herauszufinden, weshalb sie sich in diesem unheimlichen Labyrinth befindet – und was sie dorthin geschafft hat.

14 MOVIESTAR

Diesen Herrn (Julian Richings) bitte gewürfelt servieren ...

Das Labyrinth im Inneren des Würfels besteht nach allen Seiten aus einer endlosen Anordnung immer n...

Auf diese Fragen keine auch nur halbwegs befriedigenden Antworten zu finden, treibt die Gefangenen an den Rand des Wahnsinns. Deshalb geben sie die Sinnfragen auf und versuchen sich an der eher praktischen Lösung ihres Problems: Sie suchen nach einem Ausweg. Aber schnell müssen sie feststellen, daß ein zielloses Trial-&-Error-Verfahren keinen Fortschritt bringt, sondern nur Menschenleben fordert: Die teuflischen Fallen in den Würfeln töten die Unvorsichtigen auf ebenso groteske wie grausame Weise. Die Gruppe der Verzweifelten kommt der Lösung ihres Problems erst einen Schritt näher, als ihnen klar wird, daß jeder von ihnen eine ganz bestimmte Funktion in diesem mörderischen Spiel hat ...

...ole Iskra mit Vincenzo Natali ...

... der sich erst einmal schelmisch hinter MOVIESTAR verschanzt hat

Film Festivals

Cube may have found its perfect audience on the film festival circuit—other filmmakers—where it proceeded to pick up awards and praise.

GÉNÉRIQUE

Réalisateur :
Vincenzo Natali
Scénario : Vincenzo Natali, André Bijelic et Graeme Manson
Photographie :
Derek Rogers
Décors : Jasna Stefanovic
Montage : John Sanders
Costumes :
Wendy May Moore
Interprètes principaux :
Nicole DeBoer (Leaven), Nicky Guadagni (Holloway), David Hewlett (Worth), Andrew Miller (Kazan), Julian Richings (Alderson), Wayne Robson (Rennes), Maurice Dean Wint (Quentin).

35 mm. Couleur. 1,85.
Dolby SR. 1997.
Version originale sous-titrée
Durée : 1h32

Production : Mehra Meh et Betty Orr
Cube Libre
c/o Trimark Pictures
2644, 30th Street
Santa Monica, CA 90405
USA
Tel : (310) 314 20 00
Fax : (310) 452 89 09
Canadian Film Centre et Feature Film Project

Vente à l'étranger :
Trimark International
2644, 30th Street
Santa Monica, CA 90405
USA
Tel : (310) 314 20 00
Fax : (310) 452 89 09

Distribué en France par :
Metropolitan Filmexport
116 bis, av des Champs Élysées
75008 Paris
Tel : 01 45 63 53 37
Fax : 01 45 63 77 31

CUBE

de Vincenzo Natali, C[...]

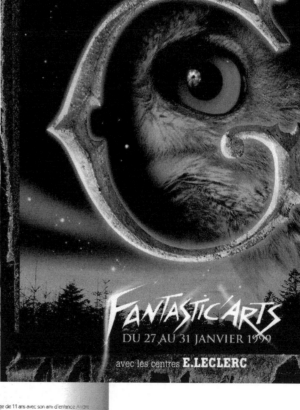

U̱n groupe de personnes se retrouve enferm[...] labyrinthe sans fin constitué de pièces cubiq[...] pièges mortels. Parmi eux, un policier, un voleu[...] mathématiques, un docteur, un autiste. Aucun d'ent[...] il se retrouve prisonnier de ce labyrinthe mortel, m[...] tion spécifique pouvant contribuer à leur évasion. [...] nalités et des luttes de pouvoir émergent rapideme[...] une la tension extrême. Il leur faudra apprendre à c[...] mortel où leurs heures sont comptés.

VINCENZO NATALI

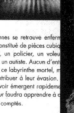

Il réalise son premier court métrage à l'âge de 11 ans avec son ami d'enfance André Bijelic. Il a depuis écrit et réalisé six autres courts métrages dont «Mouth» et «Playground» qui ont été diffusés sur CBC. Il a travaillé comme storyboardiste sur plusieurs animations télévisées et a également collaboré à ce titre à plusieurs [...] métrages dont «Johnny Mnemonic» de Robert Longo, «Blood & Donuts» de H[...] Dale et le prochain film de Bruce McDonald «Yummy Fur». «Cube» est son pro[...] long métrage.

FILMOGRAPHIE

1997   Cube

ヴィンチェンゾ・ナタリ
Vincenzo Natali

カナダ出身の29歳。カナディアン・フィルムセンター卒業。何本かの短編で映画研賞を受賞。「JM」などの大作にスタッフとして参加した他、監督・脚本を務めた長編デビュー作「CUBE」で'97年トロント映画祭最優秀デビュー賞を受賞し、世界の熱い注目を集めている。

林 隆三
Hayashi Ryuzo

東京都出身。98年の代表作に、77年新藤兼人監督の「竹山ひとり旅」、79年神代辰巳監督の「地獄」、85年森田芳光一部監督の「其春物語」、96年出目昌伸監督の「春の子午線」などがある。現在、神宮大河ドラマ「徳川慶喜」に出演中。

余 貴美子
Yo Kimiko

横浜市生まれ。主な出演映画は85年市川準監督の「会社物語」、88年代辰巳監督の「離れ家」、91年松本俊夫監督の「夢二」、93年石井隆監督の「ヌードの夜」、95年篠田正浩監督の「写楽」、97年阪本順治監督の「愛を乞うひと」、99年緒方明監督の「独立少年合唱団」、NTVの「くれない」に出演している。

安達祐実
Adachi Yumi

東京都出身。主な映画出演は89年「REX 恐竜物語」、94年「家なき子」、98年「ユメノ銀河」など。「家なき子」は「同情するなら金をくれ」という流行語を生み出し一世を風靡した人気テレビドラマの映画化。現在、テレビドラマ「ガラスの仮面」に主演し、人気を集めている。

椎名英姫
Shiina Eiki

福岡県出身。94年にベネトン・ワールドキャンペーンでモデルデビュー。またその間に振わっており、数々の雑誌のパートを飾る。コカ・コーラ「アクエリアス イオシス」、花王「ラビナス」などのCMにも出演。世界的なコンテスト「エリートモデルルック」の日本代表にも選ばれている。

松尾れい子
Matsuo Reiko

佐賀県出身。96年にソニー・ミュージックグループの「ちょっとそこまでオーディション」でグランプリ受賞。96年石井隆監督の「水の中の八月」に出演。97年には「ユメノ銀河」に出演したほか、サントリー「ビタミンウォーター」のCMでは「綺麗な存在感があるまなざし」と評された。

Michinoku International Mystery Film Festival '98 in Morioka

みちのく国際ミステリー映画祭
'98 in 盛岡

洋画新作
一挙上映
6／20（土）

V.ナタリ監督、来日

「ウェス・クレイヴンズ ウィッシュマスター」
（10：30〜／ピカデリー）

「スクリーム」「エルム街の悪夢」の監督クレイヴンが新たなる怖さを創造。オパールに封じられていた仲間ベルトの魔神が現代ロサンゼルスに甦り大暴れ。（90分）

「オースティン・パワーズ」
（15：00〜／ピカデリー）

30年の冷凍睡眠から目覚めた究極の'60'sスパイ・オースティンと蘇った悪王Dr.イーブルがカルチャーギャップにめげず、必死で合戦を展開するコメディー。（89分）

「CUBE（キューブ）」
（17：30〜／中劇2）

謎の立方体「キューブ」に閉じ込められた男女6人が、数々の殺人トラップをかいくぐり、必死で脱出を試みるが…。カナダの新鋭V.ナタリ監督渾身の作。（91分）

「普通じゃない」
（20：00〜／フォーラム1）

「トレイン・スポッティング」の監督・主演コンビ最新作。ドジな銀行員と誘拐被害の美女が、天使の導きで恋に落ちる風変わりな犯罪×恋愛劇。サントリ整も必殺。（103分）

Life After *Cube*

1: Together for *Cypher* premiere, left to right: Natali's assistant Amy Green, Natali and his wife, Kana, and writer Brian King **2:** Andrew Miller with actress Chandra West **3:** Pascal Launay, French *Cube* publicist **4:** French distributor Anne Schnitzer, Kana and Green

Cube Abroad

1: Hewlett with Japanese hero Ultraman **2:** Once you start seeing cubes, it's impossible to stop **3:** Natali later screened *Elevated* at the Fantasia Film Festival in 1999, accompanied by its co-star, David Hewlett (Note the *Cube* cap.) **4:** One of many *Cube* festival Q&A sessions

Cube **Abroad**
(continued)

5: Left: Film producer Samuel Hadida [*Resident Evil* series] who oversaw French distribution of *Cube* **6:** No matter where the *Cube* core ended up, the warmth between them was ever present **7:** Miller and Anne Schnitzer

8: Left to right: Kana, Natali, French comics writer Jean-Pierre Dionnet and Japanese horror movie director Hideo Nakata (*Ringu, Dark Water*) **9:** Director Marc Caro (*Delicatessen*) **10:** Left to right: Clusiau, Natali, unidentified man, and Naoko Tsukeda, who bought Japanese distribution rights for *Cube* **11:** Natali and Kana

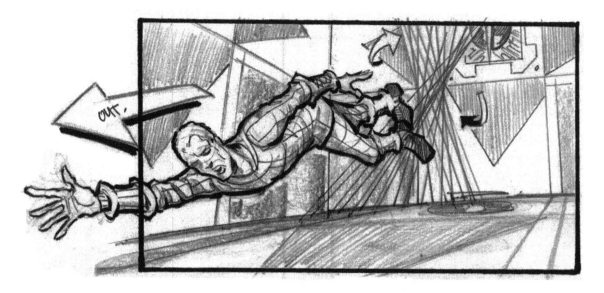

acknowledgments

AS THE PREVIOUS words and illustrations demonstrate, this book would not exist without the kindness, enthusiasm and boundless generosity of director Vincenzo Natali. From allowing the author to visit him at his then-Los Angeles home to answering countless emails and phone calls, he has been a gracious guide through the twisted world of *Cube* and its making. I'm particularly in his debt for opening his extensive archives to us, including script drafts, budgets, notes, as well as pages and pages of gorgeous illustrations and storyboards. No matter what he was working on at the time, he never failed to reply to emails promptly or to make an introduction to a member of the cast or crew. Art director/designer Pamela Norman and I are also forever grateful to him for never once, in the eight years since we first proposed this book, mentioning the fact that he shot his whole film in just 20 days.

Heartfelt thanks also go to Natali's creative partner Andre Bijelic for sharing his memories of the early days right on through the film festival premiere of *Cube*. David Hewlett's recollections of those days, as well as life in the cube, were invaluable and, let's face it, the perfect excuse to chat with one of the most entertaining screen presences of his generation: the Laurence Olivier of actors adept at portraying characters that you want to simultaneously throttle and share a beer with.

The author's indebtedness also extends to Andrew Miller for his insight into the experiences that bound the core group together and what actually happened to Kazan in the famous "lost ending"; Nicky Guadagni for her memories and for being as cool as Holloway; William Phillips for unraveling *Cube*'s "door problem" for us; VFX master Robert Munroe for taking a walk down memory lane; David Pravica for helping us with all that math; Mark Korven for conveying the challenge of creating a movie score with no discernible musical elements; Louise Mackintosh for explaining those amazing makeup effects; Colin Brunton for taking us on one last pogo; Vickie Papavs for her memories of filming *Cube* 1.0 (aka *Elevated*); and Derek Rogers for being one of the most tell-it-like-I-see-it people we've ever met. Whatever merits this book boasts is because of them; any errors are the author's own.

Omissions

For all the amazing people I had the privilege to speak with for this book, there were those that, for one reason or another, I couldn't reach. On that list are actors Maurice Dean Wint (Quentin) and Nicole De Boer (Leaven), producer Mehra Meh and production designer Jasna Stefanovic. In one case I approached an individual's management without success; in a couple of other instances I actually exchanged an email or two with the people only to lose touch as their careers intervened, or they just didn't feel like chatting with me. Fair enough.

That being the case, I decided to leave out biographical material for all involved except where it concerned the making of *Cube*, rather than including potted biographies that you can easily Google yourself. I'm painfully aware of the hole this leaves, and for that I must humbly apologize. My hope is that the epic story of the making of this classic film will more than make up for those details I failed to include.

Photo Credits

Mark Lipczynski: pp. 10, 13, 46, 230; Steve Wilkie: pp. 17, 151, 218 (bottom, right); Colin Brunton: p. 69; Gage Skidmore: p. 98; David Pravica: p. 108; 20th Century Fox Film Corp.: p. 109; Bob Monroe: p. 175; Madeline Phillips: p. 201; Nicky Guadagni (top, right): p. 309; Andre Bijelic: p. 21 (excluding top, right), 81, 105, 120, 127, 134-135, 139, 148, 162 (excluding bottom, right), 167, 309 (top, left and bottom, center), 313; Excerpt page from *Cube* comic book: p. 349 (see pp. 332-333).

this page is intentionally blank

Also by A.S. Berman

* The Gilmore Girls Companion | 480 pages
ISBN-10: 1593936168 | ISBN-13: 978-1593936167

**Soap: The
Unauthorized
Inside Story of the
Sitcom that Broke
ALL the Rules**
456 pages
ISBN-10: 1593936877
ISBN-13: 978-
1593936877

**30 Years of
British Television**
160 pages
ISBN-10: 1593931433
ISBN-13: 978-
1593931438

The New Horror Handbook
236 pages | ISBN-10: 1593931441
ISBN-13: 978-1593931445

this page is intentionally blank

Made in the USA
San Bernardino, CA
14 April 2018